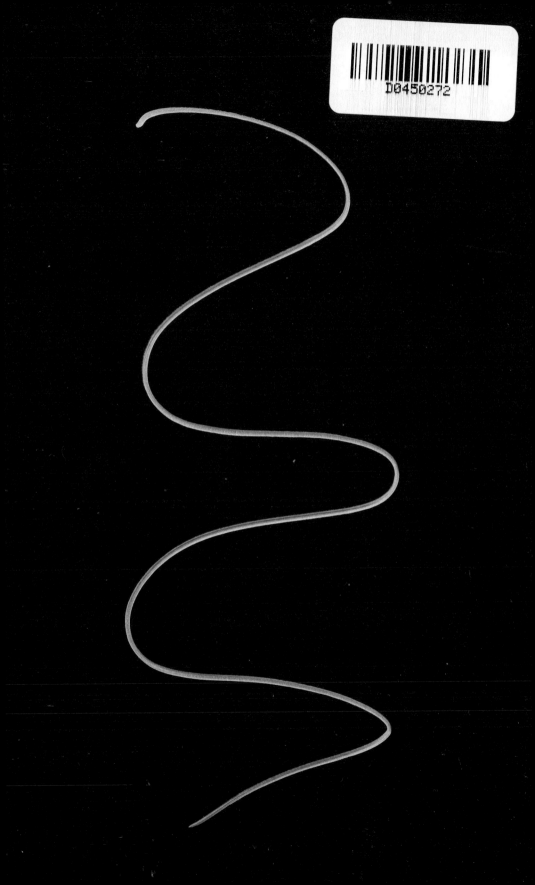

CABINET'S FINEST HOUR

Cabinet's Finest Hour

The Hidden Agenda of May 1940

DAVID OWEN

First published in 2016 by

Haus Publishing Ltd
70 Cadogan Place
London SW1X 9AH
www.hauspublishing.com

A CIP catalogue record for this book is available from the British Library.

ISBN 9781910376553
eISBN 9781910376591

Typeset by MacGuru Ltd.

Printed in Spain.

Contents

Acknowledgements

Many people have helped me at Haus Publishing. Barbara Schwep-cke, Harry Hall and Emma Henderson have been towers of strength. Once again my cousin Simon Owen has contributed criticism and advice and as always Maggie Smart has been strongly supportive. The Bodleian Library, Oxford, and the British Library have been very helpful in providing access to the writings of Arthur Greenwood who has never been the subject of a biography. His contribution with Clement Attlee to rebuilding the Labour Party from 1935 was second to none and was of particular importance to the whole nation in 1939 and 1940. It is hard to do justice to the helpful support I have received from the staff of the library at the House of Lords. I have written in other books about many of the people who feature in this work, in particular *In Sickness and In Power: Illness in Heads of Government During the Last 100 Years*[1], a work I updated for a new edition in 2016. I have used or modified the same words about these people rather than attempting to revise my own considered judgements.

I am convinced that Winston Churchill's greatness is not impaired but enhanced by demonstrating that his War Cabinet was one of collective decision-making in which his judgements were challenged and opinions changed in debate; the authority and quality of the Government was hugely improved by Churchill's wish to remain *primus inter pares*, or first among equals.

Limehouse, August 2016

---

1 Methuen Publishing Ltd, 2009.

Preface

I first sat around the Cabinet table as a junior minister for the Royal Navy at the age of 31, deputising for Denis Healey, the Secretary of State for Defence. The subject under discussion at the Defence and Overseas Policy Committee of the Cabinet was the source of much amusement in the country. A somewhat bizarre decision to authorise 'Operation Sheepskin' had been taken the previous week, on Friday 14 March 1969, by DOPC which had resulted – five days later, on 19 March at 5.30 am – in 331 paratroopers and marines wading ashore at two sites with guns at the ready only to be greeted on the sand of the island of Anguilla in the West Indies by sixty television crews and reporters. It was too early for the tourists asleep in their hotel rooms to be present.

The farcical nature of what was in Whitehall terms a successful operation to restore the authority of the British Government over local politicians was lampooned by the press who dubbed it as the 'Bay of Piglets' after President Kennedy's ill-fated and somewhat more serious invasion of Cuba in 1961.

After a Cabinet conversation accompanied by frequent references to SNOWI, the Chancellor of the Exchequer Roy Jenkins leant back somewhat languidly in his chair and, with a smile, asked Harold Wilson, the Prime Minister sitting opposite him, "Who and what is SNOWI?" The answer, to our baffled amusement, was Commodore Lacey the Senior Naval Officer West Indies!

Periodic attendances as Health Minister from 1974 to 1976, again under Harold Wilson, was followed by full Cabinet membership as Foreign Secretary under Prime Minister James Callaghan from 1977 to 1979. This period was marked by seemingly endless armed conflicts in Southern Rhodesia, the Horn of Africa, Mozambique and Angola. There was a very real danger of the Cold War between the Western democracies and the Soviet Union spilling over from Europe into the African continent. There was also an important economic agenda in the context of our membership of what was then the European Economic Community.

I do not think this book would have been possible without this Cabinet experience. As the years pass I grow evermore convinced that collective decision-making is the hallmark of a true democracy, however differently it might be organised. Also that there is nothing old-fashioned about its mechanisms that are proven to work. The worst possible form of democratic governance in my view is that which tries to make an ad hoc amalgamation of the strong powers of a US President with the UK tradition of a Prime Minister and seeks to do so without the complex separation of powers that exists in the US with checks from Congress and the Supreme Court, while retaining the fusion of power between Parliament and the Executive. The UK has suffered, with varying degrees of intensity, from that combination under three Prime Ministers and successive Cabinet Secretaries from 2001 to 2016. It is time to not just dismantle such appalling governance but to put constitutional safeguards in place that make it virtually impossible for it to re-emerge.

As with my 2014 book with Haus Publishing, *The Hidden Perspective: The Military Conversations of 1906–1914*, I attach much importance to making available to the reader original documents from the time. I have tried to select sufficient quotes so that the narrative is not dependent on reading the documents in full but is rather a matter of individual preference as to whether one chooses to do so. I have long been fascinated as to whether there was the basis for a negotiation with Mussolini in 1940 and am deeply indebted to John Lukacs' ground-breaking book *Five Days in London, May 1940*.[1] When I first read the War Cabinet minutes in full covering nine meetings of six ministers from Martin Gilbert's brilliantly edited work of scholarship and revelation, *The Churchill War Papers: Never Surrender*,[2] I

---

1   John Lukacs, *Five Days in London*, May 1940 (Yale University Press, 2001).
2   Martin Gilbert, *The Churchill War Papers, Volume II: Never Surrender May 1940–December 1940* (Heinemann, 1994).

wanted to make them available as an easy and continuous read. This is done in Chapter 4. What they bring alive is a genuine debate and clash of views mainly, but by no means exclusively, between Halifax, the Foreign Secretary, and Churchill as Prime Minister. The outcome of the debate had a profound impact on world history.

1

Speak for England

On Saturday 2 September 1939, after rushing through the Military
Service Bill, followed by a long wait until nearly eight o'clock in the
evening, the Prime Minister Neville Chamberlain made a short statement to a House of Commons expectant of a declaration of war on
Germany. Instead, according to the Conservative MP, Leo Amery,
he "came to tell us in a flat, embarrassed voice, first of all that Mussolini's project for a conference could not be entertained while Poland
was subject to invasion; secondly that we were discussing with the
French."[1] There was a deep sense of frustration in the Commons
when Chamberlain sat down. In part, such feeling stemmed from the
assumption that we were already at war. And yet here was Chamberlain ready only to speak about a delayed reply from Hitler to the British
message delivered a day before to his Foreign Secretary, Ribbentrop.

Few, if any, MPs were even the slightest bit interested to hear about
a proposal from the Italian Government for a conference, believing,
correctly, that even Chamberlain would find it impossible to take
part. It was a House of Commons seething with frustration; Poland
was being subjected to invasion, her towns under bombardment
and Danzig made the subject of a unilateral settlement by force. The
House of Commons very rarely sits on a Saturday; the only recent
precedents have been 3 November 1956 during the Suez Crisis, and 3
April 1982 when Margaret Thatcher announced that in response to
an Argentinian landing on the Falkland Islands, a task force would
sail for the South Atlantic on the Monday.[2]

---

1 Leo Amery, *My Political Life: The Unforgiving Years, 1929–1940* (Hutchinson, 1955), p 323–4.
2 Ed Iain Dale, *Memories of the Falklands* (Politico's, 2002), p 179–181.

Suddenly, though unrecorded in Hansard – the supposedly verbatim report of what is said in the Commons – Leo Amery, one of Chamberlain's foremost critics, First Lord of the Admiralty from 1922 to 1924 and a very successful Colonial Secretary from 1924 to 1929, called out to Arthur Greenwood on the opposite bench as he rose to reply to the Prime Minister, "Speak for England, Arthur!" Amery "dreaded a purely partisan speech" and afterwards felt that "no one could have done it better".[3]

Greenwood was deputising for the Labour leader, Clement Attlee, who was away from Parliament recovering from an operation on his prostate. Attlee's total trust and confidence in Greenwood is revealed through his determination to keep to his doctor's orders and not cut short his convalescence. So he was sitting on the beach with his children on 23 August 1939 when the German-Soviet Nonaggression Pact was signed; he was playing golf on 1 September when Hitler sent his forces into Poland; and was back on the beach on this day, 2 September, when Chamberlain made his statement to Parliament and Greenwood made his speech. Attlee had told Greenwood to protest furiously that Britain had not yet fulfilled its obligations to Poland. The two communicated constantly by telegram while Attlee was absent, though one rather important telegram was torn up by the Attlee family dog, Ting, and only when pieced together read "War imminent. Arthur." [4]

Amery's words carried the clear implication to everyone in the House that Prime Minister Neville Chamberlain had not spoken for England – the effect was electric. Greenwood at the despatch box was a tall and, on this occasion, a commanding figure, who only a few years later would still be able to beat off a knife attack from an assailant outside the Commons late at night. On such occasions as these the House becomes a cockpit, with a theatrical atmosphere that cannot be reproduced when it is half empty. It is a moment when reputations are made as well as broken.

Speaking with a new authority to a crammed chamber, Greenwood began, "This is indeed a grave moment. (*Cheers*) I believe the

---

3   Leo Amery, *My Political Life: The Unforgiving Years 1929–1940*, p 324.
4   Francis Beckett, *Clem Attlee: Labour's Great Reformer* (Haus Publishing, 2015), p 219.

whole House is perturbed by the right hon. gentleman's statement. There is a growing feeling, I believe, in all quarters of the House that this incessant strain must end sooner or later – and, in a sense, the sooner the better (*Cries of "Now"*). But if we are to march, I hope we shall march in complete unity and march with France." A maverick backbench MP, John McGovern, then interjected with a sneer: "You people do not intend to march – not one of you."[5] Greenwood wisely did not deal with the charge, intent on maximising unity amongst all MPs and appealing to the better nature of everyone. John McGovern had sat as an independent MP for the Scottish seat, Glasgow Shettleston, while retaining membership of the Independent Labour Party [ILP] since a by-election in 1922. He was a combative figure who maintained his passionate commitment to peace throughout the war, and was described as someone capable of causing hackles to rise on the left as well as the right.

Greenwood continued, "I am speaking under very difficult circumstances – (*Cheers*) with no opportunity to think about what I should say; and I speak what is in my heart at this moment. I am gravely disturbed. An act of aggression took place 38 hours ago. The moment that act of aggression took place, one of the most important treaties of modern times automatically came into operation (*Opposition Cheers*)". He ended by saying, "I believe that the die is cast, and we want to know in time."[6]

In a revealing letter to his sister Ida seven days later on 20 September 1939, Chamberlain explained that the "long drawn out agonies that preceded the actual declaration of war" were due to "three complications".[7] Firstly, secret communications that a neutral intermediary conducted between Hitler and Göring and himself and his Foreign Secretary Halifax which he had found "rather promising". Though "they gave the impression, probably with intention, that it was possible to persuade Hitler to accept a peaceful and reasonable solution of the Polish question in order to get an Anglo-German

---

5 HC, Hansard, *Parliamentary Debates: Official Report,* 1939, Vol. 351, p 281.
6 HC, Hansard, 2 September 1939, vol. 351, cc 280–6.
7 Neville Chamberlain, *The Neville Chamberlain Diary Letters: The Downing Street Years, 1934–1940.* Ed Robert C Self (Routledge, 2005), p 443.

agreement". Once again, Chamberlain was not ready to accept the reality that Hitler was intent on war. What Chamberlain wrote was that until Hitler "disappears and his system collapses there can be no peace ... What I hope for is not a military victory – I very much doubt the possibility of that – but a collapse of the German home front." Still in November Chamberlain thought the war would be over by the Spring with "the German realisation they can't win".[8]

Many MPs were surprised by the effectiveness of Greenwood's speech, but he was a far more significant figure in the Labour Party than many Conservative MPs and right-wing political commentators had hitherto recognised. From his position as Head of Economics at Huddersfield Technical College and the economics department at Leeds University he had written in the *Economic Journal*, the *Journal of the Royal Statistical Society* and *Political Quarterly*. Greenwood, besides a long-standing expertise in education, left Leeds to become Secretary to the Council for the Study of International Relations for which he contributed to a book *The War and Democracy*,[9] published in 1914, writing at the end: "Today is seed-time. But the harvest will not be gathered without sweat and toil. The times are pregnant with great possibilities, but their realisation depends upon the united wisdom of the people." He became a civil servant in the Ministry of Reconstruction where he worked with Christopher Addison and Arthur Henderson. Besides all this, he produced a report on adult education with R H Tawney. This gave him well-rounded experience and sufficient knowledge to deal with international crises as well as domestic issues.

In September 1916 he spoke at a conference which was written up in *The Athenaeum*, a monthly journal he was closely associated with. He spoke about the news of partially disabled soldiers and the important question of women, all in consideration to the question of Reconstruction after the war. *The Athenaeum* in January and February 1917 was critical of the five-man War Cabinet that the new Prime Minister Lloyd George had established, fearing that either

---

8 *Ibid*, pp 466–7.
9 R.W. Seton-Watson, J. Dover Wilson, Alfred E. Zimmern, Arthur Greenwood, *The War and Democracy* (Project Gutenberg, 2004).

way they must bring in other members of the Government to unify general policy or they must seek the advice of people less responsible, which would certainly lead to dissension and confusion. Greenwood was secretary of the Labour Party's research department from 1920, before being elected as MP for Nelson and Colne in Lancashire at the general election on 15 November 1922. This was precipitated by the disowning of Prime Minister David Lloyd George by his Conservative coalition partners at the earlier 'Carlton Club meeting'. That was also the same election in which Attlee became the MP for Limehouse. The two men were destined to be key partners from 1935–40 in bringing the Labour Party back to being a major political force, a force which deserved to serve again in government. They would both be ready to participate in and weld together a cross-party grouping in May 1940, among the first to remove Chamberlain as Prime Minister and then to be Labour's two members of the five-member War Cabinet formed by Churchill on 10 May 1940.

As his biographer Beckett has written, Attlee "came to socialism slowly and reluctantly, by painstakingly eliminating all possible alternatives, through his heart first and his head afterwards, mentioning (but only privately, never publicly) the 'burning anger which I felt at the wrongs which I could see around me.'"[10] Attlee quietly dropped the Christianity that had played a major role in his family life growing up, and became a social worker. But Attlee wanted political action, not talk of theory. He became a member of the Independent Labour Party and joined the only union for which he was eligible – the National Union of Clerks. When he joined it had 887 branches, 22,000 members and 30 MPs. It was not Marxist but linked to the Social Democratic Federation, and it did not talk the language of class war.

Attlee started to build a reputation in the ILP in London as a whole. Then in 1914 Britain was at war with Germany. The ILP was divided; it had previously declared that in the event of war as socialists they should refuse to fight. Ramsay MacDonald, the Labour leader, was in favour of refusing yet Arthur Henderson supported the war. Attlee enlisted in the army two days after war was declared.

---

10 Francis Beckett, *Clem Attlee*, p 33.

By September, Attlee was a lieutenant in the 6th South Lancashire Regiment in Tidworth. He became in temporary command of a company of seven officers and 250 men from Liverpool, Wigan and Warrington. He was made a Captain early in 1915 and, in June, he and his company of men set sail for Turkey stopping off en route in Valletta in Malta and in Alexandria in Egypt. After arriving at the port of embarkations, Mudros Harbour, he, as part of a battalion, went up the peninsular to find themselves in trenches stinking from Turkish corpses, and water which tasted of sand in the dreadful heat and flies. Soon the main enemy was dysentery which Attlee eventually caught; he ended up on a stretcher, unconscious, on a hospital ship where he was dropped off to recover in Malta. In his absence, the South Lancashires fought in the battle of Sari Bair and 500 of them were killed. He rejoined his men on 16 November and they held the final lines, embarking on HMS *Princess Irene* on 19 December. Attlee was the last but one to leave Gallipoli, the last being Major General FS Maude.

The fascinating and important historical consequence of Attlee's fight against the Turks and the strategy of the Eastern Front, with which First Sea Lord Winston Churchill will always be identified, was that he fully supported the concept of taking the pressure off the Western Front in France. "It was a bold strategy and controversy still rages about whether it was a good one, but Attlee never had any doubt. It gave him his lifelong admiration for Churchill as a military strategist, an admiration which contributed enormously to their working relationship in the Second World War."[11]

Attlee came back to England and was promoted to Major Attlee in February 1917. From then on many people continued to call him Major Attlee and, more affectionately, in Limehouse 'the Major'.

In June 1918 Attlee was sent to France and discharged from the army on 16 January 1919. In the 'coupon' general election called by Lloyd George, sometimes referred to as the 'khaki election', the Government list of MPs numbered 473. Three hundred and twenty two were conservative; Labour had 57. Attlee became Mayor of Stepney, appointed by the new Labour Council after the local elections in November 1919.

11   Francis Beckett, *Clem Attlee*, p 61.

In October 1922 Attlee, as the prospective candidate for Lime-house for the ILP, fought the sitting Conservative MP whose majority was 6,000. On 15 November 1922, the day after the election, it was announced Attlee had 9,688 votes – a majority of 1,899. Labour now had 142 MPs, a majority of which came from the ILP.

In 1923 there was another general election, surprisingly called by the new Prime Minister Stanley Baldwin. Attlee won his Limehouse constituency with a large majority of 6,185 and Greenwood was also successful. While the Conservatives had the largest number of MPs, at 258, it no longer had the largest overall majority. Labour, who had 191, united with the Liberals and Ramsay MacDonald became Prime Minister in January 1924 when the king asked him to form the first Labour Government, albeit a minority one. It was destined to only last for a short time.

At this point Arthur Greenwood was made parliamentary secretary to the Ministry of Health and Clement Attlee became Under Secretary of State at the War Office. Forty-nine new Labour MPs were elected and there was a considerable increase in the number of ILP members, both being part of the Labour Representation Committee first convened on 27 November 1900. It was inevitably a short-lived government but a significant milestone had been passed in that a number of Labour MPs had gained experience of government for the first time.

Four days before polling day Labour was hit by the publication of what turned out to be a forged letter in the *Daily Mail*. The various headlines were:

CIVIL WAR PLOT BY SOCIALIST MASTERS
MOSCOW ORDERS OUR REDS
GREAT PLOT DISCLOSED YESTERDAY
'PARALYSE THE ARMY AND NAVY'

and

MR MACDONALD WOULD LEND RUSSIA OUR MONEY!
DOCUMENT ISSUED BY FOREIGN OFFICE AFTER DAILY MAIL
HAD SPREAD THE NEWS.

Publication of the so-called 'Zinoviev Letter' became an issue especially for women voters troubled by the portrayal of Labour in the
press as 'bloody Bolsheviks'. MacDonald, who besides being Prime
Minister was Foreign Secretary as well, did not repudiate the Foreign
Office when they took the letter at face value but protested angrily
to the Russian Government about Zinoviev, whose real name was
Apfelbaum, Chairman of Communist International. He was allegedly writing to the British Communist Party on ways of controlling
the Labour movement. Attlee's disillusionment with MacDonald
began over his handling of the alleged Zinoviev letter.

When the general election took place on 29 October 1924, both
Greenwood and Attlee were re-elected and Hugh Dalton was elected
for the first time for Peckham. Labour lost 40 seats and Baldwin
became Prime Minister again with 412 Conservative MPs.

Herbert Morrison, after a surprise victory in the 1923 election,
lost his seat in Hackney South to a Liberal, the Conservatives having
withdrawn. Morrison was the architect of the proposals the London
Labour Party put to the Royal Commission on London Govern-
ment in 1922. During this first spell as an MP, Morrison clashed with
Ernest Bevin, the General Secretary of the Transport and General
Workers' Union, and Harry Gosling, the new Minister of Transport.
MacDonald, urged on by Bevin, had supported the London Traffic
Bill as a stop gap measure but Morrison voted against it. Bevin and
Lord Ashfield, formerly Sir Albert Stanley, President of the Board
of Trade in Lloyd George's coalition wartime government, and who
was chairman of the London General Omnibus Company, were in
cahoots and both Ashfield and Bevin were depicted as "tycoons". The
nub of it all was that Bevin thought his Transport Workers would get
"a better deal from Ashfield than from Morrison and the London
County Council, LCC; after all, Ashfield's bus workers were paid
more than LCC train workers."[12] Morrison, for his part, saw Ashfield
as wanting a "monopoly", arguing, "I would prefer local government
any day to Whitehall government".[13] There was the democratic

---

12 Matthew Worley, *Labour Inside the Gate: A History of the British Labour Party
Between the Wars* (I. B. Tauris, 2005), p 80.
13 HC, Hansard, *Parliamentary Debates: Official Report,*1931, vol. 250.

dilemma of who should wield power – central or local government? Bevin wanted a member of his union and one member from Ashfield's to represent their interests while Morrison wanted only representatives of local authorities. Bevin won out. Morrison's official biographers wrote "By standing up to Bevin, Morrison earned his everlasting hatred. Bevin was a spiteful man who looked on opposition in very personal terms. For the rest of his life Bevin was to pursue Morrison with venom."[14] Whilst Bevin's biographer wrote of the 1924 clash "there was another reason for Bevin's impatience with the politicians in the Labour Party. He lived in a world dominated by industrial conflict, a world in which he had all the time to deal with hard, often unpalatable facts and take real decisions. The politicians lived in a different world where parliamentary manoeuvres, party resolutions and conference speeches were neither taken nor meant to be taken literally, a world in Bevin's of make-believe, of shadow politics and sham decisions ... the first task of the party was propaganda; it had to appeal and win over the unconverted. After the defeat of 1931 Bevin saw this clearly enough, but in 1924–5 he was too close to the immediate industrial conflict to take a long view of the Labour Party's problems."[15]

In October 1926 Greenwood wrote an article in *The Pilgrim: A Review of Christian Politics and Religion*. It was edited by William Temple, the then Archbishop of Canterbury and a man sympathetic to Labour. The edition looked back on the General Strike and Temple, in an editorial, claimed that Prime Minister Baldwin had "acted rightly throughout" – right to refuse all arrangements that might give rise to the hope of subsidy, then yielding "rightfully" to the policy of the blank cheque. To Greenwood 'the new spirit of Industry' was the expression of a hope; the term 'class war' the expression of a fact. Describing the atmosphere in industry as "more hostile today than before", he went on to argue using Christian terms "Nevertheless a 'new spirit'" in industry "is essential on spiritual as

---

14 Bernard Donoughue, G. W. Jones, *Herbert Morrison: Portrait of a Politician* (Weidenfeld & Nicolson, 1973), pp 119–120.

15 Alan Bullock, Baron Bullock, *The Life and Times of Ernest Bevin: Trade Union Leader 1881–1940* (Heinemann, 1960), p 256.

well as material grounds". He warned that "The escape from the 'class war' does not lie along a broad and easy road". The way from the "class war to community of interest is the road from Capitalism to Socialism" and that the "spirit of co-operation cannot be born of the spirit of competition and private gain". It was felt that it was still very difficult to evaluate the full effect of the General Strike but far from helping the miners it had damaged their cause. Overall, the General Strike was another blow to Labour's claim to be able to govern. Years later Attlee told Kenneth Harris, one of his biographers, "I'd heard a General Strike discussed for fifteen years. When it came it collapsed because no one knew what to do with it, and most of them discovered they didn't really want it." In the wake of the strike, Scammell and Nephew factory owners had taken action against him and fellow Labour members because of Attlee's chairmanship of the electricity committee of Stepney Council for pulling the fuse of their factory, though they had their own generating plant. Action was not taken against Conservatives on the committee so it was a flagrantly political action. And yet the High Court ordered Attlee to pay £300; fortunately he won on appeal. Had he lost, and on an MP's salary of only £400, Attlee would have been financially embarrassed as he had been drawing down his family legacy and was from 1925–1940 always anxious about his lack of money.

In the new Parliament Attlee was appointed a member of the Indian Statutory Commission in November 1927 having been given an assurance from MacDonald that this should not give rise to any misgivings as it would not affect his inclusion in any future Labour Government. Attlee spent some months in India in early 1928 and then from October 1928 until April 1929 visiting every province. India was the occasion for Attlee's one very serious row with Churchill during the time of the War Cabinet. His real knowledge of India meant that as Prime Minister he was the driving force behind the granting of Independence in 1947 – one of the greatest acts of statesmanship in the 20th Century.

The election in May 1929 gave Labour 289 MPs, 19 short of an absolute majority. MacDonald became Prime Minister but he did not offer or even see Attlee to explain why he was not in a government job. The other Labour MP on the Indian Commission, Vernon

Hartshorn, was also excluded, whereas MacDonald gave Arthur Greenwood a big career boost and made him Minister of Health with a seat in the Cabinet. Greenwood improved widows' pensions in 1929. His Housing Act of 1930 permitted slum clearance and rebuilding. In January 1931 he warned against cuts in social services as a means for balancing the budget, an argument which he held to throughout the summer financial crisis. The only MP clearly on the left at this time was the 70-year-old George Lansbury as the Minister of Works.

It was not until 24 May 1930 that Attlee entered the Government as Chancellor of the Duchy of Lancaster owing to Oswald Mosley's resignation over the rejection of his radical proposals for dealing with unemployment. Although not in the Cabinet, Attlee for a short time had an important role as, in effect, economic adviser to MacDonald. A Cabinet paper he submitted recommended a Ministry of Industry. The appointment of Horace Wilson as industrial adviser to MacDonald meant that in March 1931, Attlee became Postmaster-General, though still not in the Cabinet. Meanwhile Philip Snowden, as Chancellor of the Exchequer, appointed an 'economy committee' under Sir George May, an accountant, to propose cuts. It was suggested an estimated deficit of £120 million for 1932–3 should be reduced by £97 million by cutting unemployment benefits and the salaries of teachers, the military and the police. By mid-August the Cabinet reluctantly agreed £56 million in cuts. In what had become a political crisis, the Conservatives and Liberals said these cuts were not enough. The Liberal Party position might have been different had Lloyd George not been out of action having a prostate operation. MacDonald, who could accept £70 million, was then persuaded by King George V to form a National Government. MacDonald took four Labour Cabinet ministers with him, including Philip Snowden and Jimmy Thomas, the National Union of Railwaymen leader, as Lord Privy Seal.[16] Oswald Mosley, earlier the scourge of unemployment and advocate of economic growth, en route to becoming a fascist and no longer supportive of the Labour Party, asked of the Labour Government, "What would we think of a Salvation Army that took to its heels on the Day of Judgement?"[17]

---

16 Robert Skidelsky, *Britain Since 1900: A Success Story?* (Vintage, 2014), p 207–8.
17 Oswald Mosley, *Last Words* (Black House Publishing, 2012), pp 44–5.

On 24 August after the National Government had already been formed, Attlee and other ministers not in the Cabinet met with MacDonald in the Cabinet Room at No. 10. Attlee described how he "made us a long and insincere speech in which he begged us to remain with the party out of regard for our careers, but really because he had all the appointments fixed up and any adhesions would have gravely embarrassed him."[18] Attlee, thereafter, had no time for Mac-Donald and unlike Morrison, who had been Minister of Transport, never even considered staying with MacDonald. Morrison's position remains to this day somewhat obscure. Sticking with the Labour Party and following Arthur Henderson into Opposition was for Attlee the only choice. Near the end of his life when interviewed on 16 September 1965, Attlee singled out for criticism how MacDonald "had no idea of treating his colleagues properly. He used to recall to me the contempt he had for his colleagues".[19] On other senior Cabinet figures he was asked:

> Q: What about Thomas?
> Attlee: Jimmy? Jimmy was a good fellow. He never knew quite where he was, like some others I've known. He hadn't any clear idea of what was right and wrong.
> Q: And how about Snowden?
> Attlee: Snowden was quite genial you know. He was a very hard set free trader.
> Q: How did you view after 1931, these same men – MacDonald, Snowden, Thomas?
> Attlee: I regarded them as traitors.

Attlee was not alone in his condemnation of MacDonald. Bevin also had little time for him: "Of all the Labour politicians, MacDonald, with his upper-class tastes, his lack of industrial experience and air of aloofness, had least sympathy with the trade union side of the movement. He and Bevin each embodied many of the characteristics which the other most disliked in the Labour movement and neither

---

18 Roy Jenkins, *Mr. Attlee: An Interim Biography* (Heinemann, 1948), p 139.
19 Clem Attlee, *The Granada Historical Records Interview* (Panther, 1967), p 12.

had much time for the other."[20] Attlee wrote to his brother Tom about how difficult it was to gauge MacDonald's mind at any time. "It is, I think, mainly fog now. I think that while at the back of his mind he realises his own incompetence for the job which he has in hand, he sees himself in a series of images in the mirror, images which constantly fade and melt into each other. Now he is the Weary Titan, or the good man struggling with adversity; anon he is the handsome and gallant leader of the nation, or the cultured and travelled patron of art and letters..."[21]

On 21 September 1931 the gold standard was suspended by the National Government and never reinstated. Britain had been impaled on it by Winston Churchill, who restored it on 28 April 1925 when Chancellor of the Exchequer and later accepted this was his greatest single mistake. The reaction of one Labour minister was "No one told us that we could do that", and in that plaintive comment about the gold standard there was a deeper reality. Labour had taken power too soon and it still lacked the experience and intellectual financial knowledge that a party needs to govern well and which takes time to acquire.

At the general election on 27 October 1931 Labour paid the price for their widely perceived incompetent handling of the financial crisis. Attlee just managed to hold on in Limehouse but with a greatly reduced majority. Greenwood lost in Nelson and Colne. Only 46 Labour MPs supported by five ILP members were elected against over 500 MPs who supported the 'National' Government. At the first meeting of the new Parliamentary Labour Party, ex-ministers like Arthur Henderson, Herbert Morrison and Arthur Greenwood, having lost, were not present. George Lansbury, who had been First Commissioner of Works in the Government for two years, a Christian Socialist and pacifist, was elected leader and Clement Attlee deputy leader. Lansbury was an early campaigner for a state-run national health service and votes for women but he was not the person to rebuild the shattered party. Attlee was beset by

---

20 Alan Bullock, *The Life and Times of Ernest Bevin: Trade Union Leader 1881–1940.* pp 256–257.
21 Francis Beckett, *Clem Attlee*, p 157.

money problems at this time and this was only relieved when Stafford Cripps, now an MP, donated £500 a year as an addition to his salary. In power terms, Cripps was too new as an MP to challenge Attlee. Attlee was now for the first time in Labour hierarchy ahead of Greenwood and it was a position he was never to relinquish. [22]

Somewhat surprisingly, Herbert Morrison, who lost his seat at Hackney South and was a potential challenger to Attlee, took time to recover his political ambition and did not put his name forward to even be a member of the National Executive Committee of the Labour Party in 1931. In 1932 Morrison took third place and first place in 1934, beating Attlee who was making his first appearance on the NEC as well as Hugh Dalton and Cripps. Even more surprising, Morrison was blocked from resuming as leader of London County Council by Lewis Silkin who people thought had been chosen "simply to keep the seat warm for Herbert". While 43 years old, Morrison had been the youngest Cabinet minister. His biographers identified his behaviour then as going some way to explain why he never later became leader of the Labour Party: "He regarded the leadership of the LCC as his ... When he was defeated, he became petulant. If rejected for the top job, he would accept no other. In 1932 he would not be deputy to Silkin, in 1935 he would not be deputy to Attlee, and in 1955 he would not be deputy to Gaitskell."[23] He did, however, agree to be deputy to Attlee from 1945 to 1955, becoming Lord President of the Council, co-ordinating the home front and Leader of the House of Commons, though he had lost the treasurership of the Labour Party to Greenwood in 1943. Nevertheless when Morrison did again become leader of the LCC in the spring of 1933 he continued to be a formidable organiser and effective administrator, though he did not return as an MP again for Hackney until the 1935 general election, leaving Attlee unchallenged. In that period Attlee quietly consolidated his position among Labour MPs as a hard-working and conscientious House of Commons man.

Herbert Morrison established Labour from the moment he

---

22 Greg Rosen, *Old Labour to New* (Politico's, 2005), pp 43–50.
23 Bernard Donoughue, G. W. Jones, *Herbert Morrison: Portrait of a Politician*, pp 180–183.

was elected to the LCC in 1922 as an independent political force in London. In the country he was crucial in demonstrating Labour was not one under the control of the far left. This triumph over the left was Morrison's enduring legacy. Unemployment was high in his borough of Hackney when he became Mayor in 1920 and Morrison immediately established a distress fund. It wasn't long however before militants started on direct action, fighting with the police and even stealing some borough council coal. Morrison disowned this action and wrote to Prime Minister Lloyd George on 4 December 1920 that he had set his face against disorder and illegality and that the great bulk of organised labour adhered to "democratic constitutionalism". This "fervour for constitutional behaviour brought him sharply into conflict with George Lansbury at Poplar. There the local Labour Party had decided, without consultation with the London Labour Party, that the local council should not levy rates for the precepts from the LCC and other local government bodies, as a protest against rising unemployment, the inadequacies of government action and the miserable scale of the relief."[24] Morrison's attitude to Lansbury was further strained in 1924 over excluding Communists from the London Labour Party [LLP] whereas Lansbury wanted no barrier against them at all.[25] In 1925 Morrison attacked Lansbury for disloyalty in still collaborating with Communists.

Arthur Greenwood, by contrast to Morrison, returned to the House of Commons through a by-election in April 1932 and patiently began to bring the skills he had learned in Cabinet to the parliamentary party. Then at the end of 1933 Lansbury fell and fractured his thigh. He spent the next eight months in hospital in constant pain and was temporarily replaced by Attlee for nine months. It was a reminder to all that a party leadership election was coming. Greenwood never wrote an autobiography and there is nothing but an unpublished, totally inadequate draft biography which is in the Bodleian Library.[26]

---

24 Bernard Donoughue, G. W. Jones, *Herbert Morrison: Portrait of a Politician* (Weidenfeld & Nicolson, 1973), p 47.
25 *Ibid*, p 100.
26 Written by Tom Moult who lived for a time in The Mill House, Finchingfield, Braintree, Essex. There is correspondence attached relating to this manuscript dated 31 January 1951 from Hutchinson & Co to Greenwood about how in May 1949 "we

It is hard to be sure, therefore, whether Greenwood really wanted the job of leader of the parliamentary party, or that of the Party National Secretary. He "most embodied the traditions of the party. A protégé of Henderson, he was a warm-hearted intellectual of modest political skills with wide support in the north of the country. He was also known to enjoy a few drinks."[27] Even then his drinking was probably becoming a factor in his failure to build up sufficient support within the parliamentary party in order to be able to defeat Attlee in 1935.

Greenwood was well aware already that Arthur Henderson, a friend, who had been National Secretary of the party since 1922, was thinking over whether to retire. Greenwood decided to stand if he did, but so did Morrison who tried and failed to win the support of Henderson himself. Dalton claimed in his diary in 1934 that Henderson, still reluctant to retire, was actually forced out by the NEC. Morrison looked the clear favourite, but Ernest Bevin along with some other trade unionists were reluctant for the Secretary to also be an MP, believing this put too much power into the hands of one person. Their call for 'one person, one job' was an important factor, not just Bevin's dislike of Morrison. It soon became clear that Greenwood was not prepared to give up being an MP and Morrison was unwilling to renounce his wish to enter Parliament as soon as possible. And yet the NEC came up with a compromise: the Secretary could be an MP, but the individual would have to resign the Secretaryship if they also decided to enter government as a minister. Bevin ensured that this compromise proposal was defeated at the conference winning only 841,000 votes against 1,449,000. When the vote was announced Morrison was described as "White, stiff-lipped

---

exchanged agreements for a volume of reminiscences to be written by yourself with the collaboration of Mr Thomas Moult" as the work had not reached them. It went on to say they had been forced to the conclusion: "In view of the very greatly changed conditions now prevailing, to cancel the agreement for the book by mutual consent." An assessment of the biography dated 14 May 1973 says "Large sections of this manuscript are clearly taken from AG's own writings (both published and unpublished)" but AG had only revised up to Chapter 12 which was called Blueprint for War and Peace. This was preceded by a note in AG's handwriting "haven't got any further." The note assessment continues "no case at all for recognising any copyright by TM."

27 Michael Jago, *Clement Attlee: The Inevitable Prime Minister* (Biteback, 2014), p 100.

and sick to the gills."[28] Bevin had outmanoeuvred him and George Middleton was elected National Secretary and wisely the post has never since been held by an ambitious politician.

In September 1935 the League of Nations met at Geneva and Sir Samuel Hoare, the Foreign Secretary since 7 June that year, declared Britain would stand firm supporting collective resistance to any aggression. On 25 September Mussolini ordered the Italian Army to enter Abyssinia from Italian Somaliland. It was the Hoare-Laval Pact, which he developed with the French Foreign Minister, detailing the partition of Ethiopian land (Abyssinia) that lead to widespread anger and Hoare's resignation on 19 December 1935. In October, the NEC at the Labour Party Conference in Brighton put down a resolution giving full support to the League. Stafford Cripps had resigned from Labour's National Executive on the eve of the conference and spoke from the floor against the resolution claiming that it risked committing Labour to supporting a "Capital-ist and imperialist war" and that sanctions might entail war. Whereas Dalton said of League of Nations sanctions: "A threat of sanctions may be enough to prevent war. If not, the actual use of sanctions, economic and financial, without any military or naval action, may be difficult to re-establish peace even if Mussolini breaks it ... Are we going to play a part of a great comrade among the nations, or are we going to slink impotently away into the shadows, impotent by our own choice; unfaithful to our solemn pledges, not a comrade but a Judas among the nations..."[29] Attlee, as deputy leader, spoke in favour. Lansbury, a Christian pacifist, made an emotional speech of his belief that "force never has and never will bring permanent peace and permanent goodwill in the world", stating that his disagreement with the official policy affected his leadership and he would raise this at the next meeting of the parliamentary party. "It may be that I shall not meet you on this platform any more."[30]

The conference ovation was warm, respecting his long-held pacifist

28 Bernard Donoughue, G. W. Jones, *Herbert Morrison: Portrait of a Politician*, p 234.
29 Greg Rosen, *Old Labour to New*, pp 91–111.
30 Chris Wrigley, John Shepherd, *On the Move: Essays in Labour and Transport History Presented to Philip Bagwell* (A & C Black, 1991), p 225.

views. This aroused the anger of Bevin who went to the rostrum and denounced Lansbury: "It is placing the Executive and the Labour movement in an absolutely wrong position to be hawking your conscience round from body to body asking to be told what you ought to do with it."[31] Morrison, summing up for the Executive, was however conciliatory, far too conciliatory for Bevin who saw what Morrison was after – namely gaining support from the left in any party leadership election which was obviously coming soon. While Morrison shook hands with Lansbury as he left the platform, saying, "Stand by your beliefs, George," and was well-received by conference, Bevin was left complaining, "I say all the nasty things, while others get the credit" considering there to be "too many namby-pambies about." When reproached for his brutality, he said "Lansbury has been going about dressed in saint's clothes for years waiting for martyrdom: I set fire to the faggots."[32]

The resolution was only able to collect 102,000 votes against 2,168,000. Stafford Cripps had been brought into government as Solicitor General by MacDonald at the end of 1930 with the traditional knighthood, but only became an MP in a by-election in Bristol East in January 1931, yet he managed to hold the seat nine months later. Dalton, who had eased his path into Parliament, called Cripps's spiral to the left as "an adolescent Marxist miasma"[33]. Attlee never really felt threatened by Cripps; he was content for him to be brought into the War Cabinet and made him Chancellor of the Exchequer when Dalton was forced to resign over the leak of Budget secrets in London's *Evening Standard*. Though irritated by some of his political stances, he was grateful for his financial support when he most needed it and regarded him as a "most warm-hearted and generous friend and a delightful companion."[34]

On 8 October the House of Commons returned and Labour's parliamentary party met to hear Lansbury say that the divisions over foreign policy were so great that he had to tender his resignation.

31 Roy Jenkins, *Mr. Attlee: An Interim Biography*, p 161.
32 Francis Williams, *Ernest Bevin: Portrait of a Great Englishman* (Hutchinson, 1952), p 196.
33 Ben Pimlott, *Hugh Dalton* (Jonathan Cape, 1985), pp 203–206.
34 Francis Beckett, *Clem Attlee*, p 161.

The question of who would replace him primarily oscillated in the press between Greenwood and Attlee. Roy Jenkins, who wrote an early biography of Attlee, summed up the differences between the two men: "Some sections of the press had put forward the claims of Arthur Greenwood to the leadership. Greenwood had been Minister of Health and a member of the second Labour Cabinet; as such he had been a more prominent member of the party than Attlee... He would have been a more colourful leader than Attlee, and at the time a figure better known to the ordinary elector. But at the meeting of the parliamentary party, the desire for some degree of continuity in the leadership combined with an appreciation of Attlee's proven ability in the House, were more weighty factors."[35] So Attlee became leader for the election campaign which within three weeks was well under way. He addressed 49 meetings, gave a broadcast address and appeared in news film. On 14 November Labour gained 102 seats, with 154 MPs up from the previous 52. It was a solid achievement in rebuilding the party after the disaster of 1931.

On 26 November the parliamentary party met at 11.30 in the Commons with Attlee in the chair. Greenwood was nominated first as leader of the Parliamentary Labour Party [PLP], then Attlee, and finally Morrison who was widely judged the favourite. Then an MP asked, "Would the candidates, if elected, give their full time to the job?"[36] This was a planted question, agreed surprisingly with Dalton, who was Morrison's campaign manager. Yet the question backfired and it was Morrison who was damaged by his own reply, as described by his biographers: the "gist was he put himself in the hands of the party. If they thought he should give up the leadership at County Hall, he would. If they thought some accommodation could be found, at least till the next LCC elections, he would fall in with that."[37] One MP shouted back at Morrison "It's not fair"; another "very slick". A mood was thereby established, not for the first or last time, that Morrison's methods were that of a machine

---

35 Roy Jenkins, *Mr. Attlee: An Interim Biography*, p 162.
36 Giles Radice, *The Tortoise and the Hares: Attlee, Bevin, Cripps, Dalton, Morrison* (Politico's, 2008), p 89.
37 Bernard Donoughue, G. W. Jones, *Herbert Morrison: Portrait of a Politician*, p 239.

politician and his fellow parliamentarians demanded more than this. Time and time again in discussing or analysing great historical events, the role of independent MPs and how they are assessed by their colleagues is underplayed. There has never been a successful Prime Minister, for example, who has not been able to 'take' the mood of the House of Commons. The House is a hard taskmaster; it does not like the too-clever-by-half member, nor the unfeeling and insensitive member, but it dislikes above all the contemptuous. This sophisticated electorate of MPs were well able to weigh each candidate up. The first ballot gave Attlee 58 votes, Morrison 44, Greenwood 33. The second ballot had Attlee with 88 and Morrison only 48. Greenwood then was elected deputy leader with Morrison declining to stand. In Dalton's language, the "non-entity" had won, and his verdict, recorded in his diary, was "A wretched, disheartening result! And a little mouse shall lead them."[38] History was to show the facile nature of this comment. Attlee was never a mouse; careful with his opinions, weighing his options, very frequently underrated, but decisive and tough when it came to the point of decision-making.

There were many reasons for Morrison's defeat, but it is likely that Greenwood had the bulk of the votes from the provincial MPs who had not been in the 1931–5 Parliament and which simply transferred to Attlee, having been put off by the Londoner Morrison's style and campaign. A fellow Labour MP, James Walker, captured Morrison's vulnerability in this satirical verse:

The man on whom the party leans,
Who never says just what he means,
Nor ever means just what he says,
As skilfully with words he plays.

In a letter of advice to incoming MPs, Morrison indirectly and unwisely attacked Greenwood by inference. "Parliament is almost the easiest place in which to become a chronic drinker ... A speech in the House becomes 'impossible' without a stimulant." There is

---

38 Hugh Dalton, *Memoirs: The Fateful Years, 1931–45* (Muller, 1957), p 82.

little doubt that Greenwood's known liking for alcohol had affected his vote. Without much evidence to support it, the signs are that thereafter Greenwood accepted that he would never stand again against Attlee. Some believed that Greenwood showed some interest in the summer of 1939, but Dalton's biographer only describes it as "The Greenwood campaign – if such there had been – was not mentioned."[39] Greenwood's "regular drunkenness had now become firmly established" according to his Oxford Dictionary National Biography [ODNB] "and many of his afternoons must have been unproductive." An NEC inquiry into the research department of the Labour Party, which he continued to run, found in a report dated June 1938 that it was "not, either administratively or psychologically, in a happy condition".[40] It was arranged Greenwood would no longer supervise detailed work and he was left with liaison function in the PLP. This might have been the shock he needed, or perhaps it was the gravity of the growing threat from Germany, as Greenwood seemed, from the little evidence around, to have been able to constrain his drinking from 1938–40. Drink was what led to Asquith's downfall,[41] George Brown's failure to beat Harold Wilson for the Labour leadership in 1963 owed something to drink,[42] and President Nixon's ousting over Watergate was, by the end, a resignation of a man too drunk too often to control the nuclear button.[43] Politicians appear to be particularly vulnerable.

Greenwood was loyal to Attlee, but he was no placeman. He was a real deputy not just a title, and in combination they provided effective leadership. There were many international challenges to the Labour Party as the official opposition in the run up to World War II. Attlee formed a Defence Committee in the 1935 Parliament with the purpose of building up a group of Labour MPs with real knowledge of defence and even began to write in the *Army, Navy and Air Force Gazette*. Attlee said in the Commons in February 1936, "Whatever arms are required, they must be for the League Policy and the

---

39 Ben Pimlott, *Hugh Dalton*, p 265.
40 Report as an appendix to the NEC minutes of 22 June 1938.
41 David Owen, *In Sickness and In Power* (Methuen, 2011).
42 Philip Ziegler, *Wilson* (Weidenfeld & Nicolson, 1993), p 151, 171.
43 David Owen, *In Sickness and In Power*.

first condition for any assent to more arms is that the Government shall be following a League Policy."[44]

In March 1936 German troops marched into the demilitarised Rhineland zone. Then, in June, sanctions were lifted that had been applied against Italy. Attlee asserted that the Government had killed the League of Nations and by July the Spanish Civil War was under way and the Government's equivocation over General Franco had begun, though Labour's policy of non-intervention was not much better, though somewhat inhibited by the stance of the French Socialist Prime Minister Léon Blum, whom Attlee admired, first in office 1931–1932, then for the second time June 1935–1936. At the end of 1937 Attlee travelled to Spain and visited the front line, inspecting the British Battalion of the International Brigade. He later accused the British Government of being "an accessory to the attempts to murder democracy in Spain".[45]

Rearmament became a huge issue and Labour's position in the summer of 1937 was defined by Attlee. "The Labour Party, therefore, has steadily opposed the rearmament policy of the Government, not on the grounds that the level of armaments of two years ago is adequate, or even that the present level is excessive, but because it is impossible to tell what the scale of armaments should be in the absence of any sound foreign policy."[46] Attlee and Greenwood were slowly, and at a pace the party as a whole could accept, but determinedly shedding from Labour any association with pacifism. Both men knew that a fight was coming with Germany. Hugh Dalton, who spoke for the party on foreign policy, was much firmer in public on defence issues. In July 1936 he had failed by a wide margin to persuade the Labour MPs to abstain on the Service Estimates and the PLP voted, as usual, against. In 1937 Dalton "canvassed hard amongst MPs urging that an abstention would greatly strengthen his hand in debate".[47] However he was met with resistance from a group led by Greenwood, yet Dalton had the support of Transport House, the

---

44 HC, Hansard, *Parliamentary Debates: Official Report, 1936,* vol. 309, p iv.
45 Zara Steiner, *The Triumph of the Dark: European International History 1933–1939* (Oxford University Press, 2011), p 221.
46 Roy Jenkins, *Mr Attlee: An Interim Biography*, p 184.
47 Ben Pimlott, *Hugh Dalton*, p 243.

party HQ, and the unions. Greenwood was supported by Attlee and Morrison. Dalton won the PLP vote 45–39 and it was a crucial step in Labour becoming fit to govern in a coalition.

Attlee had made a mistake in a broadcast on the Government's 1937 Budget that they had put "guns before butter". His mistakes, however, were rare. He was the quintessential political 'safe pair of hands' and on rearmament he was quick to readjust his position. In March 1937 Bevin had told the executive council of the TGWU, "I cannot see any way of stopping Hitler and the other dictators except by force."[48]

The new, adjusted Labour position was reinforced by the National Council of Labour, which under Bevin and Dalton's chairmanship produced a restatement of Labour views as supported at the 1937 Labour Party conference by a solid vote. The paper entitled 'International Policy and Defence' said bluntly, "In consequence of these events the League of Nations, for the time being, has been rendered ineffective ... and commands little confidence, largely owing to lack of British leadership ... A Labour Government will unhesitatingly maintain such armed forces as are necessary to defend our country and to fulfil our obligations as a member of the British Commonwealth and of the League of Nations..."[49] The conference statement, however, only said "must be strongly equipped to defend this country ... and would therefore be unable to revise the present programme of rearmament."[50]

In March 1938, when Hitler ordered his forces into Austria, Attlee and Greenwood were with Churchill and Eden in criticising the Government and strongly against appeasement. The wartime coalition could be said to have been formed at this time. Attlee and Greenwood saw Chamberlain to warn him about Hitler's aims in Eastern Europe.

Greenwood and Attlee had to be sensitive to the danger of the party splitting in Parliament and in the country over defence. But after Munich, over Czechoslovakia the Labour Party proved

---

48 Alan Bullock, *Ernest Bevin: A Biography* (Politico's, 2002), p 217.
49 *Ibid.*
50 *Ibid.*

themselves to be a governing force. When Attlee spoke in the House of Commons on defence, dissent was now minimal and the whole Labour movement could be truly said to be behind him. "It is a tremendous victory for Herr Hitler," Attlee said, "without firing a shot, by the mere display of military force, he has achieved a dominating position in Europe which Germany failed to win after four years of war ... He has destroyed the last fortress of democracy in Eastern Europe which stood in the way of his ambitions."[51]

Yet that transformation was challenged when on 13 January 1939 Stafford Cripps proposed to the Labour Executive Committee a campaign for Popular Front to include individuals from other parties, including Communist Harry Pollitt. The campaign differed significantly from the Unity campaigns and Attlee never doubted Cripps's behaviour was a serious threat to all he had done to build a credible party up since 1931 – the party as a whole agreed with him. On being rejected by the Executive Committee, Cripps proceeded to circulate his memorandum to local parties. Summoned to the Executive on 18 January, Cripps failed to appear. On 25 January Cripps was asked to reaffirm his allegiance to the Labour Party and its constitution; he refused and was expelled. Despite Attlee's friendship, exasperated though he was at times with Cripps, he fully supported the National Executive's decision to expel him, along with Aneurin Bevan and five others from the party. Writing in the *Daily Herald* in February, Attlee was unequivocal: "It is assumed that a majority can be obtained by Labour allying itself with Liberals, Communists ... I believe that any alliance with the Communists would be electorally disastrous ... In 1939 as in 1931 I reply to those who ask me to change my faith because times are difficult that socialism is not a fancy fair-weather creed but a faith."

Attlee, since Labour's special conference in Southport at the end of May 1939, had been in severe pain from his bladder due to an enlarged prostate. He used to refer to it as his 'hydraulics' problem and in June he needed to have a prostatectomy operation in the London Clinic. While convalescing with his family, criticism of his absence and of him personally was triggered by Ellen Wilkinson espousing the case

---

51 Robert Pearce, *Attlee* (Routledge, 2014), p 83.

for Herbert Morrison replacing Attlee as leader. She wrote about Attlee on 4 June in, of all places, the *Sunday Referee* – a paper full of gossip about film stars. "I wonder what Mr Chamberlain would think if he were informed that in future he would have to face daily a Herbert Morrison, that superb political organiser." But then the potential challenge became more serious with the *Daily Herald*, a newspaper funded by the trade unions, hinting at the case for a change of leaders: "Can the Labour Movement bring to the political scene during the next few months before the general election the vigorous urge which will rouse the nation". Dalton recorded in his diary at the time that, according to Sidney Webb, "Greenwood's state of mind was (a) that he is tempted by the leadership, particularly if the international situation got bad, but that (b) he could not bear to serve under anyone else, except to continue under Attlee". Dalton however was becoming increasingly convinced of a scandal relating to the Masonic Lodge in the House of Commons, of which a number of Labour MPs were members, including the deputy leader, Greenwood, alleging that members of the group were backing the deputy for leadership. Greenwood stepped into the row, believing that this challenge should not be left to hang in the air and on 14 June at the Parliamentary Party meeting, Greenwood, sensing that war was imminent, judged correctly that it was necessary to force a vote of confidence in Attlee and raised "with regret" Ellen Wilkinson's criticisms of Attlee. This was done, and with only Ellen Wilkinson abstaining, Manny Shinwell's motion expressing confidence in Attlee was given full support.

Five months later a clumsy attempt to remove Attlee was made by Alfred Edwards, the Labour MP for Middlesborough East, nominating Morrison, Greenwood and Dalton at a PLP meeting on 15 November.[52] Attlee stated that he would not resent or regard as disloyal nominations for leader. Yet, Greenwood rose and declined his nomination, saying, according to Dalton's account, "it would encourage Hitler, if we now had a contest for the leadership".[53] Morrison too declined, reading aloud a letter he had sent to Edwards reluctantly

52 Ben Pimlott, *Hugh Dalton*, pp 265–6.
53 Hugh Dalton, *The Fateful Years, 1931–1945*, p 281.

deciding not to stand; it would be neither kind nor generous given that Attlee's health was still recovering. Dalton then, too, turned down his nomination, adding that Attlee had made it clear from the Chair that if in the future the party desired a leadership contest, no resentment would be felt. Nevertheless, it was extraordinary that with the country at war such an attempt could have been launched.[54]

The leadership issue was now settled, ensuring that for the next critical five months Attlee and Greenwood had the unquestioned support of the Labour Party in the country as well as in Parliament. Such uncontested support was necessary to help create the wartime coalition government that stayed in power from 1940–1945 and paved the way for ensuring that a credible Labour Party won a massive victory in the general election of 1945.

Years later Attlee would sum up this particular short-lived leadership fracas succinctly and, I believe, accurately. "Dalton wouldn't have backed Morrison. Morrison wouldn't have backed Cripps, and Cripps wouldn't have backed Dalton. The Parliamentary Labour Party wouldn't have let Greenwood go and Greenwood was loyal to me."[55] It is also worth reflecting on the answer Attlee gave on 17 September 1965, two years before his death, which shows, perhaps surprisingly, that he did not claim being Prime Minister from 1945–51 as his greatest achievement.

> Question: What would you say yourself was your biggest single achievement?
> Attlee: Taking the Labour Party into coalition for the war and bringing them out without losing anybody.[56]

It says much for Greenwood that he stood in for Attlee to such considerable effect in 1939. Yet he would not have been so effective if Attlee had not trusted him and given him scope to decide day to day on current issues without constant back-seat driving either from a hospital bed or convalescence.

---

54 Hugh Dalton, *The Fateful Years, 1931–194*, p 281.
55 Francis Beckett, *Clem Attlee*, p 217.
56 Clem Attlee, The Granada Historical Records Interview (Panther 1967), p 54.

Immediately after his speech to the Commons in the 2 September 1939 debate, Greenwood went to see Chamberlain in his room behind the Speaker's chair. Unless the inevitable decision was taken before reassembling, Greenwood said, "neither you nor I nor anyone else on the earth will be able to hold the House of Commons."[57] Greenwood was telephoned at home on Sunday to say the Cabinet would meet at 11.00 am. On Monday 4 September he saw the Prime Minister who was about to go on the BBC to announce that the country was at war. Greenwood made a broadcast after the one o'clock news.

On 7 September, though Winston Churchill had joined the Government as First Lord of the Admiralty in a flourish of publicity, the newspapers were still being effusive about Greenwood, the new Labour political star in their midst. The *Daily Mail,* no natural supporter, wrote how it had been so "very fortunate for the country that Greenwood had stepped into the breach caused by Mr Attlee's illness. But for the latter's absence, while sick, we might never have discovered what a statesman Mr Greenwood has become and how admirably he can explain Labour's viewpoint to the world." The *Daily Telegraph* wrote "Handicapped as he was by the rules of order, Mr Greenwood won admiration for the skill with which he made a short speech disguised as a series of questions." Greenwood went on to suggest that, in future, statements should be made on a motion for the adjournment of the House so as to allow for a full debate. This procedure was adopted and later used on 7 May 1940 creating the debate that actually led to Chamberlain's downfall – an outcome Greenwood had long wanted and which is described in Chapter 2. The *Daily Herald* on 20 September referred to Labour's "enhanced effectiveness … admitted on all sides to be due in no small measure to the spirited and statesmanlike way in which Arthur Greenwood has led the Labour Party in recent weeks. He has emerged with a personal authority which extends far beyond the boundaries of the Labour Party and has surprised even some of his closest friends with unexpected reserves of strength and integrity."

---

57 Zara Steiner, *The Triumph of the Dark: European International History 1933–1939,* p iv.

Greenwood's drinking problems had been absent or well controlled during the build-up to this crisis and this had an undoubted effect on his overall performance. In his book on Churchill, Roy Jenkins writes of Greenwood "He had as great a propensity to alcohol as Churchill himself, but he held it less well. He did not make an exhibition of himself, but alcohol did not energise him as it did Churchill. He was more of a soak than a drunk. He also had a somewhat diffuse mind which was accentuated by Prime Ministers, first Churchill in 1940 and then Attlee in 1945, giving him posts of high prestige but little hard content."[58] The illness at the end of 1939 that temporarily kept him out of speaking does not appear from sketchy accounts to have been related to drink. Despite all the praise heaped upon him, the evidence points to him never allowing it to go to his head or to change his support for Attlee. It is to the credit of both men that they built such a relationship in the torrid atmosphere of party politics and, by doing so, transformed the Labour Party.

Roy Jenkins wrote in 1948 an authoritative account of one of the crucial political decisions of 1939, with excellent access to Attlee in great part because Roy's father, Arthur Jenkins, was a Labour MP and Attlee's parliamentary private secretary. "In the first few days of the war", wrote Jenkins, "the Prime Minister had made overtures to Greenwood for the inclusion of Labour representatives in the Cabinet. These had been communicated to Attlee in North Wales and he had been in full agreement with Greenwood's refusal to join under Chamberlain. The Labour members were wisely determined not to become junior partners in a weak Government, but to maintain their strength intact for a time when they could throw it more decisively into the political balance."[59]

Attlee was back in the Commons on a regular basis from 26 September and at the end of the month spoke out strongly against the consideration of any peace proposals from Berlin. Addressing a Labour Party 'Peace Aims' conference, he stressed that there must be a "fight to the finish" until the Nazis were removed from power in

---

58 Roy Jenkins, *Churchill: A Biography* (Pan Macmillan, 2012).
59 Roy Jenkins, *Mr Attlee: An Interim Biography*, p 211.

Germany and that such action was an essential pre-requisite to any Socialist reconstruction. That position he maintained consistently[60] and it was later reflected in particular in the 25–28 May 1940 War Cabinet meetings which are published in full in Chapter 4 and discussed in Chapter 5.

On 28 September 1939 Greenwood wrote to the *Daily Herald,* which as a newspaper with Labour leanings he frequently used as a vehicle for his views, on what became a persistent theme of his: that though not formally part of the coalition "Labour must be in on the ground floor". Stressing that organised Labour must be considered from the beginning, not merely because the question of Labour supply was involved, but because organised Labour had a contribution to make to the wider aspects of the question, an offering of experience which in wartime, and indeed in peacetime, could not be ignored. On 16 October he was critical of the Government saying "Lethargy and excessive caution must be replaced by vigour and courage." On 6 November "This is not the Government's war it is the people's war."

On 18 November Greenwood's doctor said there must be no more speeches until the end of the year because of prolonged work and overstrain but, nevertheless, he spoke in the Commons on 5 December saying, "Why do we fight Labour's cause." On 15 January 1940 Greenwood was hammering home his underlying message to party supporters, "Get this thought. We will never be yes-men." Greenwood was anxious that by supporting the Conservative Government Labour would lose its identity, a potential consequence at times of war when winning on the battlefield was the overriding priority. He had been disillusioned by the spirit of the trenches in 1914–18 not lasting into the 1920s and '30s. He went on to explain the spirit behind a recent decision to co-operate over any individual constituency by-elections. "Political truce no! A by-election pact yes." On 10 March he told his Yorkshire constituents in Wakefield, "Labour would support every step to secure the successful prosecution of the war, but would continue to criticise inefficiency, wavering and the lack of forethought." He knew, however, the time was coming when

---

60 *Ibid,* p 212.

there would have to be a formal coalition, but he wanted it to be on, if not equal terms, honourable terms.

It happens from time to time in the hothouse atmosphere surrounding Westminster that new stars emerge. But this is most often only temporarily established and a particular speech is soon forgotten in the reporting of Parliament. What was unusual about Greenwood's speech was that he continued to 'speak for England' and that it became the public's lasting memory of him. When he died on 9 June 1954, an obituary in the *Daily Mail* wrote about the "peak of his achievement, his shining hour, in the period when Britain was poised upon the brink of the last war, Attlee was ill, and it fell to Greenwood to lead his party in those tense and historic sittings in the House of Commons. In a situation charged with anxiety, and changing almost hourly, he made speeches, marshalled at the spur of the moment, which deserve to rank as parliamentary classics. He was inspired by the urgency of the moment to a performance altogether beyond his usual style and power." The writer concluded that though he never touched the same heights again "his voice in those days established its right to a place among the memorable voices of Britain."

Greenwood continued to be, after Attlee, an important Labour figure, though less powerful than his former rivals Bevin, Morrison, Dalton and even Bevan who was one of the few MPs opposing the Government in the House of Commons throughout the war. After Attlee, Ernest Bevin, through 1940, first in the Cabinet and later the War Cabinet as Minister of Labour, was the most powerful Labour politician. As so often in politics it was pure chance that Attlee's illness gave Greenwood the opportunity to speak in September 1939, but politics is about taking one's chances when they arrive. Greenwood capitalised on them and was still contributing when his moment in the spotlight diminished in 1942, though his wisdom and experience still had value to the Labour Party for a decade to come.

2

In the Name of God, Go!

When Neville Chamberlain took over from Baldwin as Prime Minister, on 28 May 1937, public opinion responded with some enthusiasm. He was initially a vigorous and active Prime Minister though already sixty-eight years old. Chamberlain's five and a half years' tenure as Chancellor of the Exchequer, some commentators believed, had been the most successful since Gladstone had been at the Treasury. Chamberlain was seen as competent, decisive, and at ease with figures from his experience in the manufacturing industry in Birmingham. Herbert Samuel, the Liberal leader, had, however, detected a ruthless streak in Chamberlain's character that was to become much more evident in No. 10: "What he says goes. When he puts his foot down and says something must be done, that decision settles it."[1] Halifax replaced MacDonald as Lord President of the Council. Halifax "greatly admired" Chamberlain, according to his biographer Andrew Roberts, though he would never develop as personal a relationship with Chamberlain as he had with Baldwin.

On Friday 18 February 1938 a serious rift had developed between Eden and Chamberlain over the projected Anglo-Italian Agreement. On 20 February Eden resigned. Chamberlain and Eden had had a serious row earlier in November when No. 10 briefed the press over the Berlin visit against Eden's advice; Chamberlain, by way of response, told him dismissively to go home and take an aspirin. Some put the level of Chamberlain's interference down to the age difference between the two, but 40 years later, when the age difference of Prime Minister Callaghan and the Foreign Secretary

---

1 Robert Self, *Neville Chamberlain: A Biography* (Ashgate, 2006), p 256.

was similar, there was no such interference. Halifax, after a five-day wait, was appointed the new Foreign Secretary. Churchill described Halifax as "a man to bear this burden ... although I differ from his views". Morrison denounced him as "a weakling who will merely be the servile instrument of an ignorant and reckless Prime Minister".[2] This was odd to say the least considering the way Morrison wooed Halifax in early May 1939 and seemed, at times, to favour Halifax over Churchill.

Despite their later differences, Churchill did not initially turn his fire on Chamberlain. When Anthony Eden resigned as Foreign Secretary, having widened his protest to include Chamberlain's policy of appeasement, Churchill was quick to indicate in the House of Commons support of Chamberlain's policy, and told the Chief Whip, David Margesson, on 17 March that the Prime Minister's point of view and his were not divergent.[3] Why did Churchill respond like this? It is hard to escape the conclusion that he did not want to unduly boost Eden to the extent that the latter might displace him as the most powerful backbench Conservative critic of appeasement. When assessing Churchill's image, it is a significant fact that he was the relentless and ever-watchful hawk in all debates concerning what to do about Hitler. Halifax had visited Hitler with the full support of the then Foreign Secretary Anthony Eden, on 18–19 November 1937. It signalled, according to Roberts, the high watermark of Halifax's personal appeasement. "Hitler took Halifax in both personally and politically", albeit Halifax initially mistook Hitler for a footman and was saved by the prompt of 'Der Führer! Der Führer!'[4]

Following Eden's resignation, according to Gallup, only 26 per cent favoured Chamberlain's foreign policy and 71 per cent thought Eden had been right to resign. Yet, by March, Gallup showed only 33 per cent wanted to express support for Czechoslovakia in the event of German aggression and 43 per cent opposed support in line with Chamberlain's policy. Eden's resignation, therefore, never became the parliamentary rallying point to remove Chamberlain, in part

---

2 Andrew Roberts, *The Holy Fox: The Life of Lord Halifax* (Head of Zeus, 2014), p 85.
3 David Dutton, *Neville Chamberlain* (Arnold, 2001), p 112.
4 Andrew Roberts, *The Holy Fox*.

because of Churchill's attitude, but most likely owing to the movement in public opinion.

Chamberlain's personal diplomacy during two weeks in September 1938 was disastrous and Munich still reverberates in history. 'More dangerous still was the idealism (and hubris) of a politician who believed he could bring peace to Europe.'[5] The Mass-Observation organisation sampled opinion on 15 September 1938, the day Chamberlain flew to Germany for the first time, and reported a 'sensational swing' of opinion in the Prime Minister's favour. No British Prime Minister had been to Germany since Disraeli attended the Congress of Berlin in 1878.

Chamberlain said of Hitler on 17 September that "when he had included the Sudeten Germans in the Reich he would be satisfied".[6] As Roberts described him, "Here was the hubris required by all the best tragedies before any eventual nemesis."[7]

Chamberlain revealed in a letter to his sisters written on 19 September that President Woodrow Wilson had heard that Hitler was impressed by him and continued that Hitler was a man "with whom I can do business". He also claimed: "I am the most popular man in Germany!"[8]

Yet by 22 September, when Chamberlain flew again to Bad Godesberg, opinion was hardening against further concessions and protestors booed as he flew off. On his return war seemed imminent and public opinion grew fearful. On 24 September the Foreign Office's senior diplomat, Alec Cadogan, noted in his diary about his boss, Lord Halifax (whom he abbreviates to H): "Still more horrified to find PM has hypnotised H who capitulates totally ... I gave H a note of what I thought, but it had no effect ... Cabinet at 5.30 and H got back at 8.00 completely and quite happily défaitiste – pacifist."[9] But Cadogan's bluntness did have its effect. Halifax changed his

---

5 David Reynolds, *Summits: Six Meetings That Shaped the Twentieth Century* (Allen Lane, 2007), p 91.

6 CAB 23/95 39 (38).

7 Andrew Roberts, *The Holy Fox*, p 111.

8 Neville Chamberlain, *The Neville Chamberlain Diary Letters: The Downing Street Years 1934–40*. Ed Robert C Self (Routledge, 2005), pp 348–9.

9 Andrew Roberts, *The Holy Fox*, p 115.

mind after their discussion and a night of restlessness. He told the Cabinet the next morning, 25 September, that "So long as Nazism lasted, peace would be uncertain. For this reason he did not feel that it would be right to put pressure on Czechoslovakia to accept ... he imagined that France would join in and if the French went in we should join them".[10]

Chamberlain sent Halifax a pencilled note: "Your complete change of view since I saw you last night is a horrible blow to me, but of course you must form your opinions for yourself ... If they [the French] say they will go in, thereby dragging us in, I do not think I could accept responsibility for the decision." Halifax replied: "I feel a brute – but I lay awake most of the night, tormenting myself." Chamberlain retorted tersely: "Night conclusions are seldom taken in the right perspective."[11]

Hitler responded positively on 28 September 1938 to holding a meeting in Munich. The House of Commons celebrated when the Prime Minister confirmed he would go the next day and that Mussolini and the French Prime Minister Daladier were involved as well. Members stood, cheered and waved their order papers. In the public galleries, against the rules, people clapped. When Chamberlain returned from Munich on the 29th it took the Prime Minister's car an hour and a half to drive from Heston Airport to Downing Street. During this time, according to Roberts, Halifax – who was with the Prime Minister in the car – performed the function of the slave in ancient Rome, who constantly whispered in the victorious general's ear reminders of his mortality in the hope of curbing his hubris. Chamberlain's public waving of the piece of paper carrying his and Hitler's signature was ill-advised, as was the invitation by the new king, George VI, for Chamberlain to appear with him on the balcony of Buckingham Palace where thousands of people cheered below. Yet most newspapers were overwhelmingly supportive.

Chamberlain was self-satisfied and exhausted though not depressed the day after his heady return to Heston Airport. He admitted to his sisters that he had come nearer to a nervous breakdown 'than I have

---

10 *Ibid*, pp 117–18.
11 Andrew Roberts, *The Holy Fox*, p 115, 117, 118.

ever been in my life'.[12] His mood was exultant and he had, as I argue in my book *In Sickness and In Power*, acquired Hubris Syndrome. He believed he had been successful in ending the prospect of war and having acted throughout with a small inner Cabinet marginalising any anti-opinion in the full Cabinet.

Chamberlain for a short time became a man of destiny. In the House of Commons, on 5 October 1938, Churchill however unleashed his full invective, calling the Munich settlement "a total and unmitigated defeat", and his relations with Halifax deteriorated as the policies of appeasement were progressively discredited.[13]After ambushing Chamberlain in Cabinet on the morning of 25 September, Halifax had progressively hardened his position, even when Hitler softened the arrangements at Munich which he had previously demanded in Bad Godesburg. The Kristallnacht pogrom on the night of 9–10 November, which saw Jewish shops smashed and much bloodshed, shocked the public and revolted Halifax. Although in a letter to a friend in 1952 he admitted he had "always been rather anti-Semitic", the events of Kristallnacht completed his "about face on appeasement". At the meeting of the Committee of Imperial Defence on 26 January 1939, Halifax advocated "tripling the British Expeditionary Force, doubling the Territorials and instituting immediate wide-ranging Staff talks and full military conscription".[14] Chamberlain and John Simon, the Chancellor of the Exchequer, opposed these measures. Not only were they worried about the financial implications of such policies, but, as Roberts points out, "they saw Staff talks as symptomatic of the pre-1914 mood that they were trying at all costs to avoid".

Halifax continued for the rest of the year to identify Nazism as the problem and argue for a tougher stance. He accompanied Chamberlain to Paris in late November; Chamberlain saw it as giving "the French people an opportunity of pouring out their pent up feelings of gratitude and affection towards him" in a letter to his sister dated 27 November.[15] By this stage Halifax was no longer a major appeaser,

12 David Reynolds, *Summits*, p 91.
13 Geoffrey Best, *Churchill and War* (A & C Black, 2006), p 104.
14 Andrew Roberts, *The Holy Fox*, p 128.
15 Zara Steiner, *The Triumph of the Dark: European International History 1933–1939* (Oxford University Press, 2011), p vii.

perhaps not even an appeaser, but there was something missing in his diplomacy rather like Grey in 1912.[16] He continued private meetings with Germans during the summer of 1939 but there was no steely Machiavellian purpose and the same was revealed over the more realistic option of moving to involve Russia to bolster the defence of Poland. There is something about both Grey and Halifax detectable in those who inherit power rather than struggle for the right to wield power.

The differences of opinion between Prime Minister and Foreign Secretary, evermore clear to the Cabinet, had perhaps one beneficial effect: it made it easier for Chamberlain after his resignation as Prime Minister in May 1940, and thereafter as a member of the War Cabinet, to distance himself from Halifax; he was no longer bound in "hoops of steel" in his friendship.

Exhaustion and stress were taking their toll on Chamberlain by March 1939 when R. A. Butler, usually known as 'Rab'– then a minister in the Foreign Office, but who later became Chancellor of the Exchequer under Harold Macmillan – on learning that the Italians had invaded Albania, went over to No. 10 to inform the Prime Minister. Chamberlain was at the open window of his study feeding seed to the birds, and was rather annoyed at Butler's arrival. He expressed amazement at Butler's distress at the news, saying: "I feel sure Mussolini has decided not to go against us."[17] Butler's warnings about the obvious threat to the Balkans was dismissed with a swift assertion of: "Don't be silly. Go home and go to bed", before continuing to feed the birds.[18] The capacity for self-delusion is the most worrying aspect of this story, and the fact that it was recorded by Butler, a politician who supported Munich and appeasement, renders the testimony all the more convincing. And yet it was to become increasingly apparent that Chamberlain was never going to be easy to remove and that he would have to be forced out of No. 10 by Parliament and his colleagues.

---

16 David Owen, *The Hidden Perspective: The Military Conversations 1906–1914* (Haus Publishing, 2014), pp 212–13.

17 William Manchester, *The Last Lion: Winston Spencer Churchill: Alone* (Dell, 1989), p 419.

18 William Manchester, *The Caged Lion: Winston Spencer Churchill, 1932–1940* (Michael Joseph, 1988), p 421.

Chamberlain's removal was not going to be the result of opinion polls, nor the growing criticism in the press or the rumble of dissatisfaction from the armed forces. Though these were all factors, it was the large Conservative majority in the House of Commons that buttressed Chamberlain that needed to be eroded.

It became obvious very soon after Chamberlain's reshuffle of the Government in September 1939 that his removal could only be achieved by the House of Commons as a whole, requiring MPs from all parties to come together in a unified decision. In this sense, Attlee and Greenwood became essential for the project to succeed, their refusal to act prematurely over forming a coalition was the instrument for the eventual overthrow. In an adversarial chamber where party discipline is enforced by the respective party Whips, cross-party action is not easy. But these were not normal times and, fortunately, there were a significant number of independent, principled and brave MPs across the political spectrum ready and willing to organise to remove Chamberlain after war was declared in September against Germany.

There were many factors that facilitated the creation of the cross-party political climate that allowed these groupings to flourish. The change of atmosphere was palpable shortly after Chamberlain's Munich visit in September 1938. On 3 April 1939 Churchill had noted in the House of Commons that Labour had proposed that "the attitude of His Majesty's Government towards Russia" be summed up in the phrase "The maximum co-operation possible". Churchill thought that this was "a very accurate and convenient phrase". He went on to ask, "Why should we expect Soviet Russia to be willing to work with us? No one can say that there is not a solid identity of interest between the Western democracies and Soviet Russia, and we must do nothing to obstruct the natural play of that identity of interest ... The wisest course was to forget the Bolshevik past and forge Britain, France, and Russia in a Triple Alliance..."[19] The Labour Party was thus in agreement with Churchill and his Conservative allies. It was, by any standard, a major new direction for the foreign policy of the country and was not just a vehicle for solidifying Labour's

---

19 HC, Hansard, *Parliamentary Debates: Official Report,*1938, vol. 345.

domestic political criticisms of the Chamberlain Government, but a geographically-based realignment that made sense and in which there was a window of opportunity.

The Russian Ambassador, Ivan Maisky, was in the gallery to hear Churchill speak. Prior to this, on 18 March, the Soviet Commissar for Foreign Affairs, Maxim Litvinov, three days after the destruction of Czechoslovakia, making his first attempt at rapprochement, had proposed an immediate conference in Bucharest, inviting Russia, Romania, Poland, Britain, France and Turkey, to form a "peace front" against an expanding Germany. Litvinov proposed a Soviet alliance with Britain and France, with the hope of expanding the alliance to powers under threat in the East, in order to cull further German advancement. The Quai d'Orsay made no response and the Foreign Office told the Russians that it was "not acceptable". On 19 March, Maisky called in at the Foreign Office to ask why such a proposal was not acceptable. Halifax made the excuse that no minister was available to go to Bucharest. On 23 March Chamberlain said the Government took a dim view of establishing "opposing blocs". In Chamberlain's mind Bolsheviks, not Nazis, were still the greater threat to Western civilisation.

On the 27 March at the Foreign Policy Committee Halifax, swayed by Poland's valuable military force of fifty divisions and feeling that Britain had to choose between Poland and Russia, chose Poland: "We were faced with a dilemma of doing nothing or entering into a devastating war. If we did nothing this in itself would mean a great accession to Germany's strength."[20] Halifax became the driving force behind the Polish Guarantee, which committed Britain to protecting Poland from any attack on her independence. Formally offered on 31 March 1939, Chamberlain told Parliament on this day that in the event of an attack on Poland, "His Majesty's Government would feel themselves bound at once to lend the Polish Government all support in their power."[21] Designed to act as "an assurance against forcible aggression", if successful in its intention there would be no

---

20 Sidney Aster, *1939: The Making of the Second World War* (Simon and Schuster, 1974), p 94.
21 Andrew Roberts, *The Holy Fox*, p 145.

need to carry out the guarantee at all.[22] His biographer, Roberts, put his finger on the weakness of Halifax's position: "One of the major accusations levelled at Halifax for concluding a Polish Guarantee without a concomitant understanding with Russia was that it tied London's hands whilst freeing Moscow's. Stalin was left secure in the knowledge that a German attack in the East meant help from the West. A German attack in the East however, was a war from which he [Stalin] could stand aside."[23] Another, different criticism came from Rab Butler inside the Foreign Office, who believed that the original joint British-French guarantee to Poland back in March had relieved Russia of any real anxiety about Germany's designs on her own frontier. That guarantee was, he believed, the result in the Foreign Office "of the shame engendered in some breasts by Munich". Halifax should have offered no guarantee to Poland unless they and Romania enter into the association offered by Russia. It was in this moment that Halifax's new-found recognition that Hitler was the menace floundered.

On 13 April Churchill argued again for an approach to the Kremlin:

I tried to show the House the great interest that Russia has against further Eastward expansion of the Nazi power. It is upon that deep, natural, legitimate interest that we must rely, and I am sure we shall hear from the Government that the steps they are taking are those which will enable us to receive the fullest possible co-operation from Russia, and that no prejudices on the part of England or France will be allowed to interfere with the closest co-operation between the two countries.[24]

On 15 April, the Soviet Government received formal proposals from Whitehall and the Quai d'Orsay. Britain asked Russia to follow the British example and affirm the independence of Poland and Romania. The French had proposed that Britain, France and

---

22 HC, Hansard, *Parliamentary Debates: Official Report,*1939, vol. 347.
23 Andrew Roberts, *The Holy Fox.*
24 HC, Hansard, 13 April 1939.

the Soviet Union should come to one another's aid should Germany wage war on any one of them. Chamberlain and Halifax were not prepared to spell this out. Litvinov presented a draft agreement to Britain and France. Russia would not only provide mutual assistance if either country were attacked by Hitler, the treaty would be backed by a specific commitment defining the strength and objectives of their armies, navies, and air forces. Poland was at liberty to join if she chose. The signatories would "render mutually all manner of assistance, including that of a military nature, in case of aggression in Europe" against any member of the alliance or against "Eastern European states situated between the Baltic and Black Seas and bordering on the USSR".[25] Signatories would neither negotiate nor make peace "with aggressors separately from one another and without common consent of the three Powers". Cadogan's minute, hurriedly drafted, was "we have to balance the advantage of a paper commitment by Russia to join in a war on one side against the disadvantage of associating ourselves openly with Russia. The advantage is, to say the least, problematical ... if we are attacked by Germany, Poland under our mutual guarantee will come to our assistance, i.e. make war on Germany. If the Soviets are bound to do the same, how can they fulfil that obligation without sending troops through or aircraft over Polish territory, which is exactly what frightens the Poles."[26]

Litvinov knew that Stalin would be very suspicious of any delay. Therefore he stipulated that military conversations between the three powers begin immediately. Harold Macmillan presciently felt: "This was Litvinov's last chance. It was also ours."[27] William Manchester wrote: "On 19 April the cabinet's Foreign Policy Committee considered the Litvinov initiative. The Foreign Office was startled by its airtight language; by contrast – and by design – Britain's Polish Guarantee was a sieve of loopholes ... Cadogan, in the absence of Halifax, described the Russian plan as "extremely inconvenient," suggested that Soviet military strength was trivial, and declared that

25 J. Haslam, *The Soviet Union and the Struggle for Collective Security in Europe 1933–39* (Springer, 1984), p 211.

26 Alexander Cadogan, *The Diaries of Sir Alexander Cadogan O.M. 1938–1945*. Ed. David Dilks (Cassell & Company Ltd, 1971), p 175.

27 William Manchester, *The Caged Lion: Winston Spencer Churchill, 1932–1940*, p 455.

"from the practical point of view there is every argument against accepting the Russian proposal." Yet he recognised "there is great difficulty in rejecting the Soviet offer ... The left in this country may be counted on" to exploit a refusal. There was also a "very remote" possibility that the Russians might join hands with the Germans. Nevertheless, Cadogan ended, "on balance" Litvinov's offer should be turned down.[28] This was a fatal error of judgement for which Halifax must bear full responsibility. He, not Cadogan, was in charge of Foreign Policy. It was a mistake as grave in its consequences as Grey's in 1912 when not supporting Haldane's negotiation in Berlin. Halifax then spent all his time overcoming Chamberlain's reluctance to endorse the Polish Guarantee on the well-founded ground that it meant the certainty of war at some later date.

The French Cabinet, reluctantly, had voted to accept the plan. A fortnight of silence followed from London, during which time Stalin dismissed Litvinov and chose Vyacheslav Molotov as his successor. Assurances were given that Russian policy would remain unchanged. But change it did. On 8 May, three weeks after the Soviet Union had announced its initiative, London replied in terms which had the effect of strengthening suspicions in Moscow that Chamberlain was not willing to make a military pact with Russia to prevent Hitler from taking Poland. Chamberlain revealed his opinion of the Russian proposal in the House of Commons on 19 May when Lloyd George, Eden and Churchill in his words, "pressed upon the Government the vital need for an immediate arrangement with Russia of the most far-reaching character and on equal terms".

Churchill again spoke in the House of Commons on 19 May:

> If His Majesty's Government, having neglected our defences for a long time, having thrown away Czechoslovakia with all that Czechoslovakia meant in military power, having committed us without examination of the technical aspects to the defence of Poland and Romania, now reject and cast away the indispensable aid of Russia, and so lead us in the worst of all ways into the worst

---

28 Alexander Cadogan, *The Diaries of Sir Alexander Cadogan O.M. 1938–1945*. Ed, David Dilks, p 175.

of all wars, they will have ill-deserved the confidence and, I will add, the generosity with which they have been treated by their fellow countrymen.[29]

There was a storm of criticism and Chamberlain, on 23 May, grudgingly agreed to negotiate with the Soviets on the basis of a British-French-Soviet alliance.

The Chamberlain-Halifax split was becoming ever more apparent. Halifax wanted a coalition government. He mixed socially with Churchill and it was clear that the two should have combined over Russia to make the Polish Guarantee credible. Nevertheless, between 19 and 24 May Halifax switched from distaste at Soviet "blackmail and bluff" to commending a Russian alliance to Cabinet. Cadogan was also now in favour but it was too late. The time for a deal was with Litvinov not Molotov. Churchill later wrote that a three-power coalition "would have struck deep alarm into the heart of Germany."[30] He was correct in this assessment.

Talks continued between Britain and Russia in June and July but they were looking to Germany, and Stalin soon could count on getting back what Russia lost at Versailles – Estonia, Latvia, Lithuania, Poland, Romania and the Balkans.

Near to midnight on 21 August Berlin radio announced the Reich Government had concluded a pact of non-aggression with Russia. Ribbentrop would sign in Moscow on 23 August. On 25 August Butler disagreed with Chamberlain and Halifax, overturning the Polish Guarantee in favour of a formal Treaty of Alliance with Poland. Butler, ever the appeaser, felt it "would have a bad psychological effect on Hitler and would wreck any negotiations".[31] Butler was divorced from political reality; negotiating with Hitler was not an option for any British Prime Minister by then.

The German-Russian pact focused minds across the parties in the Westminster Parliament. Poland was about to be attacked. Chamberlain alienated many MPs over Russia. More had to be done to

---

29 HC, Hansard, 19 May 1939.
30 Will Podmore, *British Foreign Policy since 1870* (Xlibris, 2008), p 91.
31 Anthony Howard, *RAB: The Life of R A Butler* (Jonathan Cape, 1990), p 85.

co-ordinate activity. Many played important roles. There were three MPs, however, whose activity in particular deserve further recognition and examination. Bob Boothby, a Conservative; Clement Davies, a Liberal; and Leo Amery, the man whose speech encouraged many of his fellow Conservative MPs in May 1940 to withdraw their support.

The Conservative MP, Bob Boothby, in what he calls his "book of memories that might otherwise be forgotten" wrote: "In the middle of September 1939, Clement Davies formed a small non-party group in the House of Commons, and asked me to be Secretary. We dined together once a week, and from time to time invited a distinguished guest to talk to us."[32] Leo Amery in his diary described in *The Empire at Bay* how Clement Davies' group was "... the most significant of the groups of dissidents in the winter of 1939–40. In the words of Alun Wyburn-Powell in his biography *Clement Davies: Liberal Leader*, the group was "...spurred by Munich and the inadequacy of the British Government's response to Hitler and constituted "... an all-party action group ... known as the 'Vigilantes'". This group either met in the House of Commons or at the Reform Club. In an interview quoted by Robert Rhodes James, Boothby recalled that "... [Clement] Attlee frequently attended these meetings".[33] The frequency of Attlee's involvement is hard to corroborate, but he was definitely supportive. The group also had three sub-committees "... to discuss economic issues, home defence and foreign policy"[34] with Davies as chair of the economic sub-committee and Boothby as secretary. Leo Amery in his memoir, *My Political Life* refers to the "little dinner group convened by Davies, originally to discuss the economic aspects of the war, which met every Thursday, first at the House and afterwards at the Reform Club".[35] On 4 April 1940 the 4th Marquis of Salisbury had also formed a 'Watching Committee' of Conservative members from both Houses of Parliament. This group met at

32 Bob Boothby, *Recollections of a Rebel* (Hutchinson, 1978), p 136.
33 Robert Rhodes James, *Bob Boothby: A Portrait of Churchill's Ally* (Hodder & Stoughton, 1991), p 245.
34 *Ibid*, p91.
35 L. S. Amery, *My Political Life: The Unforgiving Years, 1929–1940* (Hutchinson, 1955), p 339.

his flat in Arlington Street and, according to Leo Amery, gathered in order "to exchange views and make representations to the Government...", meeting "every few days in April either as a body or as a sub-committee on the military effort of which I seem to have been chairman". [36]

Clement Davies was born a Welshman on 19 February 1884 in Montgomeryshire. He developed a successful legal commercial practice in London, and having volunteered for military service in 1914, was posted instead to the office of the procurator general as adviser on enemy activities in neutral countries and on the high seas. He was later seconded to the Board of Trade. From 1919 to 1925 he was a junior counsel to the Treasury. He gave up his legal practice in 1930 when he joined the board of Unilever and became the Liberal MP for Montgomeryshire which he represented for the rest of his life. Although his work with Unilever took up much of his time, as a Liberal National he made his name in public health services and housing administration in Wales.

At the beginning of the war in 1939 Davies became an important element in the cross-party attempt to replace Chamberlain with Churchill, and according to the ODNB Bob Boothby, 'one of the architects – some may judge the principal architect' – of the coalition government. That no satisfactory place was found for him by Churchill in the coalition, "Boothby took as proof of his own belief that Churchill 'did not treat his friends well'."[37] That may be true. Davies rejoined the independent Liberal Party in 1942, becoming its leader in 1945 in succession to Sir Archibald Sinclair, who had been defeated in Caithness and Sutherland. With Frank Byers, who later joined Labour, as his Chief Whip, Davies was determined after the debacle of the Liberal Party in 1945 to maintain Liberal independence. He dismissed as 'unworthy subterfuge' Churchill's appeal for an electoral arrangement with the Conservatives before the general election of 1950. But in the absence of an electoral pact only nine Liberals were returned. That number fell to six in 1951 at which point Churchill offered him a place in his government. The Liberal

---

36 *Ibid*, p 355.
37 Robert Rhodes James, *Bob Boothby: A Portrait of Churchill's Ally*, pp 245–6.

vote had dropped to a mere three-quarters of a million and it would barely improve in 1955. At the following year's party conference in 1956, Davies surprised the assembly by announcing his intention of 'handing over the wheel' to Jo Grimond. Davies had by then long suffered from alcoholism which he kept from public view. He struggled with the conflict in the party, not least between Lady Megan Lloyd George and Lady Violet Bonham Carter who ultimately held considerable affection for Davies but who had once described him as 'a jellyfish who drifts on every tide ... and goes wherever he is pushed or pulled'.[38]

The Times newspaper described Bob Boothby on his death in 1986 as a "political maverick of unfulfilled promise". He was a hugely colourful figure – a star of the TV chat shows in later life and reviled for his links to the Kray brothers' criminal gang. For the purposes of this book, there is only one narrow, but very important, question to answer concerning these key figures: were Boothby and Davies's roles in helping to establish Winston Churchill as Prime Minister exaggerated, as the ODNB claims was the case, at least for Clement Davies's. Boothby's official biographer, Robert Rhodes James, was the Conservative MP for Cambridge from 1976–1992, and had also worked in the Clerks Department of the House of Commons providing an internal civil service for MPs. There was no one more knowledgeable on the intricate workings of the House of Commons and so it is interesting to consider his judgement that:

Although in later life Boothby often tended to exaggerate his role on certain occasions (in which he is not alone in politicians' memoirs) on this occasion it was indeed crucial, as was that of Davies.[39]

How did it come about that Boothby, only 40 years old when Churchill became Prime Minister, came to be in a position as to wield such influence? Born in Edinburgh on 12 February 1900, his parents were comfortably off. Exceptionally precocious , he entered Eton

38 V. Bonham Carter to Gilbert Murray, 6 April 1950, Lady Asquith MSS.
39 Robert Rhodes James, *Bob Boothby: A Portrait of Churchill's Ally*, p 242.

College in September 1913 and hated it, his masters and his house. Passed out of the Household Brigade Officers Cadet Battalion just before the November Armistice, he went to Oxford in 1919. His cousin was one Ludovic Kennedy, the broadcaster and lifelong member of the Liberal Party, and likewise he had been brought up to have a Liberal outlook. In his capacity as chairman of the Canning Club, he first met Churchill when he came to speak at the Oxford Union accompanied by Lord Birkenhead, better known as F E Smith. Boothby had heroes – Baldwin, Birkenhead, Lloyd George and Chaim Weizmann – but Churchill was not one of them. He fought Orkney and Shetland at the general election losing to the Liberal. Then at the age of 24, in 1924, he became the MP for East Aberdeenshire and a passionate supporter of the herring fish industry and the farmers.

In October 1926 after the General Strike, Boothby wrote a long letter to Churchill which made a deep impression. He was asked to come and have a talk with Churchill when in London, whereupon he was made Churchill's parliamentary private secretary and also a member of The Other Club – a political dining club Churchill had founded with Lord Birkenhead in 1911. In April 1927 Boothby, with Harold Macmillan, Oliver Stanley and John Loder, published 'Industry and the State' and had become a keen supporter of Keynes and a friend of Oswald Mosley. Churchill never seemed to mind his PPS taking somewhat contrarian views. Boothby won his seat in the 1929 election while his friend Macmillan lost his. Boothby invited him and his wife, Dorothy, to his father's annual shooting party and there began a love affair that lasted until Dorothy Macmillan's death in 1966. The political consequences of this relationship became apparent when James Stuart MP, who was married to Dorothy's sister, became a Scottish Whip in 1935 and Deputy Chief Whip in 1937 under David Margesson. Whips are dangerous enemies and Stuart and Boothby hated each other. Stuart also harboured a dislike for both Eden and Churchill.

Many Conservative MPs disliked Boothby intensely for his gambling and womanising and his relations with Churchill waxed and waned. Boothby saw over the years anti-Semitism building up in Hitler's Germany and warned against it and of the growing strength of Himmler. In January 1932 in Berlin, Boothby had met Hitler and sent his assessment to Churchill. Boothby reacted strongly against the Hoare-Laval Pact of 1935, describing it as "one of the most discreditable documents ever issued in the name of the people".[40] Both the French and British Foreign Ministers had underestimated the ensuing public reaction to assigning the fate of the Abyssinians to the Italians and Hoare was soon replaced by Eden. In the abdication crisis, Boothby sympathised with the King but he did not doubt, unlike Churchill, that the King's position was untenable. At Churchill's Chartwell home on 6 December 1936, Churchill, the Liberal leader Sinclair, and Boothby prepared a declaration for the King saying he would not contract a marriage against the advice of his ministers. On 7 December, according to Boothby, was the only time he saw Churchill the worse for wear in public due to drink. Churchill made a disastrous intervention following Baldwin's statement to a question in the House of Commons. Boothby wrote a letter to Churchill which he came to believe, according to Rhodes James, was fatal to their relationship. Churchill took five days to reply. "The old intimacy was never to return."[41]

Dear Winston,
I understood last night that we had agreed upon a formula, and a course, designed to save the King from abdication, *if that is possible.*

I thought you were going to use all your powers – decisive, as I believe, in the present circumstances – to secure a happy issue on the lines that were suggested.

But this afternoon you have delivered a blow to the King, both in the House and in the country, far harder than any that Baldwin ever conceived of.

You have reduced the number of potential supporters to the minimum possible. I should think now about seven in all.

And you have done it without any consultation with your best friends and supporters. I have never in my life said anything to you that I did not sincerely believe. And I never will.

40 Robert Rhodes James, *Robert Boothby: A Portrait of Churchill's Ally,* p 161.
41 *Ibid,* p 170.

What happened this afternoon makes me feel that it is almost impossible for those who are most devoted to you personally to follow you blindly (as they would like to do) in politics. Because they cannot be sure where the hell they are going to be landed next.

I am afraid this letter will make you very angry.

But not I hope irretrievably angry.

I could not leave what I feel unsaid.

Yours ever
Bob[42]

After he became Prime Minister, Churchill appointed Boothby as junior minister to Fred Woolton, the Minister for Food, a role that was well below what Boothby considered to be his right. It was not, however, an insignificant position as it rendered him the lead spokesman in the House of Commons. On 9 October 1941 Boothby received a letter from Churchill informing him that he had seen documents that disclosed a financial association to Richard Weininger, who was born in July 1887 in the old Austro-Hungarian Empire at Baden near Vienna and had been interned under Regulation 18B. There was never any question of Boothby being prosecuted but, nevertheless, there was a *prima facie* case of allegedly discreditable behaviour by a Member of Parliament with an alien. On 17 October Churchill told the House of Commons that a select committee would be appointed to determine the fate of Boothby, who was not asked to resign his office but was suspended from ministerial duties. The committee concluded "Mr Boothby's conduct was contrary to the usage and derogatory to the dignity of the House and inconsistent with the standards which Parliament is entitled to expect from its members."[43] Boothby resigned as minister but not from the House of Commons. His career never recovered. His relationship with Churchill continued its "hot-cold pattern". Perhaps one of the

---

42 Robert Rhodes James, *Robert Boothby: A Portrait of Churchill's Ally*, pp 166–167.
43 Matthew Parris, Kevin Macguire, *Great Parliamentary Scandals: Five Centuries of Calumny, Smear and Innuendo* (Robson, 2004), p 119.

most generous gestures ever made in politics was Harold Macmillan's decision to offer him one of the first life peerages in 1958.

After the abdication crisis, Churchill was bound to face a major reappraisal in the House of Commons from MPs of all parties. Many had witnessed his performance in confronting Baldwin, sensed he was drunk and were bound to ask themselves should and could this man ever become Prime Minister. Few doubted that he was as the military historian Carlo D'Este wrote many years later in his book *Warlord*: "... first a soldier. War and soldiering were in his blood, inspiring his earliest fantasies as a child and his greatest adventures as a young man."[44] What ministers now had to ponder in the midst of war was whether he was more than that: was he a Premier with the make-up and character, not of a warrior but of a leader of men and women who lived their lives as civilians; people for whom war was anathema, something to only contemplate as a last resort; people who wanted as their Prime Minister, while not an appeaser, someone capable of finding a real peace. A man of composure in his person, not at war with himself, a man not prone to excessive mood changes, not manic nor depressive. Of course, they knew he was not an ordinary leader but these were times so testing that normality was a handicap. They could settle for his exceptional personality but as MPs they had to be sure that he was not unstable.

There was a certain admiration for the way he had donned uniform as Lieutenant Colonel Churchill on 5 January 1916, taking command in the field of the 6th Battalion, Royal Scots Fusiliers, having gone to Flanders to fight after resigning from the Cabinet on 11 November 1915 as Chancellor of the Duchy of Lancaster. Nevertheless, he was greatly diminished in political stature following his dismissal from the prestigious post of First Lord of the Admiralty following the debacle of the Dardanelles and Gallipoli campaign. It was not until he served in the Army for over eighteen months that Lloyd George, as Prime Minister, was able to overcome the resistance of the Conservatives in the coalition government and appoint his fellow Liberal, as he then still was, to join his Cabinet.

---

44 Carlo D'Este, *Warlord: A Life of Winston Churchill at War 1874–1945* (Allen Lane, 2009), p xv.

Out of government since 1929, as a Conservative, and almost the whole of the 1930s, a period often referred to as his 'wilderness years', Churchill began not only to warn against appeasement but became the best-informed MP on all matters related to German rearmament. He studied Hitler with great attention, and his military experience as the serving First Lord of the Admiralty was the crucial factor when on 10 May 1940, aged sixty-five, he took over as Prime Minister and Minister of Defence. It was a moment of national peril. Yet MPs from across all parties knew Churchill, his weaknesses as well as his strengths; they had weighed them up by May 1940 from watching him in and out of government. They had assessed particularly what they all knew of his mood changes or cyclothymic personality. Cross-party soundings had revealed that a majority of MPs from all political parties believed that he was the man to lead a wartime coalition.

He was undoubtedly highly emotional and some of his critics in Parliament thought him mentally unstable. A cyclothymic temperament consists of numerous hypomanic episodes but without clear evidence of a major manic episode. In the mild hypomanic state a person can be highly creative, energetic and productive; in the mildly depressed state they can be agitated and restless and can sleep badly.

Churchill called his mood changes his 'Black Dog'. Sometimes they lasted only for hours, at other times for months. An early reference to 'Black Dog' appears in a letter Churchill wrote on 11 July 1911 to his wife, Clementine, about a friend:

> Alice interested me a great deal in her talk about her doctor in Germany, who completely cured her depression. I think this man might be useful to me – if my black dog returns. He seems quite away from me now – it is such a relief.[45]

Churchill talked about past suicidal feelings when young and married. He didn't like to stand near the edge of a platform when an express train was passing through the station, he claimed, and if

---

45 Winston Churchill, Clementine Churchill, *Speaking for Themselves: The Personal Letters of Winston and Clementine Churchill*. Ed. Mary Soames (Doubleday, 1998), p 53.

possible he preferred to get a pillar between him and the train, for a second's action could end everything. Churchill's family, including his wife, believed his mood changes were not as significant as Lord Moran, his personal doctor, and some psychiatrists have suggested. Martin Gilbert, Churchill's biographer, quotes a letter from John Colville, Churchill's long-serving private secretary:

> I suppose that this hypothetical state of depression into which Lord Moran alleges Sir Winston used to fall will become accepted dogma. I therefore, some time ago, took the trouble to ask Lady Churchill about the theory. She was quite positive that although her husband was occasionally depressed – as indeed most normal people are – he was not abnormally subject to long fits of depression.[46]

Churchill in his early years had, by any standard, clinical depression, with notable episodes after the failed Dardanelles Campaign in 1915, the loss of his parliamentary seat in 1922 and after his exclusion from the National Government in 1931.

Churchill's daughter, writing sensitively about his times of depression and deep frustrations, also used the term 'Black Dog' and wrote that it had 'been his companion too often in earlier years for him not to know the power of such feelings'.[47]

Some later psychiatrists have diagnosed Churchill as having bipolar-I disorder. To make the diagnosis of bipolar-I there is merit in sticking to the criterion dominant when Churchill was alive, that there should be at least one clear manic disturbance sufficiently severe to cause marked impairment in occupational functioning or in usual social activities or relationships with others, often sufficient to necessitate hospitalisation to prevent harm to oneself or others. Usually there is also at least one family member with a history of severe depression. In Churchill's case the family of his father, also named Randolph, had a history of depression, which was apparent

---

46 Martin Gilbert, *In Search of Churchill: A Historian's Journey* (Harper Collins, 1994), pp 209–10.
47 Mary Soames, *Clementine Churchill* (Doubleday, 2003), p 253.

in many Dukes of Marlborough. But his father's bizarre, somewhat manic behaviour, which was thought at one time to be the result of general paralysis of the insane, the terminal stage of syphilis, looks as though it may have been caused by a brain tumour. Some commentators have considered as manic behaviour Churchill dictating to a secretary while in the bath – and certainly he was unselfconscious about being in the nude – but a casual approach to nudity was quite common in his social class.

Churchill, by the time he had become Prime Minister, appeared to have flattened out the violence of the mood swings of his youth. In that sense, his depression was rather like that of another hyperactive politician, Theodore Roosevelt, who was diagnosed in a recent study as having bipolar-I disorder.[48] Neither of Churchill's doctors, Lord Moran nor Lord Brain, in their writings came anywhere near to labelling their patient a manic depressive and nor I believe should doctors decades later.

After a long life in politics Churchill had formidable enemies, but the House of Commons is an extremely intimate place and across party lines, amongst MPs, there is often a fair measure of agreement about an individual's overall qualities. They desperately wanted Churchill's inspirational abilities and judged this to be his all-important attribute. The force of his personality was elemental, suited to a wartime leader and head of government.

After the abdication crisis, Rhodes James wrote, "Seldom has there been such a dramatic reversal of political fortunes. Churchill's reputation fell to its nadir, Baldwin's rose to its zenith."[49] Boothby's relations with Churchill were not improved by Boothby's criticism of Churchill during the debate that followed Eden's resignation on 22 February 1938. On 12 March, Hitler annexed Austria. At this time Boothby admitted he "fell under the spell" of Halifax for a time. Even his relations with Chamberlain were good. On 19 September Boothby met the Russian International Commisar in Geneva and

48 Jonathan R T Davidson, Kathryn M Connor, Marvin Swartz, 'Mental Illness in US Presidents between 1776 and 1974: A Review of Biographical Sources', *Journal of Nervous and Mental Disease* (2006), vol. 194, pp 47–51.
49 Robert Rhodes James, *Robert Boothby: A Portrait of Churchill's Ally*, p 167.

discovered that the British Government had not even had political talks, let alone staff talks with Russia. But despite that, if the French fulfilled their obligations to the Czechs they would fight.

It was Munich that changed Boothby's attitude to the Chamberlainites and he told a friend "this Cabinet must be hurled from power, whatever happens".[50] This guided him in every action that he took from then on until Churchill became Prime Minister. He would go on to abstain with over 30 Conservative MPs at the 8 May vote as well as combine with Amery. The Whips' Office began to attack the anti-Munich Conservatives who opposed appeasement, and Boothby was put under increasing pressure in East Aberdeenshire; even Churchill had trouble in his own constituency. But all this allowed Boothby to exploit his position and, through Davies, establish relations with Labour and Liberal people in the country and amongst MPs. His ups and downs with Churchill by the spring of 1940 were all forgotten; Churchill was the man for the job and he did not consider any other candidate.

Churchill's position was strengthened outside of the House of Commons at this time by one other important relationship. Churchill had developed a significant bond with Ernest Bevin surrounding the negotiations and drafting of the first Orders under the Road Haulage Wages Act, which were not ready for enforcement until 1940. Bevin was having to deal with the growing employment of women in roles previously occupied exclusively by men and tasked with negotiating the 'rate for the job'. The fishing industry, hard hit by the Admiralty requisitioning trawlers for minesweeping and other naval duties, also demanded time and reorganisation. Bevin took the initiative in persuading five different Ministries, one of which was the Admiralty, to come together. Churchill agreed on 19 October 1939 to take the chair and Churchill and Bevin, "brought into co-operation for the first time in their lives, rapidly took the measure of each other. There could hardly have been a greater contrast: the patrician politician, master of the suspect arts of war and diplomacy, and the working-class leader, immersed in the social and

---

50   Robert Rhodes James, *Robert Boothby: A Portrait of Churchill's Ally*, p 167.

industrial problems of trade unionism".[51] As Alan Bullock went on to note "Bevin found in Churchill a politician capable of the prompt and bold action which he could never obtain from other government departments to his satisfaction. Churchill marked in Bevin a breadth of mind and natural authority which he had never before met in a working-class leader."[52]

An address to the Institute of Transport by Bevin in January 1940 in which he argued for a single authority for transport, came to Churchill's notice and he asked for a copy which Bevin sent him at once. This relationship was no secret in Labour Party circles and, indeed, encouraged other Labour figures to talk to Conservatives like Boothby, who was probably thought to have a closer relationship to Churchill at that stage than he really had. During these early months of 1940, a far better relationship was apparent in the House of Commons between Labour and some Conservative MPs, all of whom were dissatisfied with the way the war was being handled. It was the Norwegian Campaign that finally made clear how extensive this mishandling really was. On 1 May 1940 at Stoke-on-Trent, Bevin's anger was made public: "The time has come when there must be no mincing of words. It is no use disguising the fact that those who, like myself, have been constantly in touch with Government departments, are intensely dissatisfied with the kind of obstruction, lack of drive, absence of imagination and complacency which exists... But the damnable thing is they cannot put in the extra energy to give the soldier what he needs without also having to give bigger profits to the capitalists in control. The British working class want this war won. They know what is at stake. It is their liberty. But they want a Government that is going to please the nation before its friend and private interests."[53]

On 9 February 1940, President Roosevelt announced that the Under Secretary of State Mr Sumner Welles would shortly visit Italy, France, Germany and Great Britain, solely for the purpose of advising

---

51 Alan Bullock, *Ernest Bevin: A Biography* (Politico's, 2002), p 243.

52 *Ibid*, p 243.

53 Alan Bullock, Baron Bullock, *The Life and Times of Ernest Bevin: Trade Union Leader 1881–1940* (Heinemann, 1960), p 650.

the President and Secretary of State as to conditions in Europe. Welles travelled to Naples on the symbol of fascist achievement – the luxury liner SS *Rex* leaving New York on 13 February. Europe was still in the phoney war. It was Welles who had persuaded Roosevelt to make Italy not just a last minute handwritten addition to the countries he should visit but the top priority. Mussolini knew that public opinion was overwhelmingly in favour of Italy remaining neutral, though he preferred to label the stance as non-belligerent. Washington increasingly worried that Italy was growing closer to Japan. Galeazzo Ciano, the Italian fascist Foreign Minister and Mussolini's son-in-law, made a speech in December 1939 seen by the American Ambassador Philips as being deliberately anti-German and this was a big factor in Welles's thinking. Italy welcomed Welles's visit, Britain was negative, and France less so. On that first meeting Welles wrote: "Ciano made no effort to conceal his dislike and contempt for Ribbentrop or his antagonism towards Hitler".[54]

Welles was told emphatically when meeting with Mussolini that a negotiation with Germany could be successful in bringing about a peace proposal, but not once a 'real' war had broken out. The price for his help was also clearly implied; the British would have to curb their aggressive behaviour in the Mediterranean. But later Mussolini was very negative when confiding in Ciano, stating "Between us and the Americans any kind of understanding is impossible", owing to the US propensity to "judge problems on the surface" in contrast to Italy's deeper consideration.[55] In London after Welles had visited Hitler, Chamberlain told him that he was strongly opposed to offering any territorial incentives to Italy. On 10 March Ribbentrop visited Rome to see Mussolini and Ciano. When Welles returned to Rome via Paris where he met Paul Reynaud, as he had promised he would on 15 March, Mussolini had already been told that Hitler did not feel Welles's visit had brought any new elements to bear by Ribbentrop. When Welles saw Mussolini he made one remark, "You may

---

54   J. Rofe, *Franklin Roosevelt's Foreign Policy and the Welles Mission* (Springer, 2007), p 110.
55   Ray Moseley, *Mussolini's Shadow: The Double Life of Count Galeazzo Ciano* (Yale University Press, 1999), p 92.

wish to remember that while the German-Italian pact exists, I never-theless retain complete liberty of action."[56] Mussolini had requested authorisation to pass onto Hitler Welles's impressions following his visits, but when Welles checked by telephone with Roosevelt this was withheld to avoid giving the impression that the US President was participating in any peace initiative.

Mussolini met Hitler on the Brenner Pass on 18 March, on the same day that Welles met Pope Pius XII in the Vatican. Ciano was aware of all that had passed between Welles and Roosevelt as there was a phone tap in operation when Roosevelt told Welles 'No' when he reported back. The truth is Ciano was duplicitous and a dissem-bler. He was aware that on the Brenner Pass Hitler had confirmed he would attack the West and Mussolini had said he would come into the war, though he told Welles on 19 March Italy would not enter the war on the side of Germany as long as he was Foreign Minister.

Welles later reported to the President on Mussolini, "Mussolini is a man of genius, but it must never be forgotten that Mussolini remains at heart and in instinct an Italian peasant. He is vindictive and will never forget an injury or blow to his personal or national prestige. He admires force and power. His own obsession is the recreation of the Roman Empire ... I do not believe there is the slightest chance of any successful negotiation at this time."[57] Welles was correct.

The question which has never been fully answered is why, after the Welles visit, did Halifax think in May that Ciano was a credible figure and interpreter of Mussolini's thoughts and actions? Halifax's official biography gives little space or attention to Welles's mission. Did Halifax dismiss it as another Roosevelt attempt to keep the Isolationists happy? But there were important lessons to be learned from it which appeared not to have been picked up by Lothian, our ambassador in Washington, or Philips in Rome from their contacts. Welles certainly believed he was reporting only to the President, but it was the first and most credible attempt to gauge Italian intentions.

---

56 Stephen Borsody, *The Tragedy of Central Europe: The Nazi and Soviet Conquest of Central Europe* (Cape, 1960), p 121.

57 Robert L. Miller, *The Welles Mission to Rome: February – March 1940*. Lecture given at the Casa Italiana Zerilli Marimò, NYU, 27 May 2008.

In May 1940 it was Leo Amery who would prove to be the catalyst for bringing together all the groups working to topple Chamberlain. Anxiety on the Conservative backbenches was growing and about more than just what was happening in Norway. The sheer folly of not bombing German airfields while British troops in Norway were facing German air superiority seemed extraordinary. Yet since the war had started, the design of a heavy tank had not been agreed. The British Expeditionary Force had seventeen light and 100 'infantry' tanks. Lord Salisbury made representations to Chamberlain personally which failed to move him into specific action. Lord Halifax met a deputation from the Salisbury Group which led Salisbury to say bluntly of the Government "we are not satisfied".[58]

The April Budget was attacked by Amery for expenditure on war purposes of £2,000,000,000, while Germany was spending £3,200,000,000 – a gap that was bound to widen unless Britain increased its expenditure to something like £3,600,000,000 a year. Amery's diary entry for 29 April reads:

It is all terrible, and must mean the end of the Government and, perhaps, of Winston as well. But if so, what on earth have we left? My only conclusion is that we cannot do worse than with the present lot, and that if we only change often enough we shall end by finding someone who can lead us to victory."[59]

Norway was to provide the political tipping point more than its military equivalent. In François Kersaudy's *Norway 1940*, the secretary of the Chiefs of Staff Committee, Major-General Hastings Ismay, is quoted receiving "In the very early hours of 9 April... [a] report ... brutal in its simplicity. The Germans had seized Copenhagen, Oslo, and all the main ports of Norway."[60] The ensuing Allied

58 John Kelly, *Never Surrender: Winston Churchill and Britain's Decision to Fight Nazi Germany in the Fateful Summer of 1940* (Simon and Schuster, 2015), p 110.
59 Reginald William Thompson, *Winston Churchill: The Yankee Marlborough* (Doubleday, 1963), p 270.
60 François Kersaudy, *Norway 1940* (University of Nebraska Press, 1998), p 81.

expedition in Norway was described by Kersaudy as "ill-founded"[61] with some British units suffering an "unmitigated disaster".[62] In his history of the Second World War, Churchill described Norway as "... this ramshackle campaign".[63] According to Boothby "... everything drifted gradually from bad to worse; and the Norwegian campaign, botched by Churchill, brought matters to a climax";[64] a Leo Amery diary entry for 17 April 1940 added that any action was "'too little and too late' as usual".[65] In his memoir, he wrote that on the 2 May 1940 "...at a meeting with Clement Davies and his group ... we decided to see if we could not make the two days' Whitsun adjournment debate on 7 May the occasion for a trial of strength".[66] In his diary Amery describes this meeting on 2 May as "... an emergency conclave convened by Clem Davies (more or less his Economic dinner group) ... to discuss the line for next week's debate. I urged 'national government and War Cabinet' which was generally agreed while it was also agreed that we should press for no Whitsun holiday".[67] The account of this day, 2 May, by the biographer of Clement Davies wrote that Davies "met the Labour leadership to encourage them to press for a vote of confidence in the adjournment debate scheduled for 7 May".[68] In his memoir, Amery also writes that "... Davies accordingly tried to persuade Attlee to raise the direct issue of confidence. Attlee hesitated, wisely, as the event proved, for it made it much easier for Conservatives to be influenced by the opening day's debate".[69] Once again one sees the Labour Party carefully using their power as the official opposition to reinforce Conservative backbench MPs who were not able to put down motions or to influence when and how votes would take place. They all knew each needed the other.

To himself Amery concluded: "this muddle cannot go on any

61 *Ibid*, p 142.
62 *Ibid*, p116.
63 Winston Churchill, *The Gathering Storm* (Houghton Mifflin, 1948), p547.
64 Bob Boothby, *Recollections of a Rebel* (Hutchinson, 1978), p 142.
65 John Barnes, David Nicholson, *The Empire at Bay: The Leo Amery Diaries*, 1929–1945 (Hutchinson, 1980), p587.
66 L. S. Amery, *My Political Life: The Unforgiving Years*, p358.
67 John Barnes, David Nicholson, *The Empire at Bay*, p 591.
68 Alun Wyburn-Powell, *Clement Davies: Liberal Leader,* (Politico's, 2003), p990.
69 L. S. Amery, *My Political Life: The Unforgiving Years*, p 358.

longer". At all costs and at the earliest possible moment the Chamberlain Government must be forced to go. On 7 May the House of Commons met and Amery was poised to speak.[70] Arthur Greenwood, he wrote, truly expressed the mood of the House quoting him as saying:

> I have never known the House in graver mood. Its heart is troubled. It is anxious; it is more than anxious, it is apprehensive.

Somewhat surprisingly, Chamberlain, in opening the debate, made what Amery felt was "a skilful statement, but it entirely misjudged the temper of the House which was not concerned with the scale of our failure, but with its nature".[71] Attlee posed what Amery felt were some shrewd questions, but it was the Liberal leader, Sinclair, who went to the heart of the matter according to Amery with the assertion that "the Government is giving us a one-shift war while the Germans are working a three-shift war".[72] It is appropriate to give much attention to Amery's own account of the debate. He sat through it all, and it is rightly judged by history as his debate owing to the drama of his speech. But it could well have been a relatively boring occasion with Amery squeezed out by the Speaker and the Conservative Whips. He describes the waiting period in the middle of the debate that many MPs have to endure:

> Then followed for me two hours of that agonised discomfort which only members of the House know, divided between perfunctory listening to unimportant speeches which never seem to end, and vainly trying to remember the all-important points of the all-important speech one hopes to make oneself. This time I knew that what I had to say mattered and, what was more, was desperately anxious that it should have its intended effect. So I followed impatiently the alternation between speakers who declared that

---

70 *Ibid*, pp 358–369.
71 *Ibid*, p 359.
72 Gerard J. DeGroot, *Liberal Crusader: The Life of Sir Archibald Sinclair* (C. Hurst & Co. Publishers, 1993), p 153.

all was well with the best of governments which had just won a successful campaign and those who dwelt on the military disaster which was the natural climax of years of incompetence. The only note of colour, for eye as well as for mind, was afforded by Roger Keyes, who had come down in all the splendour of his uniform as Admiral of the Fleet, in order to speak for those "officers and men of the fighting, seagoing Navy" who shared his unhappiness over the failure to take Trondheim.[73]

As a Privy Councillor Amery had a certain customary right to be called. But the choice of when lay with the Speaker, who was sympathetic to Chamberlain. Amery realised that the Speaker meant to postpone calling him until the dinner hour in the knowledge that Amery was out to create difficulties for the Government. Amery needed a packed House. Members had however steadily slipped away from the Chamber with a dozen or so remaining. Amery nearly decided to speak for a few minutes at most. But Clement Davies came in and while he was speaking said that he would go off to bring in MPs from the Smoking Room and Library. Gradually the Chamber began to fill up and Amery felt sufficiently confident to make a direct attack on Chamberlain.

The Prime Minister gave us a reasoned, argumentative case for our failure. It is always possible to do that after every failure. Making a case and winning a war are not the same thing. Wars are won, not by explanation after the event, but by foresight, by clear decision and by swift action. I confess that I did not feel there was one sentence in the Prime Minister's speech this afternoon which suggested that the Government either foresaw what Germany meant to do, or came to a clear decision when it knew what Germany had done, or acted swiftly or consistently throughout the whole of this lamentable affair.[74]

After a while Amery turned to military questions.

73 L. S. Amery, *My Political Life: The Unforgiving Years,* pp 359–360.
74 HC, Hansard, 7 May 1940, vol. 360, cc1073–196.

The Prime Minister, both the other day and today, expressed himself as satisfied that the balance of advantage lay on our side. He laid great stress on the heaviness of the German losses and the lightness of ours. What did the Germans lose? A few thousand men, nothing to them, a score of transports, and part of a Navy which anyhow cannot match ours. What did they gain? They gained Norway, with the strategical advantages which, in their opinion at least, outweigh the whole of their naval losses. They have gained the whole of Scandinavia. What have we lost? To begin with, we have lost most of the Norwegian Army, not only such as it was but such as it might have become, if only we had been given time to rally and re-equip it ... What we have lost, above all, is one of those opportunities which do not recur in war. If we could have captured and held Trondheim, and if we would have rallied the Norwegian forces, then we might well have imposed a strain on Germany which might have made Norway to Hitler what Spain once was to Napoleon.[75]

Now the House was listening to his arguments and he could hear murmurs of approval from his own Conservative benches:

We cannot go on as we are. There must be a change. First and foremost, it must be a change in the system and structure of our governmental machine. This is war, not peace ... In war the first essential is planning ahead. The next essential is swift, decisive action.

We can wage war only on military principles. One of the first of these principles is the clear definition of individual responsibilities – not party responsibilities or Cabinet responsibilities – and, with it, a proper delegation of authority ... What is our present Cabinet system? There are some 25 Ministers, heads of Departments, who have no direct chief above them except the Prime Minister. How often do they see him? How often can they get from him direct advice, direct impulse, direct drive? Who is to settle disputes between them?[76]

---

75 HC, Hansard, 7 May 1940, vol. 360, cc1073–196.
76 HC, Hansard, 7 May 1940, vol. 360, cc1073–196.

Amery advocated, as he had been doing for months, a real War Cabinet, such as Lloyd George had created in the First World War and which the Committee of Imperial Defence had laid down as axiomatic:

We must have, first of all, a right organisation of Government. What is no less important today is that the Government shall be able to draw upon the whole abilities of the nation. It must represent all the elements of real political power in this country, whether in this House or not. The time has come when hon. and right hon. Members opposite must definitely take their share of the responsibility. The time has come when the organisation, the power and influence of the Trades Union Congress cannot be left outside. It must, through one of its recognised leaders, reinforce the strength of the national effort from inside. The time has come, in other words, for a real National Government. I may be asked what is my alternative Government. That is not my concern: it is not the concern of this House. The duty of this House, and the duty that it ought to exercise, is to show unmistakably what kind of Government it wants in order to win the war. It must always be left to some individual leader, working perhaps with a few others, to express that will by selecting his colleagues so as to form a Government which will correspond to the will of the House and enjoy its confidence. So I refuse, and I hope the House will refuse, to be drawn into a discussion on personalities.[77]

By now the atmosphere was becoming tense. Amery came to his conclusion:

Somehow or other we must get into the Government men who can match our enemies in fighting spirit, in daring, in resolution and in thirst for victory. Some 300 years ago, when this House found that its troops were being beaten again and again by the dash and daring of the Cavaliers, by Prince Rupert's Cavalry, Oliver Cromwell spoke to John Hampden. In one of his speeches

---

77 HC Deb, 7 May 1940, vol. 360, cc1073–196.

he recounted what he said. It was this: "I said to him, 'Your troops are most of them old, decayed serving men and tapsters and such kind of fellows' ... You must get men of a spirit that are likely to go as far as they will go, or you will be beaten still." It may not be easy to find these men. They can be found only by trial and by ruthlessly discarding all who fail and have their failings discovered. We are fighting today for our life, for our liberty, for our all; we cannot go on being led as we are.[78]

Amery admitted later that he then hesitated for a moment as to whether to quote the words of Cromwell when he dismissed the Rump of the Long Parliament. He knew that to go "beyond the sense of the House, above all beyond the feeling of my own friends, would be not only an anti-climax, but a fatal error of judgement. I was not out for a dramatic finish, but for a practical purpose; to bring down the Government if I could."[79] He described feeling himself swept forward by the surge of feeling which his speech had worked up on the benches around him. Across the floor of the House, he caught the "the look of admiring appreciation on the face of that old parliamentary virtuoso, Lloyd George".[80] So he ventured:

I have quoted certain words of Oliver Cromwell. I will quote certain other words. I do it with great reluctance, because I am speaking of those who are old friends and associates of mine, but they are words which, I think, are applicable to the present situation. This is what Cromwell said to the Long Parliament when he thought it was no longer fit to conduct the affairs of the nation: "You have sat too long here for any good you have been doing. Depart, I say, and let us have done with you. In the name of God, go."[81]

When he sat down he knew he had done what he meant to do. He could see on the faces of the ministers who had come in to crowd

---

78 HC Deb, 7 May 1940, vol. 360, cc1073–196.
79 L. S. Amery, *My Political Life: The Unforgiving Years*, p 364.
80 J. S. Bromley, E. H. Kossmann, *Britain and the Netherlands, volume 5: Some Political Mythologies* (Springer, 2012), p 162.
81 HC, Hansard, 7 May 1940, vol. 360, cc1073–196.

the front bench, that they knew it too. In his conviction that the Chamberlain Government must go he had carried with him far more Conservatives than he had been able to in recent months. Lloyd George told him afterwards that in 50 years he had heard few speeches to match it in sustained power and none with so dramatic a climax. This much was also clear to the Opposition, Greenwood pointed out later in the evening:

> Members of this House know perfectly well, and it is no good pretending to hide it, that there is a feeling in this country against the Government. [Hon. Members: "Nonsense."] I hope I have never talked any nonsense in this war. I have spoken what I believe to be true …
>
> It is perfectly clear that there must be an active, vigorous, imaginative direction of the war. Up to now, our record in this war, despite magnificent exploits which will remain in the annals of our history as long as there is a Britain, does not redound to the credit of the Government. I turn again to the words which I quoted at the beginning of my speech: "Should there be confused councils, inefficiency and wavering, then other men must be called to take their place." That is what we ask. The responsibility for any change lies, not with the minority; it lies with the majority whose responsibilities are, far and away, greater than ours.[82]

Roy Jenkins, in his biography of Attlee, quotes him as saying that the debate on the adjournment on 7 May "revealed that discontent had gone far deeper than we thought and I was assured that if a division were called we should get a lot of support from the Conservatives, especially from the serving soldiers, sailors and airmen".[83]

Herbert Morrison's biographers quote the Labour MP, Jim Griffiths, as saying that Morrison "… saw the chance to destroy the Government. He saw that they could take a division at the end of

---

82 Ibid.
83 Roy Jenkins, Mr. Attlee: An Interim Biography (Heinemann, 1948), pp 215–6.

an adjournment debate..."[84] They also quote Clement Attlee remembering that "I presided at the party meeting and I, not Morrison, proposed that we should call a vote against the Government".[85] It seems that Herbert Morrison pressed for a division at a meeting of Labour's Parliamentary Executive Committee, while Attlee proposed a division at a full meeting of the Parliamentary Party. It turned out to be a tactical triumph and an example of how parliamentary procedure has to be mastered if its full potential is to be harnessed.

On the next day, 8 May, Herbert Morrison opened the debate for the Labour Party. At the very end, he asked for a vote which should "represent the spirit of the country".[86] Chamberlain rose to say that, at a time when national unity was essential in the face of a relentless enemy, this challenge had made a grave situation graver. He continued:

> I do not seek to evade criticism, but I say this to my friends in the House – and I have friends in the House. No Government can prosecute a war efficiently unless it has public and parliamentary support. I accept the challenge. I welcome it indeed. At least we shall see who is with us and who is against us, and I call on my friends to support us in the lobby tonight.[87]

The reference to 'my friends' was judged by most MPs as a very unwise choice of words, making it a party, or even a personal, issue. Amery wrote later that "The Conservative benches shivered at so crude an error of judgement. There was, no doubt, real anxiety behind the appeal. The Whips had discovered that the discontent in the Conservative ranks was far more widespread than they had imagined, and were frantically busy trying to stem it."[88]

In his memoir, Boothby records that "Clement Davies immediately sent for me ... asked me to arrange a meeting of dissident Conservative members ... I had no difficulty in persuading Amery

84 Bernard Donoughue, G. W. Jones, *Herbert Morrison: Portrait of a Politician* (Weidenfeld and Nicolson, 1973), p272.
85 *Ibid*, p 272.
86 L. S. Amery, *My Political Life: The Unforgiving Years*, p 366.
87 HC, Hansard, 8 May 1940, vol. 360, cc1251–366.
88 L. S. Amery, *My Political Life: The Unforgiving Years*, p 366.

to take the chair at the meeting, several being in uniform, which extended beyond the various 'groups'. At this meeting the fateful decision was taken to vote against the Government".[89] Amery mentions a "... meeting of our lot"[90] on 8 May, which in his memoir he refers to as "... an emergency meeting".[91] Clement Davies's biographer wrote that before the division, the Vigilantes, joined by other dissenters, meant that the Commons committee room swelled to over 100, and they made their final decision to vote against the Government".[92]

Now all the work in the groups bore fruit and some thirty or forty MPs had announced their intention of voting against the Government. Lord Dunglass (Alec Douglas-Home), the Prime Minister's parliamentary private secretary, managed to persuade some of them to hold off, promising that Chamberlain would meet with them the next day to tell them of his plans for a drastic reconstruction of the Government.

Lloyd George had been busy making notes at the beginning of the debate as if he was intending to speak, but had disappeared. Noting his absence, Davies had found him and brought him back to the House in time to hear a good part of Hoare's speech. Lloyd George then began with a general indictment of the Government's unreadiness on every critical occasion in recent years and then went on to Norway. A suggestion that the First Lord was not entirely to blame for all that happened there at once brought Churchill to his feet to claim his full share of responsibility. But Lloyd George replied:

> The right hon. Gentleman must not allow himself to be converted into an air-raid shelter to keep the splinters from hitting his colleagues.[93]

In this way Lloyd George not only highlighted the feeling which ran through the debate, that whether Churchill had, or had not,

89 Bob Boothby, *Recollections of a Rebel*, p 142–3.
90 John Barnes, David Nicholson, *The Empire at Bay: The Leo Amery Diaries 1929–1955*, p 611.
91 L. S. Amery, *My Political Life: The Unforgiving Years*, p367.
92 Alun Wyburn-Powell, *Clement Davies: Liberal Leader*, p104.
93 HC Deb, 8 May 1940, vol. 360, cc1251–366.

made mistakes over Norway he was not responsible for the underlying incompetence which was the real issue. His speech was powerful, but Amery thought his closing appeal to Chamberlain to set an example of sacrifice by sacrificing the seals of office, struck a false note, and was not helpful from the point of view that mattered most, namely securing his fellow Conservative MPs votes. By contrast, Duff Cooper a Conservative, was far more persuasive and declared that "this is not a time when any man has the right to wash his hands like Pontius Pilate", stating bluntly that he would show his lack of confidence in the Government by his vote. Duff Cooper continued:

> Tonight we shall no doubt listen to an eloquent and powerful speech by the First Lord of the Admiralty. I almost wish it was going to be delivered from the now empty seat which he used to occupy below the Gangway here. He will be defending with his eloquence those who have so long refused to listen to his counsel, who treated his warnings with contempt and who refused to take him into their own confidence. He will no doubt be as successful as he always has been, and those who so often trembled before his sword will be only too glad to shrink behind his buckler.[94]

Churchill, in winding up the debate and speaking for forty-five minutes, made the point that the enemy air supremacy prevented Britain from dealing with the German advance on land or, except by submarine, with the transport of her troops by sea. Everyone knew well enough that he, at least, was not to blame for that. Narvik was the place which had interested Churchill and which might still lead to some decisive achievement. Then for three minutes Churchill turned to the vote of confidence.

> The first part of the debate was concerned with Norway, but about five o'clock this afternoon we were told there was to be a Vote of Censure taken in the form of a vote on the Motion for the Adjournment. It seems to me that the House will be absolutely wrong to take such a grave decision in such a precipitate

---

94 HC Deb, 8 May 1940 ,vol. 360, cc1251–366.

manner, and after such little notice. The question of the dismissal of a Government has always been open to the House of Commons, and no Minister would condescend to hold office unless he had the confidence and support of the House. But if the Government are to be dismissed from office, and that is the claim which has been made without scruple, then I think that in time of war at least there should be a solemn Resolution put down on the Paper and full notice given of the debate. Exception has been taken because the Prime Minister said he appealed to his friends. He thought he had some friends, and I hope he has some friends. He certainly had a good many when things were going well. I think it would be most ungenerous and unworthy of the British character, and the Conservative Party, to turn in a moment of difficulty without all the processes of grave debate which should be taken.[95]

The speech, for all its skill, made little impression. Amery thought that "what really mattered was that it strengthened Churchill's position with the defenders of the Government without weakening it in the eyes of those of us who saw in him the obvious successor to Chamberlain".[96]

Amery then describes the most dramatic division in which he had ever taken part. "So unexpectedly large was the number of Conservatives voting against the Government – we were forty-four in all – and so many remained ostentatiously in their seats determined to abstain, rather than vote, that, for a moment, some half thought they might have an actual majority."[97] Yet as the Whips marched up to the table, bowing their heads three times, the Government Whips, as expected, were on the right meaning the Government had won. David Margesson read out the figures: 281 to 200 instead of the normal majority of over 200. Gasps, and shouts of "resign, resign" were then heard from MPs. Confidence was obviously no longer held in Chamberlain's

95 HC Deb, 8 May 1940, vol. 360, cc 1251–366.
96 L. S. Amery, *My Political Life: The Unforgiving Years*, p 368.
97 Asa Briggs, *They Saw It Happen: An anthology of eye-witnesses' accounts of events in British history, 1897–1940, vol.3.* (B. Blackwell, 1960), p 500.

Government. It was a devastating blow demonstrating that winning in the division lobby is not always the real test.

The House of Commons is a place of moods, mostly rather drowsy and slow moving, but when roused its power collectively applied is formidable. Even Chamberlain now began to recognise that either Halifax or Churchill must form a real War Cabinet on an all-party basis. The Government benches tried to raise a cheer while the Socialists shouted, "Go, in God's name go!"

The House met next day on 9 May. Davies, having presided earlier over an all-party meeting of MPs, had found an overwhelming majority would not support the existing government and would only support a National Government comprising all parties. This conclusion was at once communicated to the Prime Minister.

Also meeting on 9 May was Lord Salisbury's Watching Committee, including the Conservative MP Harold Macmillan and the National Labour MP Harold Nicolson, and amongst them peers, with Paul Emrys-Evans as secretary and Amery as chairman of its sub-committee on military matters. It was agreed that, irrespective of how people had voted the night before, it was now essential that Chamberlain resign. Davies moved that the House of Commons should reassemble on 14 May, instead of 21 May. But the Speaker limited discussion so narrowly to the question of date that neither Davies nor other speakers could really raise the main issues with which they were concerned. In his diary entry for 9 May 1940 Leo Amery records that there was an "early meeting of Salisbury's Watching Committee at which the general feeling was, including those who had voted with the Government, that Neville should now resign and either Halifax or Winston form a real War Cabinet on National Lines".[98]

Chamberlain, who had seemed the night before to be reconciled to the necessity of an all-party government to restore confidence, was influenced by Churchill, to whom he had spoken immediately after the division in the House of Commons, and who expressed a doubt as to whether resignation was necessary. He offered Amery the choice of Chancellor of the Exchequer or Foreign Secretary the next morning, but he refused. Halifax that morning was quite definite with

---

98 John Barnes, David Nicholson, *The Empire at Bay*, p 611.

Chamberlain that a coalition government had become inevitable. Chamberlain then arranged for Churchill and Halifax to come and discuss the situation at four-thirty that afternoon in Downing Street.

There are many different accounts of what happened in Downing Street in the aftermath of 9 May. All the participants had different perceptions and conflicting stories emerged in varying diary entries and books. One can, however, piece together a narrative based on probability. When Attlee and Greenwood eventually arrived at Downing Street after a long lunch at the Reform Club with Clement Davies, they went to the Cabinet Room where Chamberlain was flanked by Halifax and Churchill. Chamberlain began by saying that he thought the time had come for him to renew his invitation of the previous autumn to join his government. Attlee left it to Greenwood to firmly explain that the Prime Minister completely misunderstood the situation, insisting "there was not the slightest prospect of the Opposition joining a government under him; they not only disliked him but regarded him as something evil".[99] Whether the term "evil" was actually uttered is not clear, but one can be certain that Greenwood and other Labour MPs felt resentful about the way that Chamberlain had treated them and blamed him for the mess the country was in. Many years later, Attlee would allude to these feelings in an interview for Granada:

> Q: But had you made up your mind then that if this should happen you would not serve under Chamberlain?
> Attlee: I don't know that was ever suggested, He always treated us like dirt.

Churchill at once leapt to Chamberlain's defence with an eloquent tribute; he had found him charming to work with as well as most efficient in the despatch of business. Greenwood cut in, "We haven't come here to listen to you orating, Winston",[100] before continuing that whilst this all may be true it was irrelevant to the fact

---

99 John Barnes, David Nicholson, *The Empire at Bay*, p612.
100 William Manchester, *The Caged Lion: Winston Spencer Churchill, 1932–1940*, p 668.

that Labour leaders could only join with the approval of the Party Conference that was meeting at Bournemouth next day. There is some dispute as to whether it was Attlee or Chamberlain who then scribbled on a slip of paper the questions that would be put to the Labour Conference next morning on 10 May. Was Labour prepared to support a government under (a) the present Prime Minister, (b) another Prime Minister? There is no doubt, whatever its provenance, that Attlee agreed with the formula, but added, as he took it away with him, according to Amery, that there was not the ghost of a chance of the Conference accepting the first alternative which sounds a very typical example of both Attlee's brevity and style. When interviewed in 1965, Lord Attlee remembered saying at that same meeting, "I have to be quite frank with you Prime Minister, our party will not serve under you. They don't want you, and in my view the country doesn't want you."[101]

When Attlee and Greenwood left the Cabinet Room David Margesson joined the meeting as the Conservative Party Chief Whip. The Chief Whip traditionally played a role in deciding who would emerge as party leader prior to the now established procedure of an election. There is little doubt that Chamberlain, now having full knowledge of Attlee and Greenwood's position, here admitted that it was impossible for him to continue.

Writing in September 2013 on a new edition of *The Holy Fox*, its author, Andrew Roberts, writes in his introduction:

There has only been one piece of brand new information that has come out about the crucial meeting of 9 May 1940 in which it was decided that, on his resignation, Neville Chamberlain would recommend Winston Churchill to King George VI as his successor rather than Chamberlain's (and indeed the King's) first choice of Lord Halifax. That is to be found on page 476 of Amanda Smith's 2001 edition of *Hostage to Fortune*, her edition of the private papers of her grandfather Joseph P. Kennedy, the American Ambassador to London from 1938 to 1940.

---

101 Alan Watkins, *The Road to Number 10: from Bonar Law to Tony Blair* (Duckworth, 1998), p 45.

Knowing he was dying of cancer – indeed he had less than three weeks to live – Chamberlain invited Kennedy to his home in the country on 19 October 1940 to say farewell. According to Kennedy's diary, they discussed the May meeting, and Chamberlain told Kennedy that after the Labour Party leaders had indicated that they would not serve in a National Government under him, 'He then wanted to make Halifax P[rime] M[inister] and said that he would serve under him. Edward, as [is] his way, started saying "Perhaps I can't handle it being in the H[ouse] of Lords" and finally Winston said, "I don't think you could." And he wouldn't come and that settled it.[102]

Other accounts have Churchill saying nothing when asked by Chamberlain, "Can you see any reason, Winston, why in these days a peer should not be Prime Minister?"[103] We are told that Churchill had been warned that this trick question would be posed by Kingsley Wood in a private conversation before the meeting and took his advice to say nothing. Churchill's account admits his silence was out of character: "Usually I talk a great deal but on this occasion I was silent ... As I remained silent, a very long pause ensued. It certainly seemed longer than the two minutes which one observes in the commemorations of Armistice Day".[104] Halifax writes, "Winston wore suitable expressions of regard and humility, [and] said he could not but feel the force of what I had said" when earlier Halifax had referred to having "no access to the House of Commons".

For Roberts, who has studied Halifax in depth and with objectivity, Kennedy's is the authentic account of what was said; Churchill did say it would be difficult to be in the Lords. This does not mean that membership of the House of Lords was the real reason for Halifax not taking on the premiership however. The king had said that Halifax's peerage could be put into 'abeyance', and only four months previously Chamberlain had contemplated an enabling bill

102 Andrew Roberts, *The Holy Fox*, p xv-xvi.
103 Anthony Dix, *The Norway Campaign and the Rise of Churchill 1940* (Pen and Sword, 2014), p 152.
104 Winston S. Churchill, *The Gathering Storm: The Second World War, vol.1* (Rosetta Books, 2010), p 597.

to allow Lord Stamp to be Chancellor of the Exchequer and speak in the Commons.

Halifax's own account is probably best encapsulated within Butler's, whom he saw immediately after the meeting: "He told me that he felt he could do the job. He also felt that Churchill needed a restraining influence. Could that restraint be better exercised as Prime Minister or as a minister in Churchill's Government? Even if he chose the former role, Churchill's qualities and experience would surely mean that he would be running the war anyway and Halifax's own position would speedily turn into a sort of honorary Prime Minister".[105] Roberts writes that "to restrain Churchill from below rather than above" was a strategy understood by Chamberlain and a significant reason why he did not push Halifax to become Prime Minister.[106] Ambition is not the simple pursuit of personal power on every occasion. At a time when your country is in peril and close to invasion, it is perfectly possible that Halifax was ambitious above all to maximise the war effort and prepared to forgo the premiership in order to provide, along with the military, the control and restraint required from below. Attlee was to provide, not control of Churchill, but a persistent, well-judged restraining influence.

Halifax had had a formidable career. As Viceroy of India he had ruled over more than 300 million people, and had exercised political power under both Baldwin and Chamberlain. He undoubtedly wished to continue to exercise power on 10 May. He did not resign, as well he might have, after being defeated in the War Cabinet, as the reader will discover in the next two chapters. He defied with great intensity being pushed out of exercising real power in December 1940 by resisting being sent to Washington. There is a very good case for concluding that Halifax's ambition was to exercise as much control over Churchill, when he thought it was needed, as he could. Given Churchill's formidable gifts, he was right to conclude that this should be done from below.

Churchill had his own sources of information as to the attitude of the Labour Party before hearing from Attlee and Greenwood.

---

105 Andrew Roberts, *The Holy Fox*.
106 *Ibid*, p 200.

Amery claims that dining with Brendan Bracken, a Conservative MP who later became the proprietor of the *Financial Times,* on 7 May, Attlee had expressed the view that, if there was a change of government, his people, who had never forgiven Churchill for Tonypandy, would expect it to be under Halifax with Churchill as Minister of Defence. Bracken, entirely on his own responsibility, had insisted that Churchill could not and would not serve under Halifax, incurring all the blame if things went wrong, and with no real control of the situation, and had persuaded Attlee at any rate not to refuse to serve under Churchill, if the occasion arose. Churchill however knew that evening of 9 May that he was going to become Prime Minister the next day. At a dinner that evening, he told his companions Eden and Sinclair that he thought Chamberlain "would advise the King to send for him. Edward [Halifax] did not wish to succeed. Parliamentary position too difficult."

On the evening of 9 May, Boothby wrote urgently to Churchill to keep him up with developments, but Churchill knew the die was cast. The note is nevertheless important for showing where Churchill's support was coming from:

Dear Winston,

I have been in the House all day. This is the situation, as I see it.

(1) The Labour Party won't touch Chamberlain at any price.

(2) Nor will Archie [Sinclair].

(3) Nor will our group.

Therefore it is inconceivable that Chamberlain can carry through a reconstruction of the Government.

A majority of the House is, nevertheless, determined on a *radical* reconstruction, which will involve (inter alia) the elimination of Simon and Hoare.

(4) Opinion is hardening against Halifax as Prime Minister. I am doing my best to foster this, because I cannot feel he is, in the circumstances, the right man.

At the moment of writing, our group would oppose his appointment, unless it commanded universal assent. It is quite a powerful group. It is now led by Amery and includes Duff Cooper, Eddie Winterton, Belisha, Hammersley, Henderson-Stewart,

Emrys-Evans, Mrs Tate, R. Tree, Russell, Harold Nicolson, [Derrick] Gunston, Clem Davies, & [Stephen] King-Hall.[107]

Next morning, 10 May, the world woke up to the shock news of a double invasion of Holland and Belgium. Chamberlain's first reaction when the War Cabinet met at 8.00 am was to feel that the change of situation made it necessary for him to stay in office, until the immediate crisis was over, according to Amery's account. Corroboration of Chamberlain's assumption that he would temporarily remain Prime Minister is available in that even before the meeting of Cabinet he had told Reith, formerly the head of the BBC and now Minister of Information, that he was to attend all future Cabinet meetings. The news of his intention to stay on was simultaneously given out by the Whips' Office. On getting wind of this, Davies at once telephoned Attlee and Greenwood, urging them to lose no time in getting an immediate decision from the Labour Conference in Bournemouth. That Labour were willing to serve in a National Government, but not under Chamberlain, was, by then, a foregone conclusion, but it was only communicated by telephone to staff in No. 10 early that afternoon.

The War Cabinet met again that morning at 11.30 am with the issue of Labour's attitudes still not confirmed officially, though a wire report describing the mood of the Conference was handed in while the Cabinet was sitting. Churchill went back to the Admiralty not knowing when the task of forming a government would fall on him. Attlee, before leaving for Bournemouth, issued a statement about the "latest series of abominable aggressions by Hitler".[108] He went on to say that he was "firmly convinced that drastic reconstruction of the Government is vital and urgent in order to win the war" and which "reaffirms its determination to do its utmost to achieve victory. It calls on all its members to direct all their energies to this end." Attlee's statement, drafted with Greenwood and Dalton, had deliberately not endorsed Chamberlain staying on and was soon

---

107 Samantha Heywood, *Churchill* (Psychology Press, 2003), p 80.
108 Alan Watkins, *The Road to Number 10: From Bonar Law to Tony Blair* (Duckworth, 1998), p 48.

followed after the 3.00 pm National Executive Committee meeting in Bournemouth with an even clearer statement: Labour would serve in a coalition government but on specific conditions. The formal confirmation of the Labour Party's conditions were eventually conveyed by Chamberlain to the Cabinet after Attlee had read the statement at dictation speed to one of Chamberlain's secretaries over the telephone. Labour would serve only "as a full partner in a new Government under a new Prime Minister which would command the confidence of the nation."[109] Wisely, Labour did not articulate who should be Prime Minister.

Chamberlain told the Cabinet he was going to see the King to advise that Churchill should be sent for. Churchill saw the King soon after 6.00 pm. Later that evening at 9.00 pm Churchill saw Attlee and Greenwood at Admiralty House on their arrival from Bournemouth and invited them to join his War Cabinet. This was constitutionally the correct way of proceeding. Churchill was installed as Prime Minister by Conservative Party informal mechanisms; no formal votes were cast but soundings of key people in the party were heeded. Attlee would be Lord Privy Seal and Greenwood Minister without Portolio. Churchill would be his own Minister of Defence and Chamberlain would be Lord President of the Council, able to cover international and domestic policy. Halfax was already Foreign Secretary, and the three service ministers would be Anthony Eden, responsible for the army as Minister of War; Sinclair, the Liberal Party leader, as Minister for Air; and A.V. Alexander would reassume the role of First Lord of the Admiralty, which he had been in the last Labour Government.

Chamberlain, in a farewell broadcast that evening, announced that he would be in the War Cabinet and Leader of the House, in effect Deputy Prime Minister. Many Labour MPs had hoped that Chamberlain would be kept out altogether. Attlee and Greenwood saw Churchill next morning and protested against Chamberlain being Leader of the House and formally Deputy Leader. They were to meet with Churchill again in the afternoon; in the meantime, the Conservative Watching Committee and Amery's group, including Clem

---

109 Ben Pimlott, *Labour and the Left in the 1930s* (CUP Archive, 1977), p 191.

Davies, learnt of the exasperation of the Labour leaders and of their grave doubts as to whether they could join the Government on this basis. Amery and Davies explained the situation to Salisbury on the telephone, who was deeply disturbed by the thought that Churchill's insistence on the retention of Chamberlain could conceivably wreck the prospect of a real National Government. He promised to ring up Churchill at once to convey the strong objection felt by himself and his Conservative associates, as well as by the Opposition, to such an arrangement. Amery had no doubt that, due to Salisbury's intervention, when the Labour leaders returned to see Churchill later that day, it would be agreed that Chamberlain should be President of the Council but with no departmental responsibilities. Churchill had also made clear that, of the Labour people he wanted to serve in the Government, foremost on the list was Bevin, along with Morrison and Dalton. This was a clear indication of Churchill's respect for Bevin since he was then not even an MP.

Though Churchill looked to be in a powerful position he knew that he was doubted or disliked by most Conservative MPs, and yet they were the source of his power. William Spens, the Conservative Chairman of the 1922 Committee of Backbench MPs, succinctly spelt it out. Three quarters of Conservative MPs were ready to oust Churchill and bring back Chamberlain. It was no more than common prudence therefore for Churchill to keep Chamberlain and Halifax in the War Cabinet. A few purists might be upset in the Conservative Party but Churchill was a pragmatist, and certainly no purist. He knew where power lay at least for the next few months and he had to harness it. Hostility was not just the language of the hard right. Rab Butler, Halifax's deputy, records Halifax saying to him in his room in the Foreign Office, "'it is all a great tragedy, isn't it?' I replied, 'that is because you did not take the premiership yourself.' He said, 'you know my reasons, it is no use discussing that – but the gangsters will shortly be in complete control'".[110] By "gangsters" Halifax was alluding to the Churchill entourage, such figures as Beaverbrook, Brendan Bracken and Professor Lindemann, later Lord Cherwell. Butler, a moderate one-nation Conservative, never quite lived down

---

110 Anthony Howard, *RAB: The Life of R A Butler*, p 94.

his reputation as an appeaser with a sharp tongue; he was reported as saying, "Surrendering to Winston and his rabble was a disaster and an unnecessary one. It was like mortgaging the future of the country to a 'half-bred American' whose main support was that of inefficient but talkative people of a similar type."[111]

In the House of Commons, on 13 May, for the first time as Prime Minister, Churchill moved a vote welcoming a government representing the united and inflexible resolve of the nation to prosecute the war with Germany to a victorious conclusion. He said, with Clement Attlee sitting beside him on the front bench:

> I have nothing to offer but blood, toil, tears and sweat. We have before us an ordeal of the most grievous kind. We have before us many, many long months of struggle and of suffering. You ask, what is our policy? I can say: it is to wage war, by sea, land and air, with all our might and with all the strength that God can give us; to wage war against a monstrous tyranny, never surpassed in the dark, lamentable catalogue of human crime. That is our policy. You ask, what is our aim? I can answer in one word: it is victory, victory at all costs, victory in spite of all terror, victory, however long and hard the road may be; for without victory, there is no survival.[112]

This magnificent injunction to fight had more resonance, however, outside the House of Commons. Inside, while he had a promising reception from Labour, Conservative MPs listened to Churchill in 'sullen silence'.

---

111 Boris Johnson, *The Churchill Factor* (Hodder & Stoughton paperback, 2014), p 33.
112 Alan Axelrod, *The Real History of World War II: A New Look at the Past* (Sterling Publishing Company, Inc., 2008), p 66.

3

The Politics of the Coalition Government

Prime Minister Churchill, seasoned politician that he was, knew from the start he had to pay attention personally to four political figures: Chamberlain, Lloyd George, Bevin and Roosevelt. Their goodwill was urgently needed; their ill will could be fatal for victory. Parliament, for the purpose of debate and legitimacy, was essential, but in a three-party coalition votes were unlikely to be very frequent or important. If Churchill was to run into trouble it was going to be instigated by the Conservative MPs who had never wanted him; ever in his memory was what Conservative MPs had done to Lloyd George in 1922. Two people in the House of Commons that Churchill felt could have perhaps the most significant bearing on his standing and authority was, most obviously, Neville Chamberlain; the other, more surprisingly, was Lloyd George and Churchill persisted throughout 1940 in trying to bring him into the fold.

We have some insight into what Chamberlain was actually feeling on 11 May, the day after Churchill took over, through a personal letter he wrote to his sister, Ida. The so-called 'phoney war' was over; Germany had now invaded the Low Countries of Belgium, the Netherlands and Luxembourg, and the first major air attack on mainland Britain had started. In the letter, Chamberlain refers back to the debate on 7–8 May in his final days as Prime Minister, which ended in the reduced majority of 81:

My dear Ida,
....The serving members were acutely conscious of various deficiencies, not realising apparently that though you can double your T[erritorial] A[rmy] with a stroke of the pen, you can't do

the same thing with its equipment. The Amerys, Duff Coopers & their lot are consciously or unconsciously swayed by a sense of frustration because they can look on ... They don't want to believe that the real reason is our comparative weakness because we haven't yet anything like caught up with the German start, but as that fact remains whatever the administration I am afraid they will presently be disappointed again.

It did not take me long to make up my mind what to do. I saw that the time had come for a National Government in the broadest sense. I knew that I could not get it, but it was necessary to get an official confirmation of the Opposition attitude, if only to justify my resignation to my own party ... Winston & Halifax ... agreed with my view and I sent for Attlee & Greenwood that afternoon to ask the definite question whether the Labour Party would join a Government under me or, if not, under someone else. I did not name the someone else to them but I had understood that they favoured Halifax, and I had him in mind. He declared however that, after careful reflection, he would find it too difficult, being in the Lords, whereas troubles always arose in the Commons. Later I heard that the Labour Party had changed their minds and were veering towards Winston and I agreed with him and Halifax that I would put Winston's name to the King.[1]

Chamberlain went on to say that Winston had been most handsome in his appreciation of Chamberlain's own willingness to help and ability to do so, paraphrasing Churchill's letter to him, "My fate depends largely on you". He then went on to refer to Lloyd George:

It has been suggested to me by the way that Ll.G.'s speech yesterday in the Commons in which he sought to justify Hitler on the grounds that we had broken faith with Germany was deliberately made to separate himself from the new Government and stake out a position from which ultimately he might be called to make the peace. This seems to me so characteristic of Lloyd George that

---

1   Neville Chamberlain, *The Neville Chamberlain Diary Letters: The Downing Street Years 1934–40*. Ed. Robert C Self (Routledge, 2005), pp 528–530.

I think it is very likely true. I know that he thinks we shall be beaten in the war.[2]

Another interesting vignette was that Winston had told him not to move from No. 10 for a month or even longer, and he tells his sister "if the Govt still stands" we will go back to No. 11. This sensitivity to Chamberlain's feelings shows Churchill at his strategic best, working to build a positive and indeed productive relationship with Chamberlain.

Then on 17 May, writing from Downing Street to his older sister, Hilda, as part of his practice of alternating letters which each sister passed on to the other, his reserve is set aside when he confides:

All my world has tumbled to bits in a moment. The national peril has so swamped all personal feelings that no bitterness remains. Indeed I used to say to Annie before war came that if such a thing happened I thought I should have to hand over to someone else, for I knew what agony of mind it would mean for me to give directions that would bring death & mutilation & misery to so many. But the war was so different from what I expected that I found the strain bearable and perhaps it was providential that the revolution which overturned me coincided with the entry of the real thing. I confess that I am thankful that the primary responsibility is off my shoulders, though of course it is quite impossible for me to detach myself from the knowledge I have of the possibilities in the immediate future.

I must say that Winston has shown up well so far. After one or two hectic nights when we were kept up till the small hours, he has reverted to morning sittings of the Cabinet. He does take the opinions of the staff and doesn't attempt to force different views upon them or to shoulder off his colleagues. Our own relations are admirable and I have no difficulty with any of my colleagues in the Cabinet. I have agreed to let Attlee be Deputy Leader in the House.[3]

---

2 *Ibid*, p 530.
3 Neville Chamberlain, *The Neville Chamberlain Diary Letters: The Downing Street Years 1934–40*. Ed. Robert C Self, pp 531–532.

The Labour Party had objected to Chamberlain being Leader of the House of Commons but:

I am to retain the Leadership of the Party which I think was essential if Winston was to have wholehearted support. There has been much resentment among those who are personally devoted to me, both at my treatment and at the way the "Treachery Bench" has been given office.[4]

On 1 June Chamberlain, still in Downing Street, wrote to Hilda, after the evacuation from Dunkirk:

There seems to have been hardly any mistake that the French did not make and they invariably started retiring about six hours before the time they had arranged with us so that they constantly uncovered our flank. Their generals were beneath contempt & with some notable exceptions the soldiers would not fight & would not even march. The Belgians were better but not steady and in short as usual the brunt of all the hard fighting and the hard work fell upon the British.[5]

He went on to tell his sisters that what truly worried him was:

...that the people who have been building up a "hate" against me have not in any way given it up. I hear for instance that a party meet every evening at the Reform Club under the chairmanship of Clement Davies, that treacherous Welshman who ratted from the last Government & worked his hardest to whip up opposition to it. The party includes Amery, Macmillan & Boothby among those critics who are now in Winston's Government and it has been attended by Attlee, Greenwood and Sinclair.

Chamberlain was also worried about Lloyd George, who had written to Churchill saying he wanted to give the nation the benefit of his services by entering the Government and was now complaining

---

4 *Ibid*, p 532.
5 *Ibid*, p 535.

THE POLITICS OF THE COALITION GOVERNMENT   83

that Chamberlain was the sole cause of his so far being excluded. Chamberlain admitted this:

> It is true that Winston did ask me what I would think about Ll.G. entering the Government last week. He did not specify any office or mention the War Cabinet in particular. But he did say that he himself distrusted Ll.G.

Chamberlain went on to say:

> Frankly, if at any time Winston thought Ll.G. would be more useful to him than I, I should be quite ready to retire. But I could not work with him. I did not trust him, or believe his word, or feel convinced that his motives were the same as mine. Winston said at once that there was no question of any comparison between Ll.G. & myself. We had gone in together & would if necessary go down together.[6]

Then, on 8 June, Chamberlain wrote his final letter from Downing Street:

> In the H. of C ... Winston announced that there would be a secret session on Tuesday [.] I saw at once by the demeanour of the Labour Party (who still sit in their old seats opposite to us) that they meant to seize this occasion for a direct attack."

Chamberlain went to see Churchill the next day, and said:

> ..if he felt me to be an obstacle instead of a help he must say so & I should be ready to resign without reproaches. I thought it possible that he would, in the most delicate terms he could find, convey to me that it would help him out of certain difficulties if I did go and in that case I should of course have handed in my demission. However he said just the contrary. While professing some

6 Neville Chamberlain, *The Neville Chamberlain Diary Letters: The Downing Street Years 1934–40*. Ed. Robert C Self, pp 535–536.

surprise that I was taking things so seriously, he declared that he certainly wanted me to stop. I was giving him splendid help and he wasn't going to have the Government which he had only just formed knocked about.[7]

Winston said to him that he would certainly speak for the Government himself. Chamberlain then called upon Winston to appeal to Attlee and Greenwood to help prevent the *Herald* newspaper attacks; and Churchill promised he would talk to the "press generally and warn them off scalp-hunting".

In the secret session on 10 June Churchill warned that seeking scapegoats for the past was "a foolish and pernicious process".[8] Winston then reverted to the Lloyd George issue and said if he had to choose between them he would choose Chamberlain. But Chamberlain explains that Churchill had then asked him

to consider whether it was right to force such a choice on him. He developed this proposition with great earnestness saying that personal differences ought not to count now & he was quite sure that L.G. would work loyally with me. Finally I asked him to let me think it over & we parted amicably.[9]

Next morning the attacks were continuing and Chamberlain writes of a letter he had received from the Prime Minister, saying that he had been much encouraged by their talk and again pressing Chamberlain to withdraw his opposition to having Lloyd George in the Cabinet. Chamberlain writes about his reply:

I could not resist his appeal, difficult though I found it to accept. But I made two conditions. First that he should obtain a personal assurance from L.G. that he would drop all personal feuds & prejudices and second that the press campaign against me should

---

7 *Ibid*, p 537.
8 William Manchester, *The Caged Lion: Winston Spencer Churchill, 1932–1940* (Michael Joseph, 1988).
9 Neville Chamberlain, *The Neville Chamberlain Diary Letters: The Downing Street Years 1934–40*. Ed. Robert C Self, p 537.

be stopped before any announcement about L.G. was made, lest it should be said that I had made a bargain to let him in if I were protected against attack.[10]

Churchill accepted Chamberlain's conditions, passing him a note in the War Cabinet, and they later had a discussion in which Chamberlain pointed out that "he had nothing to complain of in the behaviour of my colleagues" present but that "I was bound to ask myself what they were doing to allow these venomous attacks by members of their parties to go on while we were all supposed to be working harmoniously to win the war."[11] Chamberlain wrote: "I got satisfactory assurances from all concerned & since then the campaign has stopped even more suddenly than it began."

Meanwhile Churchill once more saw Lloyd George, who wished to think over the offer of conditions before accepting. Churchill passed Chamberlain a note saying, "The Wizard [Lloyd George] remains silent."[12] In a talk with Beaverbrook, the Minister of Aircraft Production, Chamberlain asked why Lloyd George hated him. He records Beaverbrook's answer that Lloyd George

thought I was chiefly responsible for keeping him out of office for 18 years. He had counted on the collapse of Bonar Law's Government in 1922 & it had been saved by my joining it and in Baldwin's time he had always looked on me as the real power in the Govt & the one which was most hostile to him.[13]

Lloyd George had been out of office since 1922. He had since then developed an admiration for presidential government, which had begun with Theodore Roosevelt before extending to his fifth cousin, Franklin Roosevelt. He went on to admire Hitler too much for his own good. Ribbentrop, as German Ambassador in 1935, with

---

10 *Ibid.*
11 Richard Toye, *Lloyd George and Churchill: Rivals for Greatness* (Pan Macmillan, 2008), p 351.
12 *Ibid*, p 363.
13 Neville Chamberlain, *The Neville Chamberlain Diary Letters: The Downing Street Years 1934–40*. Ed. Robert C Self, p 538.

a combination of attention and flattery, prepared the visit by Lloyd George to Hitler's 'eyrie' high in the Bavarian Alps. Lloyd George met first with Ribbentrop in Munich for dinner. The meeting with Hitler began on the afternoon of 4 September 1936 for two hours, after which Lloyd George asserted, "He is a great man. Führer is the proper name for him for he is a born leader, yes and a statesman."[14] Hitler had, in *Mein Kampf*, written a few words of praise for Lloyd George's speeches. By having his old civil servant, Tom Jones, now working with Prime Minister Baldwin, accompany him, Lloyd George avoided criticism of undermining the Government.[15] Lloyd George was still writing admiringly of Hitler as late as December 1937 to Professor Cornwell Evans, "I have never doubted the fundamental greatness of Herr Hitler as a man, even in moments of disagreement... I only wish we had a man of his supreme quality at the head of affairs in our country."[16] When Lloyd George spoke in the House of Commons debate in May 1940 it was not the speech of a man of power. He nevertheless savaged Chamberlain with, what Dingle Foot, a Liberal MP called, "the accumulated dislike and contempt of twenty-five years".[17]

On 12 May Churchill invited Lloyd George to lunch at Admiralty House. On 16 May they spoke again. On 28 May Churchill asked to meet him in the House of Commons, after which Lloyd George wrote a letter to Churchill the following day, saying:[18]

> Secret and Personal
> My dear Winston,
> You were good enough to ask me if I would be prepared to enter the War Cabinet if you secured the adhesion of Mr Chamberlain. It is the first time that you have approached me on the subject and I can well understand your hesitancy, for, in the course of our

14 Hugh Purcell, *Lloyd George* (Haus Publishing, 2006), p 109.

15 Roy Hattersley, *David Lloyd George* (Little Brown, 2010), pp 623–625.

16 Peter Rowland, *David Lloyd George: A Biography* (Pan Macmillan: 1976), p 744.

17 *Ibid*, p 772.

18 Martin Gilbert, *The Churchill War Papers, Volume II: Never Surrender May 1940–December 1940* (Heinemann, 1994), pp 194–195. An invaluable record of events, brilliantly edited by Martin Gilbert, from which I draw all documents from the period of May 1940–December 1940, unless otherwise indicated.

interview, you made it quite clear that if Chamberlain interposed his veto on the grounds of personal resentment over past differences you could not proceed with the offer. This is not a firm offer. Until it is definite I cannot consider it.

I am sure you will be just enough to realise that the experience I have already had in this war justifies my reply to your conditional inquiry. Since the war began I have in public thrice offered to help the Government in any capacity, however humble. No notice has been taken of my tenders. I have never been consulted. I have never been invited even to sit on a committee. Since you became Prime Minister I offered to do my best to help in organising the food supplies of this country. I have acquired considerable knowledge and experience both in peace as well as in war in that line. At the request of your personal friends I put forward alternative proposals for the intensive production of food in this country, and I suggested the part I might play in directing this essential branch of national service. Nothing came of this scheme. I have not even been informed of the reason for its rejection. I say this in order to show that it was due to no unwillingness on my part that you found it impossible to utilise my services. I apprehend that party and personal considerations frustrated your wishes. I cannot be put in that position again. I am no office seeker. I am genuinely anxious to help to extricate my country from the most terrible disaster into which it has ever been plunged by the ineptitude of her rulers. Several of the architects of this catastrophe are still leading members of your Government, and two of them are in the Cabinet that directs the war.

Like millions of my fellow countrymen I say to you that, if in any way you think I can help, I am at your call. But if that call is tentative and qualified I shall not know what answer to give.

Believe me,
Ever sincerely,
D. Lloyd George

Churchill replied that same day.

My dear LG,

I have just received your letter of today. I am sorry that the same difficulties in regard to persons which you mentioned to me are also only too present elsewhere. I cannot complain in any way of what you say in your letter. The Government I have formed is founded upon the leaders of the three parties, and like you I have no party of my own. I have received a very great deal of help from Chamberlain; his kindness and courtesy to me in our new relation have touched me. I have joined hands with him, and must act with perfect loyalty. As you say, the inquiry I made of you yesterday could only be indeterminate, and I could not ask you to go further than you have done in your letter.

With regard to the organisation of the food supplies of this country, of which my personal friends had some talk with you, I can assure you that no personal or party difficulties have frustrated its consideration. The Ministry of Agriculture was discussed and one of my friends made representations to you. It was only after you had taken the decision that you did not at that time contemplate sharing responsibilities involved in joining the administration, that I made another selection, without making any stipulations with the new Minister. The alternative project of organisation of food supplies could well be taken up on another occasion. I have simply been so over-pressed by terrible events, that I have not had life or strength to address myself to it.

Thank you very much for what you say in your last paragraph and I trust that we shall keep in personal contact, so that I may acquaint you with the situation as it deepens. I always have the warmest feelings of regard and respect for you.

Yours ever,
Winston S Churchill

This letter is particularly interesting for one claim: "like you I have no party of my own". This is more than stretching the truth; Churchill was a Conservative MP, elected as such and eligible to become, as he did, the Conservative Party choice for Prime Minister. He had asked Chamberlain to stay as leader of the party, but that was a tactical manoeuvre, and when Chamberlain died he became leader of the Conservative Party himself. However, what is true is that Churchill respected the Lloyd George Liberals and wanted to attract them to the Conservative Party under his leadership, as particularly apparent in his readiness to include in his government his deputy from his service as Colonel in the regiment for which they had both fought in France, Archibald Sinclair. Churchill stressed that his government was "founded upon the leaders of the three parties".

Still Churchill persisted. On 6 June, Lloyd George was offered by Churchill at a hurriedly convened meeting an unconditional offer of a seat in the War Cabinet. Despite advice to accept by Tom Jones and his by-then wife, Frances Stevenson, and his friendly talk with Churchill, he refused, telling his wife he would not share in the guilt of defeat, a message he repeated in a letter to his 12-year-old daughter, Jennifer:

1. I do not believe in the way we entered the war – not in the methods by which it has been conducted. We have made blunder after blunder and are still blundering. Unless there is a thorough change of policy we shall never win.
2. I do not believe in the way or in the personnel with which the War Cabinet is constituted. It is totally different to the War Cabinet set up in the last War. It is not a War Directorate in the real sense of the term. There is therefore no real direction.

I am convinced that unless there is a real change in these two matters it would be a mistake for me to join up with the present lot.[19]

Even so, and again very surprisingly, in December 1940 Churchill asked Lloyd George, first, if he would consider going to Washington as ambassador when Lothian died.

Lloyd George refused and thereafter he paid everyone less and less regard, and even lost his respect for Parliament and they for him. Very unwisely, he took part in a no-confidence debate on 7 May 1941

---

19 Roy Hattersley, *David Lloyd George: The Great Outsider* (Hachette UK, 2010).

and said that talk of invading the European mainland was "fatuous". Churchill angrily replied that his speech was not helpful. "It was the kind of speech with which I imagine the illustrious and venerable Marshal Pétain might well have enlivened the closing days of M. Reynaud's Cabinet."[20]

It is very hard, in retrospect, to understand why Churchill was so determined to have Lloyd George enter his government. Lloyd George, 'the Welsh Wizard', or 'the Big Beast of the Forest', or 'the Goat', as he was variously called, was by 1940 a shadow of his former self. His eloquence was still on display in the debate on 8 May, with his reference to Churchill not allowing himself to be an air-raid shelter. However, apart from sentiment, it is difficult to understand why Churchill, so soon after becoming Prime Minister, tried so hard to bring Lloyd George into his government. There is no shadow of doubt that the War Cabinet Churchill constructed in May 1940 owed much to what he knew from Lloyd George's Cabinet, which he had rejoined on 17 May 1917 as Minister of Munitions, a position he held until 10 January 1919 when he became Secretary of State for War and Secretary of State for Air until 1921. The intimate exchanges the two men had shared at a time of peril were not easily forgotten.

However, though seemingly sentimental, it is probable that Churchill's concern to keep Lloyd George in a job was largely driven by his fear that if he, Churchill, ever became vulnerable after military defeats, his opponents would likely turn to Lloyd George, despite his age and ill health. Churchill perhaps perceived Lloyd George as a potential figurehead ripe to be used in a plot to overthrow him with Conservative votes.

When Lloyd George died on 26 March 1945, all was forgiven by Churchill in a most generous eulogy in the House of Commons two days later: "As a man of action, resource and creative energy, he stood, when at his zenith, without a rival."[21] There is little doubt that as Prime Minister Lloyd George was the man who Churchill most

---

20 Roy Hattersley, *David Lloyd George*, pp 629–633.
21 Winston S. Churchill, *Never Give In! Winston Churchill's Speeches* (A & C Black, 2013), p 317.

admired. For all Churchill's persistence however, one is left with the conclusion that he, Churchill, was lucky Lloyd George never came into his Cabinet; it was far more important for him to retain Chamberlain as long as he did.

Attacks on the 'Men of Munich', the agents of a failed act of appeasement, continued. On 5 July 1940 – under the pseudonym 'Cato' – *Guilty Men*, an indictment of the failures of Baldwin, Chamberlain and their colleagues from 1931 to 1940, was published. Chamberlain warned his sister Ida in a letter on 20 July to remember:

> when you read of the "Men of Munich who brought us into this mess", that the exploits of the Navy, RAF and BEF must have been made possible by the "Men of Munich". For no one can suppose that our equipment has all been turned out in the last six weeks. However it would be foolish to expect from these blind partisans either reason or logic since those things are not allowed to interfere with their emotions.[22]

Sadly in personal terms in that same letter, Chamberlain wrote he was "having considerable trouble" with his "inside" which "hadn't been working properly for a long time" and "is getting worse". In another letter to his sisters on 27 July, now from 11 Downing Street, he wrote again about his health:

> I mentioned in my last letter that I was having trouble in my inside. As a matter of fact it has been going on for some time, gradually getting worse and Horder at last thought it best that I should be X-rayed. That was done this week and the result is that I am to enter a nursing home next Monday for an operation that afternoon. It is not in itself a serious operation and I should be out again in a fortnight but the consequences will not be altogether pleasant.[23]

---

22 Graham Macklin, *Chamberlain* (Haus Publishing, 2006), p 98.
23 Neville Chamberlain, *The Neville Chamberlain Diary Letters: The Downing Street Years 1934–40*. Ed. Robert C Self, p 554.

This was a deliberate understatement to protect his sisters. In his diary on 27 July 1940 Chamberlain noted it was a major operation and he had 'even chances'.

Aside from Lloyd George and Chamberlain, the other figure whom Churchill had singled out on becoming Prime Minister was Ernest Bevin, who was not even in Parliament. The initial approach came from Attlee who rang Bevin on 11 May at his headquarters at Transport House. He started by asking him what he thought of Labour joining the coalition. Bevin's unhesitating reply was, according to his biographer Bullock, "In view of the fact that you helped to bring the other fellow down, if the party did not take its share of responsibility, they would say we were great citizens but cowards."[24] Having been informed that Churchill wanted four Labour men in high office immediately, and top of the list was Bevin himself, Attlee asked if he would indeed be willing to join the Government. "You have sprung it on me," Bevin said, to which Attlee replied, "It is sprung on all of us." Bevin asked for time to think. Then, at 3.00 pm that same day, he walked over to the House of Commons and told Attlee he was willing to serve, but only if he had the support, apart from his own Executive, of the TUC General Council and the party's National Executive. It was only then that he asked Attlee what job he was expected to take, and the answer was Minister of Labour. He spoke to Churchill sometime that day, probably by telephone, since he referred to it in his letter of acceptance.

Bevin, in fact, was criticised by some of his trade union friends for not holding out for Ministry of Supply, taken by Morrison, or Ministry of Economic Warfare, a position assumed by Dalton. Bevin, however, had an instinct that Ministry of Labour would, as he said to Arthur Deakin, give him "the chance to lay down the conditions on which we will start again after the war was over." Bevin nevertheless warned Churchill in his letter, "I feel it is imperative that [the Ministry's] position and place should be strengthened to deal with the

---

24 Alan Bullock, Baron Bullock, *The Life and Times of Ernest Bevin: Trade Union Leader 1881–1940* (Heinemann, 1960), pp 651–652.

problem of labour organisation and supply..."[25] Churchill showed the importance he attached to the trade unions writing to Bevin on 24 May with a message which he intended to be read out at their annual conference, though stating he would have welcomed, under conditions of less urgency, to speak to them himself:

> The country's needs are imperative, inescapable and imperious and we shall pay dearly if we fail to meet them. We can meet them now as a Government founded upon a new unity of national purpose ... Trade unionists with their tradition of sacrifice in the service of freedom, cannot hesitate to throw their full strength into the struggle.[26]

Bevin, from 1926 to 1931 had played an important role in national affairs in the Mond-Turner talks after the General Strike, with industrialists Sir Alfred Mond and Lord Weir, and serving on the Macmillan Committee on Finance and Industry. From 1931 to 1940, however, he was an outsider with no influence on government but a growing influence throughout the Labour Movement. Now at the age of 59 he was to start to assert a crucial influence in the government of the country. Bevin was returned unopposed as an MP at the end of June 1940 when a vacancy arose for the constituency of Central Wandsworth. In October 1940, he came into the War Cabinet.

Beaverbrook, someone Attlee once said Churchill used as a "kind of stimulant or drug", had been initially impressive but on 2 August 1940 came into the War Cabinet as Minister of Aircraft Production. It was not a successful appointment as Roy Jenkins argued, "he was never nearly enough of a team player to be either happy or useful in the War Cabinet. He was frequently wanting to resign on grounds of asthma or pique".[27] Beaverbrook also had frequent turf wars with Cripps in Moscow, Bevin on manpower allocation, Sinclair on pilot training and coastal command. Gradually the War Cabinet "moved

---

25 Richard Toye, *The Labour Party and the Planned Economy* (Boydell & Brewer, 2003), p 118.

26 Ernest Bevin, *The Job to be Done* (Heinemann, 1942), p 16.

27 Roy Jenkins, *Churchill* (Pan Macmillan, 2012), p 634.

well away from its original tight-knit group of non departmental ministers". Yet for the first three months Beaverbrook and Bevin had one essential task: to increase aircraft production at almost any cost. Churchill knew how Lloyd George had taken on the role of Minister of Munitions in May 1915, giving up the Exchequer, and he knew speed depended on drive, energy and a readiness to cut red tape and think unconventionally. These two men were for a short period a galvanic force, and the trade unions responded unreservedly for the war effort and more readily to the call of Bevin than anyone else. Employers were browbeaten by Beaverbrook to cut every possible corner. Two other newcomers came into the War Cabinet besides Bevin; Sir John Anderson in place of Chamberlain and Sir Kingsley Wood, the Chancellor of the Exchequer. Bevin was never out of an influential position in the Cabinet room until his death. Under both Churchill and Attlee he was a hugely powerful figure; only Attlee, Eden and Anderson equalled him in length of service in the War Cabinet.

The full War Cabinet met on 15 May at 11.00 am and Churchill began with an alarmist message that he had received from M. Reynaud earlier in the morning. The Germans had broken through at Sedan and the road to Paris was open. He had also heard from Admiral Sir Roger Keyes, a Conservative MP sent by Churchill to Brussels, who was famous for being in command of the Dover Patrol and the Zeebrugge raid in 1918. Keyes anticipated a strong German attack on Antwerp. The meeting was a significant one as the Foreign Secretary, Halifax, made an intervention noted under the heading 'Italy', which was to become very important ten days later.

> Continuing, the Foreign Secretary said that it might be of value if the Prime Minister, on assuming office, were to send a communication to Signor Mussolini. Perhaps the general heads of the message might be communicated to Sir Percy Loraine [ambassador in Rome] by telegram, with authority for him to cast the message into the most appropriate form, having regard to the situation in Rome.
>
> The Prime Minister said that he was quite ready to send such a message, and had already thought of doing so. He would propose to say that, on assuming the office of Prime Minister, he wished

to assure Signor Mussolini of his hope that this country and Italy should not be divided by bloodshed; we were finding the war hard, but we were confident of ultimate victory; it would be a disaster of the first magnitude if any irrevocable steps were taken, but, if this should happen, we should have no choice but to pursue the matter to the end, and this we should do. The Prime Minister said that he would draft a message and then consult with the Foreign Secretary.

The War Cabinet took note:

(a) Of the statement by the Secretary of State for Foreign Affairs.
(b) That the Prime Minister proposed to send a personal message to Signor Mussolini on the lines indicated in the discussion.

The Prime Minister then said to the War Cabinet that there remained two important questions to be decided that morning in regard to air operations:

(1) Whether we should send any more fighter squadrons to France in response to M. Reynaud's appeal.
(2) Whether we should attack military objectives in the Ruhr and elsewhere in Germany east of the Rhine.

As regards the former, he suggested that the War Cabinet would have little difficulty in deciding against the despatch of further fighter squadrons in view of the fact that no demand for these had been received from the military authorities in France.

The Prime Minister then asked Sir Archibald Sinclair, leader of the Liberal Party and an old friend, who had served under him in WW1 in France, and was now Secretary of State for Air, what was his view on the question of an attack against military objectives in the Ruhr and other similar targets. Sinclair warned that the experience of the last few days in France pointed to the fact that, at the present rate of losses, it would be extremely difficult for the Royal Air Force to maintain its present effort in support of the land battle by daylight bombing operations.

The meeting also minuted an important intervention from the Lord Privy Seal, Clement Attlee, who considered that the moment had arrived when it was essential for Britain's counter-attack. The proposed attack on the German railways and oil refineries seemed to provide the best and most effective means of carrying this out, and he was accordingly in favour of initiating these operations forthwith.

The War Cabinet then agreed:

(1) That no further fighter squadrons should, for the present, be sent to France, and to invite the Prime Minister so to inform M. Reynaud.

(2) To authorise the Chief of the Air Staff to order Bomber Command to carry out attacks on suitable military objectives (including marshalling yards and oil refineries) in the Ruhr as well as elsewhere in Germany; and that these attacks should begin that night with approximately 100 heavy bombers.

(3) That the French Government should be informed, through the normal channels, of our intention to carry out these operations.

On 16 May the War Cabinet met at 11.30 am and records show that the previous day's decision was changed after a request from the French for additional fighter squadrons had been received.

The Prime Minister said that an urgent appeal had been received from France for the despatch of additional fighter aircraft. The War Cabinet would have to decide, as a matter of urgency, whether this request should be met. German armoured fighting vehicles appeared to have broken through and reached the area Hirson-Montcornet-Neufchâtel.

The Prime Minister said that to despatch fighter aircraft from this country, at a time when we were most likely to be attacked ourselves in response to the attacks on military targets in the Ruhr the previous night, was taking a very grave risk, but it seemed essential to do something to bolster up the French. Armoured fighting vehicles could not conquer the whole of France, but there was a danger of their spreading panic behind the lines. The first necessity, therefore, was to support the French morale and give them a chance to recover themselves and deal with German armoured forces by the use of their own army. He favoured withdrawing the two fighter squadrons allocated to the defence of Scapa Flow, and sending six squadrons in all. More than that we could not do. If the fighters were taken away from Scapa Flow the fleet might have to be sent round to the Clyde, but Scapa was heavily defended by anti-aircraft artillery in addition to the ships' batteries.

The Prime Minister said that the main reason for the despatch of fighters was to give the French moral support. Provided their ground troops further back put up some opposition against them, it should be possible to deal with German armoured forces in comparatively small numbers. They would surely not be allowed to reach Paris altogether unopposed.

The War Cabinet agreed:

(i) That arrangements should be made for the immediate despatch of the equivalent of four fighter squadrons to France.

(ii) That preparations should be made for the despatch of two additional fighter squadrons, at very short notice, if it was so decided.

(iii) That a decision whether to send the two additional squadrons to France should be taken in the light of Air Marshal Joubert de la Ferté's report later in the day.

(iv) That the French should be informed of the decision at (i) only.

The Prime Minister flew to France, and while the minutes give an impression of an orderly process, the real chaos of the situation was described by Lt General Sir Harold Redman much later in a letter dated 14 July 1980:

Mr Churchill quite certainly was the figure, & personality around whom the proceedings revolved [on 16 May 1940]. This was but natural, as he was the head of a visiting delegation, and newly come to power, and aggressively seeking to find out the exact state of affairs – which Reynaud, Gamelin & the others hardly knew themselves.

The truth of the matter was, that after several months of com-plete inactivity on the Western Front, the violence & strength of the air attacks & armoured thrusts of the Germans had caught them unprepared; & after the first rude shock, all the French could think of was that air reinforcements, particularly in fighter aircraft, simply must be found & at once, & where could they come from but from Britain, who must stand or fall with France.

But you will have all of this sized up better than I ever could.

I can only add that while this meeting was indeed rather crucial, and although it has been dignified with the title of 'Supreme War Council', it was in fact just a hurried get-together of principals, called at the instigation of an over-optimistic newly appointed Prime Minister, rightly determined to go & find out for himself, at the chief danger point, the exact state of affairs.

What a wonderful man he was.

At 9.00 pm a message came from Churchill in France to the War Cabinet:

I shall be glad if the Cabinet could meet immediately to consider following. Situation grave in the last degree. Furious German thrust through Sedan finds French Armies ill-grouped many in North, others in Alsace. At least four days required to bring twenty divisions to cover Paris and strike at the flanks of the Bulge, which is now fifty kilometres wide.

Three armoured divisions with two or three infantry divisions have advanced through gap and large masses hurrying forward behind them. Two great dangers therefore threaten. First that the BEF will be largely left in the air in taking no action to make a difficult disengagement and retreat to the old line. Secondly that the German thrust will wear down the French resistance before it can be fully gathered.

Orders given to defend Paris at all costs, but archives of the Quai d'Orsay already burning in the garden. I consider the next two three or four days decisive for Paris and probably for the French Army. Therefore the question we must face is whether we can give further aid in fighters above four squadrons for which the French are very grateful and whether a larger part of our long-range heavy bombers should be employed tomorrow and following nights upon the German masses crossing the Meuse and flowing into the Bulge. Even so results cannot be guaranteed; but the French resistance may be broken up as rapidly as that of Poland unless this battle of the Bulge is won. I personally feel that we should send squadrons of fighters demanded (i.e. six more) tomorrow, and concentrating all available French and British aviation, dominate the air above the Bulge for the next two or three days, not for any local purpose but to give the last chance to the French Army to rally its bravery and strength. It would not be good historically if their requests were denied and their ruin resulted. Also night bombardment by a strong force of heavy bombers can no doubt be arranged. It looks as if the enemy was, by now, fully extended both in the air and tanks. We must not underrate the increasing difficulties of his advance if strongly counter-attacked. I imagine that if all fails here we could still shift what is left of own air striking force to assist the BEF should it be forced to withdraw. I again emphasise the mortal gravity of the hour, and express my opinion as above. Kindly inform me what you will do. Dill agrees. I must have answer by midnight in order to encourage the French. Telephone to Ismay at Embassy in Hindustani.

What a wonderful way to defeat German intelligence, to rely on Major General Ismay's service in India and fluency in Hindustani.[28]

The War Cabinet met at 11.00 pm under the chairmanship of Neville Chamberlain, an early demonstration of the wisdom of allowing him to take the chair as part of Churchill's injunction as he left for France to "mind the shop". What was at issue was how to respond rationally to a very emotional Prime Minister still in France.

---

28 Major General Ismay, known as 'Pug', was born in 1887. After Sandhurst, he started active service in India in 1908, and Somaliland from 1914–20. He was Military Secretary to the Viceroy of India from 1931–33; Deputy Secretary to the Committee of Imperial Defence 1936–38; Secretary in Succession to Sir Maurice Hankey in 1938; and Chief of Staff to the Minister of Defence Winston Churchill 1940–45.

The War Cabinet were informed that of the four squadrons already promised two had left during the day and the other two were leaving at dawn. If six more were sent, we should be down to 29 squadrons in all in the United Kingdom. Everything was being done to make up fighter aircraft received from production with the necessary accessories, which were being stripped from aircraft which had been damaged in action.

The Chief of the Air Staff said that there would be no difficulty in putting heavy bombers on to the Meuse crossings. The provision of the additional fighter squadrons was more difficult. We had at present seven fighter squadrons operating in the north of France and three in the south, but the latter had moved their bases and were somewhat disorganised. The bases in the north could not receive six more squadrons; three was the most they could take. There remained in the United Kingdom at the present time only six *complete* Hurricane squadrons. He proposed to move all these down to aerodromes in Kent, and to send servicing parties over to the aerodromes in northern France used by the Air Component. Three of the six squadrons to be sent to Kent would work in France from dawn until noon, and then return to Kent, being relieved by the other three for the afternoon. The effect would be the same as if the whole of the six squadrons were sent to work from French aerodromes, but they would be in less danger of attack on the ground in Kent and the crews would have better facilities for rest. The timings of the move would have to be worked out, and it would not be possible to get them all down to Kent tomorrow, since some squadrons would have to move in from distant parts.

The War Cabinet instructed the Chief of the Air Staff:

(a) To put in hand immediate arrangements, on the lines which he had proposed, for making available six Hurricane squadrons for operations in France as early as possible.

(b) To arrange for heavy bombers to attack the Meuse crossings on the night 17–18 May, and following nights.

This documented account demonstrates, at a time of peril, the case for orderly process and for keeping to proven procedures. It is to

Churchill's credit that he recognised this, and did not try to impose his will from France, divorced from all the essential background information.

The fourth key political figure who Churchill already had significant dealings with was the President of the United States. It had started on 3 October 1939 when Churchill, then First Lord of the Admiralty, told the War Cabinet that he had received a personal message of a very friendly character from Franklin Roosevelt, who had stated that he would be glad to receive any personal message which Churchill wished to bring to his notice. He proposed that their exchange of correspondence should take place in sealed envelopes conveyed by diplomatic bag. It was part of the constitutional position of the President that he was Commander in Chief of the United States Navy. Chamberlain agreed they should correspond, and this did indeed continue intermittently in what is now called the "Naval Person" correspondence, superseded by the Former Naval Person correspondence when Churchill became Prime Minister.

Isolationism was still strong in the US in May 1940. Roosevelt was slowly winning ground amongst his liberal friends and colleagues in developing an understanding of the deadly peril to American security that lurked in the deteriorating world situation. When the war broke out in 1939 Roosevelt had said, "This nation will remain a neutral nation, but I cannot ask that every American remain neutral in thought as well. Even a neutral has the right to take account of facts. Even a neutral cannot be asked to close his mind or his conscience ... I hope the United States will keep out of this war. I believe that it will. And I give you assurance and reassurance that every effort of your Government will be directed toward that end."[29] It is also important to recognise that Roosevelt was wary of the imperialist within Winston Churchill, and always on the alert lest Churchill should try and enlist America, and him personally, in perpetuating the British Empire. On the day that Germany attacked the Low Countries, Harry Hopkins, who was Roosevelt's closest adviser in the White House and who had been very ill for some time, went to

29 Franklin D. Roosevelt, *Public Papers of the Presidents of the United States: F. D. Roosevelt, 1939* (Best Books, 1941), p 463.

the White House for dinner and was persuaded by the President to spend the night – he remained living in the White House for three and a half years.[30] He was described as "quick, alert, shrewd, bold and carrying it off with a bright Hell's bells air ..., the inevitable Roosevelt favourite", and his influence on Roosevelt was a profound one.[31] That night Churchill and the President had a brief phone call, but as far as is known no matters of substance were discussed. On 15 May Churchill wrote to President Roosevelt:

Although I have changed my office, I am sure you would not wish me to discontinue our intimate, private correspondence. As you are no doubt aware, the scene has darkened swiftly. The enemy have a marked preponderance in the air, and their new technique is making a deep impression upon the French. I think myself the battle on land has only just begun, and I should like to see the masses engage. Up to the present, Hitler is working with specialised units in tanks and air. The small countries are simply smashed up, one by one, like matchwood. We must expect, though it is not yet certain, that Mussolini will hurry in to share the loot of civilisation. We expect to be attacked here ourselves, both from the air and by parachute and airborne troops in the near future, and are getting ready for them. If necessary, we shall continue the war alone, and we are not afraid of that. But I trust you realise, Mr President, that the voice and force of the United States may count for nothing if they are withheld too long. You may have a completely subjugated Nazified Europe established with astonishing swiftness, and the weight may be more than we can bear. All I ask now is that you should proclaim non-belligerency, which would mean that you would help us with everything short of actually engaging armed forces. Immediate needs are: First of all, the loan of 40 or 50 of your older destroyers to bridge gap between what we have now and the large new construction we put in hand at the beginning of the war. This time next year we shall have plenty.

---

30 Robert E. Sherwood, *The White House Papers of Harry L Hopkins: An Intimate History, Volume I, September 1939–January 1942* (Eyre and Spottiswoode, 1948), p 3.
31 *Ibid*, p 125.

But if in the interval Italy comes in against us with another 100 submarines, we may be strained to breaking point. Secondly, we want several hundred of the latest types of aircraft, of which you are now getting delivery. These can be repaid by those now being constructed in the United States for us. Thirdly, anti-aircraft equipment and ammunition, of which again there will be plenty next year, if we are alive to see it. Fourthly, the fact that our ore supply is being compromised from Sweden, from North Africa, and perhaps from Northern Spain makes it necessary to purchase steel in the United States. This also applies to other materials. We shall go on paying dollars for as long as we can, but I should like to feel reasonably sure that when we can pay no more, you will give us the stuff all the same. Fifthly, we have many reports of possible German parachute or airborne descents in Ireland. The visit of a United States squadron to Irish ports, which might well be prolonged, would be invaluable. Sixthly, I am looking to you to keep that Japanese dog quiet in the Pacific, using Singapore in any way convenient. The details of the material which we have in hand will be communicated to you separately.

With all good wishes and respect.

Churchill was well aware that he was skating on ice with such requests, particularly "the loan of 40 or 50 of your oldest destroyers". He had an American mother and often in years past had travelled to the US. He knew the constitutional impediments facing the President and the formidable political impediments he faced against a mood of mounting isolationism. Yet Churchill felt Britain had to have more destroyers, several hundred warplanes, anti-aircraft guns and steel to survive. An assessment from Robert Sherwood, a close friend of both Harry Hopkins and Franklin Roosevelt, who had access to all the papers of Harry Hopkins and interviewed many people including Churchill on three occasions said: "Roosevelt did not discount these requests and subsequent cabled reports from Churchill were not dismissed as exaggerations. During these weeks when horror was piled upon horror, Roosevelt believed that if Churchill erred at all in his estimates he erred on the side of optimism; but Roosevelt rarely objected to that kind of error."[32]. Yet Sherwood was at pains to declare openly, "no one will ever know just what finally went on in Roosevelt's complex mind to determine his decisions."[33] All Churchill could and did do was to grab his attention by writing frequent and riveting letters. They are every bit as important as War Cabinet decisions in producing increasing US assistance in 1940 and 1941.

Roosevelt repeated not once, but several times to Churchill that, for constitutional reasons, he could not give any assurance that the United States would declare war no matter what the provocation, short of direct attack upon the United States itself. But he well knew that if Britain and the Royal Navy went down then the Monroe Doctrine, let alone security in the Atlantic Ocean, and the principle of the freedom of the seas and the solidarity of the Western hemisphere would be threatened as never before.

By contrast, Churchill wrote on 13 May: "The public don't in the least realise the gravity of the situation. Walking round the lake (in St James's Park) today it was heartbreaking to see the people enjoying the sunshine as they lolled in their chairs or watched the little ducklings darting about in the water. We will try and bring them a little nearer to a sense of reality, though I dare say events will do more towards that end than anything else I can think of."

On 17 May Churchill received a reply from Roosevelt which he read out to the War Cabinet at 10.00 am, the Prime Minister having flown back from France that morning:

I have just received your message and I am sure it is unnecessary for me to say that I am most happy to continue our private correspondence as we have in the past. I am of course giving every possible consideration to the suggestions made in your message. I shall take up your specific proposals one by one.

First: With regard to the possible loan of 40 or 50 of our older destroyers. As you know a step of that kind could not be taken except with the specific authorisation of the Congress and I am

32 Robert E Sherwood, *The White House Papers of Harry L Hopkins: An Intimate History*, p 143.
33 *Ibid*, p xii.

not certain that it would be wise for that suggestion to be made to the Congress at this moment. Furthermore, it seems to me doubtful from the standpoint of our own defence requirements, which must inevitably be linked with the defence requirements of this hemisphere and with our obligation in the Pacific, whether we could dispose even temporarily of these destroyers. Furthermore, even if we were able to take the step you suggest, it would be at least six or seven weeks as a minimum, as I see it, before these vessels could undertake active service under the British flag.

Second: We are now doing everything within our power to make it possible for the Allied Governments to obtain the latest type of aircraft in the United States.

Third: If Mr Purvis may receive immediately instructions to discuss the question of anti-aircraft equipment and ammunition with the appropriate authorities here in Washington, the most favourable consideration will be given to the request made in the light of our own defence needs and requirements.

Fourth: Mr Purvis has already taken up with the appropriate authorities here the purchase of steel in the United States and I understand that satisfactory arrangements have been made.

Fifth: I shall give further consideration to your suggestion with regard to the visit of the United States squadron to Irish ports.

Sixth: As you know, the American fleet is now concentrated at Hawaii where it will remain at least for the time being. I shall communicate with you again as soon as I feel able to make a final decision with regard to some of the other matters dealt with in your message and I hope you will feel free to communicate with me in this way at any time.

The best of luck to you.

Churchill replied to President Roosevelt on 20 May.

Lothian has reported his conversation with you. I understand your difficulties, but I am very sorry about the destroyers. If they were here in six weeks they would play an invaluable part. The battle in France is full of danger to both sides. Though we have taken heavy toll of enemy in the air and are clawing down two or three to one of their planes, they have still a formidable numerical superiority. Our most vital need is, therefore, the delivery at the earliest possible date of the largest possible number of Curtiss P-40 fighters now in course of delivery to your Army.

With regard to the closing part of your talk with Lothian, our intention is, whatever happens, to fight on to the end in this Island, and, provided we can get the help for which we ask, we hope to run them very close in the air battles in view of individual superiority. Members of the present Administration would likely go down during this process should it result adversely, but in no conceivable circumstances will we consent to surrender. If members of the present Administration were finished and others came in to parley amid the ruins, you must not be blind to the fact that the sole remaining bargaining counter with Germany would be the Fleet, and, if this country was left by the United States to its fate, no one would have the right to blame those then responsible if they made the best terms they could for the surviving inhabitants. Excuse me, Mr President, putting this nightmare bluntly. Evidently I could not answer for my successors, who in utter despair and helplessness might well have to accommodate themselves to the German will. However, there is happily no need at present to dwell upon such ideas. Once more thanking you for your goodwill.

Hard and fast major decisions were continuously being taken by the War Cabinet. Their meeting on 18 May at 5.30 pm details how Ernest Bevin that morning had stressed that authority to apply measures for the control of labour would have to be vested in the Ministry of Labour if they were to be practicable. He contended that such authority should not be distributed among a number of Departments, as in the case of the measures which applied to the control of property. He had also taken the view that it would be essential that the control of profits should be put into operation simultaneously with that of labour.

The Prime Minister then said that the proposed powers would be transitory and would be related to the declaration of a supreme emergency. When this emergency arose, the Government would claim the right to take service and property as it might think right. When the emergency had passed, the reinstatement of former rights would be considered in accordance with the constitutional usages of the country. The request for the necessary powers should be presented to Parliament in the simplest terms and the details of the scheme should be worked out under the guidance of Neville Chamberlain, Lord President of the Council, in association with the ministers and officials concerned. The War Cabinet's formal decision was recorded as follows:

(1) Invited the Lord President of the Council to proceed with the working out of a scheme conferring on the Government drastic powers for the control of property, business, labour and services, on the lines indicated in his Report.

(2) Agreed that the institution of these measures should be linked to a declaration of a supreme emergency.

(3) Agreed that the draft Bill, containing the necessary powers, should be couched in the simplest terms.

(4) Invited the Prime Minister to broadcast a statement on the following day, on the lines suggested by the Lord President.

Chamberlain's notes for the Prime Minister's broadcast suggested it should be used to make "an urgent call for a great intensification of effort on the part of everyone who can contribute to the winning of the war. The hour is grave. A great and critical battle is being fought in France and Flanders. The men of the BEF and of the armies of our Allies are withstanding with magnificent courage the shock of a fierce and bitter assault. Their self-sacrifice and resolution must be matched by equal constancy and sacrifice at home."[34]

The coalition government was now seen to be combining the weight of Bevin and Chamberlain on a very sensitive issue of human rights and using Parliament with no attempt to bypass its authority. Without the coalition, this legislation would have been very hard to achieve and certainly would not have been done so quickly and with so great a consensus.

---

34 Martin Gilbert, *The Churchill War Papers*, p 75.

Churchill wrote to Chamberlain describing the "relations of perfect confidence which have grown up between us..." on 16 May 1940:

16 May 1940

My dear Neville,

You have been good enough to consult me about the leadership of the Conservative Party. I am of course a Conservative. But as Prime Minister of a National Government, formed on the widest basis, and comprising the three parties, I feel that it would be better for me not to undertake the leadership of any one political party. I therefore express the hope that your own leadership of our party will remain undisturbed by the change of government or premiership, and I feel sure that by this arrangement the cause of national unity will be best served.

The relations of perfect confidence which have grown up makes this division of duties and responsibilities very agreeable to me.

Yours ever,

Winston S. Churchill

Neville Chamberlain wrote back to Churchill on 18 May an important acceptance on the style of the coalition. In truth many Conservative MPs were still very unhappy with having Churchill as Prime Minister and would not have taken kindly to him becoming party leader.

18 May 1940

My dear Winston,

Thank you for your letter about the leadership of the Conservative Party. I can quite understand that in your present position as Prime Minister in a Government embracing all three parties it might seem inappropriate that you should at the same time be leader of one party, even though that party be your own.

I shall therefore very gladly fall in with your suggestion that I should retain the leadership, in the belief that this course will best enable me to help you in serving the cause of national unity, to which we both attach primary importance.

Yours ever
Neville Chamberlain

That same day, the Prime Minister's private secretary John Colville made a note in his diary that Churchill had met with A.V. Alexander, the new Labour First Lord of the Admiralty, who came in and showed him the sharp and uncompromising reply Mussolini had sent to Churchill's "firm but very polite telegram on becoming Prime Minister". Alexander thought that as Italy's involvement in the war was now practically unequivocal (an opinion Colville did not share) "we should seize the initiative and occupy Crete". Colville noted, "Winston answered that our hands were too full elsewhere to enable us to embark on adventures; such is the change that high office can work in a man's inherent love of rash and spectacular action."[35]

At a War Cabinet meeting on 18 May at 11.30 am, Halifax said that he felt the Soviet Government were uneasy at the German advance, and that it might be possible to make some arrangement with them. The possibility of such an arrangement had to be ascertained and Halifax had been in a long conversation with Sir Stafford Cripps,[36] who had flown from China to Moscow to enter into discussions with Molotov. The minutes noted that "Sir Stafford Cripps took the view that we had been at fault in our handling of the Soviet Government and felt convinced that we could reach an agreement with them on trade and possibly on political questions. For this purpose personal discussions were essential. Sir Stafford did not ask to be entrusted with this task, but if the Government felt he could be of service and chose to send him to Moscow to find out what the possibilities were, no harm would be done and the Soviet Government would see that we were in earnest".[37]

---

35 Martin Gilbert, *The Churchill War Papers*, p 78.
36 Richard Stafford Cripps, Labour MP 1931–50. Ambassador to Moscow, 1940–2. Minister of Aircraft Production, 1942–5. President of the Board of Trade, 1945. Minister for Economic Affairs, 1947. Chancellor of the Exchequer, 1947–50.
37 Martin Gilbert, *The Churchill War Papers*, p 72.

Halifax and Churchill had discussed the matter with the Minister for Economic Warfare, Hugh Dalton, and agreed that it would be of advantage to invite Sir Stafford Cripps to undertake this mission, provided it was clearly understood by him that his functions were to ascertain from the Soviet Government their attitude on various questions in which the Ministry of Economic Warfare and other departments were interested, and to report back. Churchill, however, had doubted whether it would be desirable to announce Britain's intention of sending an ambassador to Moscow; surely this could be left till a later stage. It is interesting to observe Labour and Conservative, Dalton and Halifax, working together to put Cripps's visit into operation. Only a year earlier, the party divide had been fierce when Churchill, Dalton and Cripps had been in favour of involving Russia in a triple alliance in the spring of 1939, before the German-Soviet Non-Aggression Pact formed, and Halifax and Chamberlain had opposed it. Now, within eight days, the value of the cross-party coalition was becoming ever more apparent; there was the start of a meeting of minds on the issue of how to handle Russia as our new partner against Hitler, helped by the gravity of the situation facing them all.

John Colville, whom Churchill had inherited as private secretary from Chamberlain, had earlier admitted in a diary entry that he had some difficulty initially in transferring both loyalty and affection. In time, however, he became devoted to Churchill; his diary entry for 19 May is worth quoting for the sense it gives of the spirit of working with Churchill:

> After the Cabinet I went to Admiralty House and found Mrs Churchill, who said that the preacher at St Martin-in-the-Fields had preached such a pacifist sermon that morning that she got up and left. "You ought to have cried 'Shame', said Winston, 'desecrating the House of God with lies!'" Then he came back and said to me, "Tell the Minister of Information with a view to having the man pilloried." It is refreshing to work with somebody who refuses to be depressed even by the most formidable danger that has ever threatened this country.

That night – Trinity Sunday – Churchill gave his first radio broadcast to the country. He quoted a centuries old religious call:

> Arm yourselves and be ye men of valour and be in readiness for the conflict; for it is better for us to perish in battle than to look upon the outrage of our nation and our altars. As the will of God is in Heaven, even so let him do.

At the War Cabinet meeting on 20 May, Churchill agreed that Britain had reached the limit of the air assistance it could provide to France, and that the further despatching of resources permanently to France could not be considered "thus denuding our defences at home".[38] This followed an insightful report received two days earlier, 'The Air Defence of Great Britain'[39] by Newall, Pound and Ironside. Churchill was ensuring a process of carefully organised information for those members of the War Cabinet, such as Attlee and Greenwood, who had not had the benefit of such papers as MPs in opposition. It stated:

> If we decline to send any further fighter assistance to France or to continue the support which we are now affording with these squadrons in England for more than a few days at a time at most, then it is not beyond the bounds of possibility that the French Army may give up the struggle. If, on the other hand, we continue to accept this constant drain on the vital defences of this country in order to sustain French resistance, then a time will arrive when our ability to defend this country will disappear. We do not believe that to throw in a few more squadrons, whose loss might vitally weaken the fighter line at home, would make the difference between victory and defeat in France.

On 21 May, Churchill made a statement to the House of Commons:

> With regard to the Business of the House, tomorrow, as already announced, we shall take the Second Reading of the Treachery

---

38 Martin Gilbert, *The Churchill War Papers*, p 97.
39 Cabinet papers, 66/7.

Bill. I think it is desirable that we should ask the House not only to take the Second Reading, but the Committee and remaining stages so that the Bill may become law as early as possible.[40]

The Bill passed through the House of Commons without dissent on the evening of 22 May 1940, only the second sitting day after the Labour Party and the Liberals had joined the Government. The Treason Act made it possible to detain without trial anyone suspected of treasonable activities. As a result, many German spies were arrested and subsequently shot, though some were turned into spies to work against their first masters. That evening an amendment to Regulation 18B of the First World War Defence of the Realm Act (DORA) was also passed, which made possible the arrest of Sir Oswald Mosley[41] and other members of the British Union of Fascists. Yet another example of how controversial this legislation would have been in the Commons without a cross-party coalition government.

On the morning of 22 May, Chamberlain informed the War Cabinet that, in light of the grave news from France and owing to the difficulty of ascertaining exactly the circumstances of the country, the Prime Minister had decided to go, and was now on his way to Paris to meet M. Reynaud and General Weygand. During his absence, the Prime Minister had requested that Chamberlain should take his place, endorsing "whatever decision might be taken in his absence in regard to the assumption of such additional powers by the Government as might be considered necessary to meet the present situation".

The first of these additional powers concerned the approval of Defence Regulation No. 54B, which gave the Government power over local authorities. The Regulation had been discussed the previous evening by a Committee which included all the Members of the

---

40 William George Andrews, *European Political Institutions: a comparative government reader* (Van Nostrand, 1966), p 475.
41 Sir Oswald Mosley, principally known as the founder of the British Union of Fascists (BUF). MP for Harrow 1918–24 and Smethwick 1926–31. Chancellor of the Duchy of Lancaster in the Labour Government of 1929–31. Formed the New Party which merged with the BUF (also known as the Blackshirts) in 1932. Interned in 1940, released in 1943.

War Cabinet, with the exception of the Prime Minister, and it had been unanimously agreed to submit the Regulation to His Majesty for approval.

Churchill reached Vincennes Grand Quartier Général (GQG) about midday, accompanied by the British Ambassador to Paris Sir Ronald Campbell, General Sir John Dill, Air Vice-Marshal Peirse, and General Ismay. M. Paul Reynaud was accompanied by Captain de Margerie, Cabinet Secretary April–June 1940. General Weygand welcomed the two Prime Ministers to his General Staff Headquarters and conducted them to the Map Room. Lt.-Col. de Villelume, Reynaud's private military adviser, who, according to General Spears, Reynaud had great confidence in, wrote in his diary for 22 May:

> After having called on Simon to explain the situation, General Weygand, using a map, showed that the combined Anglo-Franco-Belgian force amounted to forty divisions. Whilst the Belgian army would provide cover to the East and North, available French and British forces would have to attack in the general direction of Saint-Quentin to reach the flank of the German armoured divisions. At the same time, the Frère army would sort out the latter by launching an offensive in a northerly direction.
>
> Churchill and Dill fully approved what Weygand had said. The Prime Minister added that Gort's force only had four days of provisions left and that re-supplying these via the Channel ports had become risky. His assessment was that it was all the more necessary to attack in the direction of Arras-Bapaume.
>
> General Weygand then advised the British with firmness that their fighters and bombers should fully engage only in that battle and renounce actions further afield. [Air Vice-Marshal] Peirse objected as some of the bombers, namely the Wellingtons, could only fly at night. It was finally agreed that the RAF would wholly support troops on the ground. Fighter Command would attack in successive waves. As they were starting on English soil they would only have twenty minutes flying time left over enemy lines.
>
> Churchill complained in private that over four days Billotte had not given any orders to Gort. General Weygand replied that he had suffered a serious accident and had been replaced by Blanchard.

The following was finally agreed: 1. The Belgian army would move back, to be in line with the Yser and would maintain that position – with the river locks open. 2. The British and French armies would attack with approximately eight divisions in the direction of Bapaume and Cambrai after having reached their closest position – without doubt the following day. 3. As the battle was vital for both armies, and British communications depended on the liberation of Amiens, the Royal Air Force would provide all possible support both day and night for the duration of the battle. 4. The new French army group, which was advancing towards Amiens and forming a line along the Somme would move northwards and link up with the British forces who were attacking southwards in the general direction of Bapaume.

At 5.00 pm, General Weygand came to see M. Paul Reynaud to give him details on a map of the offensive. At my prompting the President advised him that secrecy surrounding the operation had not been good enough. At the end of the meeting Weygand stated that Frère's army would be able to engage more personnel than he had envisaged that morning.[42]

Churchill arrived back from Paris at about 6.30 pm that evening and the War Cabinet met at 7.30 pm. The Prime Minister gave his account of his visit to France with the Vice Chiefs of Staff and General Ismay. He had first seen M. Reynaud. He had gathered that former Prime Minister M. Daladier was considerably shaken by the serious defects which had been disclosed in the French military machine, particularly in view of the fact that he had been Minister for War for the past four years. The party had then gone on to see General Weygand, who had made a most favourable impression by his vigour and confidence. General Weygand had given them his full appreciation of the situation, and it was clear that his views coincided exactly with those expounded by the Chief of the Imperial General Staff to the War Cabinet. During Weygand's visit to the

---

42 Recent English translation from Paul de Villelume, *Journal d'une défaite (23 août 1939 – 16 juin 1940)*. Preface de René Rémond (Grandes Études Contemporaines Fayard, 1976), pp 344–346.

armies in the north on the previous day, the Belgians had agreed to withdraw to the line of the Yser. General Weygand had issued orders for the sluices in that area to be opened in order to cover the Belgian front.

The War Cabinet met again the following day, 23 May at 7.00 pm. The Prime Minister said that he had been giving further consideration to the observations made by Attlee, the Lord Privy Seal, that morning on the danger of falling between two stools, and that it might be best for the BEF to fall back on the Channel Ports. Churchill had spoken to M. Reynaud and had told him that the position of the BEF was very difficult. M. Reynaud had replied that the French operations were continuing.[43] He had then spoken to General Weygand at 6.00 pm and General Weygand had also had a conversation with the Chief of the Imperial General Staff. The gist of the latter conversation had been summarised by the Chief of the Imperial General Staff as follows:

(1) He (General Weygand) had taken Amiens, Albert and Péronne, and the manoeuvre was continuing under good conditions.

(2) He considered that the only solution was to continue the manoeuvre. The rest was disaster.

(3) He was quite unmoved when I told him of the weight of the forces moving up on the line Béthune–St-Omer. He said that the German Armoured Division were reduced by casualties.

(4) He talked of studying the question of feeding Blanchard from the sea. I told him that we knew the difficulties and had little chance of doing much.

(5) Weygand was confident.

General Weygand had demanded that the operation should continue. The Chief of the Imperial General Staff and the Vice Chief of the Imperial General Staff had both been of the view that it was

---

43 According to Reynaud, he had told Churchill, "Weygand is satisfied. We ought not to change anything. We must follow the path which we have traced out. *We must go on.*" Paul Reynaud, *In the Thick of the Fight* (London, 1955), p 369. The italics were Reynaud's own.

better that the operation should continue, since, if the BEF were to retire on the Channel ports, it was unlikely that more than a small part of the force could be got away.

In France Lt.-Col. de Villelume's diary for 23 May reads:

> Thursday 23 May
> At 16.00, General Weygand informed Baudouin in that he was very satisfied at the way operations had proceeded since the morning. He added that our troops had reached Amiens. Less than half an hour later, Churchill phoned Paul Reynaud to advise him that, as there had been no news of General Blanchard and in view of the position of the German armoured divisions, he wondered if it would not be better for the British troops to retreat to the Channel ports. The President replied that Weygand was satisfied with the situation and that we must not change our plans. "We must go on".[44]

In King George VI's diary the following entry appears for that same day, 23 May, written that evening:

> The Prime Minister came at 10.30 pm. He told me that if the French plan made out by Weygand did not come off, he would have to order the BEF back to England. This operation would mean the loss of all guns, tanks, ammunition, & all stores in France. The question was whether we could get the troops back from Calais & Dunkirk. The very thought of having to order this movement is appalling, as the loss of life will probably be immense.[45]

A historical reminder of the danger of Britain threatening to withdraw from World War I came from Lt.-Col. de Villelume's entry in his diary for 24 May:

---

44 Recent English translation from Paul de Villelume, *Journal d'une défaite (23 août 1939 – 16 juin 1940)*.
45 David Duff, *George and Elizabeth: A Royal Marriage* (Sphere, 1984), p 177.

THE POLITICS OF THE COALITION GOVERNMENT 117

At 9.15, Paul Reynaud received Campbell.[46] He arrived to comment on a letter by Churchill, which at 3.00 am he had passed on to the duty officer. In it, the Prime Minister complained that Gort had not received any orders from the French High Command. He then mentioned the necessity of defending the Channel ports. In front of the President, I reminded the ambassador of the demand for a withdrawal expressed by the French in August 1914 – both were unaware of this historical point. I strived to convince him that if that had been put into effect it would have led to our defeat.

At 11.30, the 4th Bureau of the Ministry of the Navy and the Director of Le Havre Industrial Oil Company advised me that the British were evacuating heavy units from their base in the port. The result was that panic seized the local population of the Seine-Inférieure department, leading to mass evacuation. I immediately sent forceful instructions via Mandel to the "préfet" (TN) of Rouen and the vice "préfet" of Le Havre.

The War Cabinet met in London on 24 May at 11.30 am. The minutes[47] read with particular poignancy since my father in the BEF left Boulogne the day before, sailing through the night and arriving in Plymouth Sound. With only the clothes he had on, he knocked on the door of our house in Plymouth for it to be opened by my mother. I was just under two years old.

BOULOGNE

(1) The Prime Minister said that Boulogne had been evacuated on the previous night. 1,000 had been got away, but 200 had been left behind.

(2) Our destroyers taking part in the operations at Boulogne the previous day had suffered a certain amount of damage from bombing, and machine-gun and battery fire. They had been fired at by some twenty German field-guns north of the harbour. The destroyers had replied, and believed they had succeeded in putting seven of these guns out of action.

46 Sir Ronald Campbell: Ambassador in Paris since 1939.
47 Cabinet papers, 65/7.

CALAIS

(3) We had the following troops in Calais:-

1 Tank Regiment, including cruiser and light tanks;

2 Rifle Battalions, the majority of whose equipment had now been landed; and

1 Battalion of Queen Victoria Rifles.

These were holding a position through the town, which was being shelled. The tanks had had an engagement with German tanks on the previous afternoon which had resulted in a stalemate. Their instructions had been to try to clear the forward roads, but this they had been unable to do, and in consequence the food convoy from Calais had failed to get through to St-Omer.

(4) As regards the Naval 12-pounder guns which were being prepared for use at Calais, the First Lord of the Admiralty said that mountings were being improvised, and that all possible steps were being taken to accelerate the necessary work. It was hoped to have six of the guns ready by the following afternoon, i.e., they might reach Calais in the evening.

DUNKIRK

(5) Considerable numbers of French troops were in Dunkirk, but no English troops had as yet been sent there, with the exception of certain small units sent back to this area from the BEF. The port was functioning quite well. One supply ship had been unloaded on the previous day. An ammunition ship was due to arrive there that day.

The Confidential Annex to the War Cabinet minutes of that same meeting read:

Secretary of State for Foreign Affairs Halifax said that just before the meeting he had seen the Belgian Ambassador[48] who had been accompanied by a Belgian minister. They had brought an urgent message pointing out that it was imperative that the King of the Belgians should not be captured. They suggested that the situation was such that arrangements should be made, if necessary, to

---

48 Emile de Cartier, Baron de Marchienne.

bring him and his staff, comprising 30 or 40 persons, to England that night. Before the King would consent to leave, however, it would be necessary that a message should be sent to him by the British Government. They had suggested that his departure should be made either by boat or plane from Ostend, Nieuport, or Dunkirk. He (the Foreign Secretary) was certainly of the opinion that the King of the Belgians should on no account run the risk of being taken prisoner.

The Prime Minister considered that such a move would be premature. The Belgian Army was still holding the line of the Scheldt, and it would be regrettable that the King should leave his Army at this stage. When the time came, however, it would be perfectly possible to send a message which would clear the King's conscience.

The Chief of the Imperial General Staff Ironside agreed. There was no sign as yet of any break in the Belgian Army, and therefore no grounds for immediate alarm.

The War Cabinet agreed to invite the Foreign Secretary to inform the Belgian Ambassador that in the opinion of His Majesty's Government the situation was not yet so critical as to justify the proposed departure of the King of the Belgians, but meanwhile, that close touch would be kept with Sir Roger Keyes, and all arrangements would be made to evacuate the King of the Belgians and his staff at short notice should this become necessary.

The situation was looking desperate. Churchill wrote to General Ismay:

VCNS[49] informs me that order was sent at 2.00 am to Calais saying that evacuation was decided in principle, but this is surely madness. The only effect of evacuating Calais would be to transfer the forces now blocking it to Dunkirk. Calais must be held for many reasons, but specially to hold the enemy on its front. The Admiralty say they are preparing 24 Naval 12-pounders, which

---

49 Vice-Chief of the Naval Staff 1939–41, Tom Spencer Vaughan Phillips. Drowned when his flagship, the *Prince of Wales*, was sunk by Japanese torpedo bombers on 10 December 1941.

with SAP[50] will pierce any tank. Some of these will be ready this
evening.

In a further memo to General Ismay later that day, Churchill
wrote very critically of Gort:

I cannot understand the situation around Calais. The Germans
are blocking all exits, and our regiment of tanks is boxed up in
the town because it cannot face the field guns planted on the out-
skirts. Yet I expect the forces achieving this are very modest. Why,
then, are they not attacked? Why does not Lord Gort attack
them from the rear at the same time that we make a sortie from
Calais? Surely Gort can spare a Brigade or two to clear his communications and to secure the supplies vital to his Army. Here is
a General with nine Divisions about to be starved out, and yet he
cannot send a force to clear his communications. What else can be
so important as this? Where could a Reserve be better employed?
This force blockading Calais should be attacked at once by Gort,
by the Canadians from Dunkirk and by a sortie of our boxed-
up tanks. Apparently the Germans can go anywhere and do anything, and their tanks can act in twos and threes all over our rear,
and even when they are located they are not attacked. Also our
tanks recoil before their field guns, but our field guns do not like
to take on their tanks. If their motorised artillery, far from its
base, can block us, why cannot we, with the artillery of a great
Army, block them? Of course if one side fights and the other does
not, the war is apt to become somewhat unequal. The responsibility for cleansing the communications with Calais and keeping
them open, rests primarily with the BEF.[51]

The Defence Committee minutes of the meeting held that day, 24
May, at 5.00 pm read as follows:

The Chief of the Imperial General Staff read out a message which

---

50 Sonic Armour Piercing ammunition.
51 Martin Gilbert, *The Churchill War Papers*, p 139.

had just been received to the effect that German tanks had pene-
trated past the forts on the west side of Calais and had got between
the town and the sea. The Brigadier[52] was organising his forces
on an inner line of defence. He thought that it would be useless
to dribble more infantry reinforcements into Calais, since they
would not have the weapons with which to deal with the heavy
tanks. The brigade which was already there and the tank regiment
had been ordered to fight it out in their present positions.

The Prime Minister agreed that this force must fight it out in
the town and endeavour to engage the Germans in street fighting,
which they would be very anxious to avoid if possible.[53]

What is clear is that there was no reporting to the War Cabinet of
any intelligence about Hitler's visit to his troops that day 15 miles away
from Calais (see Chapter 5) where a crucial decision was taken.

Chamberlain wrote on 25 May 1940 from Downing Street to his
sister Ida, what could be described as the case for his defence, and
perhaps the self-justification, for him starting to distance himself in
the next few days in the War Cabinet from Halifax:

There is no pleasure in life for us just now. Weekends cannot be
distinguished from weekdays: one works through each day wondering what new crisis will arise and only during the hours of
sleep is the mind at rest ...

... if we had had to fight in 1938 the results would have been
far worse. It would be rash to prophesy the verdict of history, but
if full access is obtained to all the records it will be seen that I
realised from the beginning our military weakness and did my
best to postpone if I could not avert the war. But I had to fight
every yard against both Labour & Liberal Opposition leaders
who denounced me for trying to maintain good relations with
Italy and Japan, for refusing to back Republican Spain against

---

52 Brigadier C N Nicholson, Commanding the four battalions of the 30th Brigade,
Calais 1940. Captured by the Germans on the late afternoon of 26 May, he was taken
prisoner and died in a German prisoner-of-war camp.
53 Martin Gilbert, *The Churchill War Papers,* pp 137–138.

Franco and for not "standing up to Hitler" at each successive act of aggression.

On that day of 25 May, as Churchill records in *Their Finest Hour* and as the adverse battle drew to its climax, "I and my colleagues greatly desired that Sir John Dill should become CIGS [Chief of Imperial General Staff]". [54] Late that night Churchill, the present CIGS, General Ironside, Dill and Ismay, met at Admiralty House, and Churchill records that General Ironside volunteered the proposal that he should cease to be CIGS but was ready to take command of British Home Forces. Churchill described it as a "spirited and selfless offer" which he accepted; it was agreed Sir John Dill would become CIGS on 27 May. It was a dramatic change; a clear demonstration of how dire the situation had become and of Churchill's readiness to take the risk of making this most crucial military command change.

In France, de Villelume was writing at length that day, of which only a few extracts are included here: [55]

On completion of yesterday's inspection I had urged General Picquendar[56] to do his utmost to find cannons, even outdated ones, which could be used against tanks in the absence of anything better. He told me today that there were only one hundred 75mm units in reserve and that the generalissimo had set them aside for other uses. At my instigation he ordered that an inventory be made on de Bange cannons in all depots in France. He only found 50, which he then made available to GQG (General Headquarters of the French Army)[57].

After I had stirred them into action with some vigour, Army

54 Winston Churchill, *Their Finest Hour* (Houghton Mifflin Harcourt, 1986), p 65.
55 Recent English translation from Paul de Villelume, *Journal d'une défaite (23 août 1939 – 16 juin 1940)*. Preface de René Rémond (Grandes Études Contemporaines Fayard, 1976), pp 349–354.
56 Head of Artillery
57 Sub-Lieutenant Imbert of the 41st Artillery Regiment assured me later that on about 20 June he had seen at least one hundred de Bange cannons at the Clermont-Ferrand artillery yard.

Staff Headquarters will provide General Héring[58] with some telephone lines, missiles and motorcycles.

Mr Banet-Rivet brought me some tables, showing in a more detailed way than Dautrey had done the previous day, the effect on the Army stocks of armaments as well as those of the Navy caused by the invasion of part of the territory.

The President held a meeting at midday, which included Marshal Pétain, General Weygand, Admiral Darlan, Baudouin and Mandel. General Weygand gave a record of the orders and reports exchanged the previous day between General Blanchard and himself. Whilst this was in progress, Commandant Fauvelle arrived to join the meeting. He was from Staff Headquarters of the North Army Groups. His description of the situation was one of the utmost pessimism: one day of bread and one unit of firepower left hence no way of mounting an attack.

As a result of that meeting, Paul Reynaud sent a telegram at 15.30 to Churchill, quoted in part here:

The withdrawal of a number of British units from the Arras area towards the Deûle canal led to General Weygand issuing yesterday Friday at 16.00 the following order to General Blanchard "If you consider that British withdrawal from the Arras area makes it impossible for you to carry out your Southern offensive, you must at least ensure that withdrawal is towards the sea thus safeguarding Dunkirk, which is vital for supplies". 4. At first light this morning, General Blanchard cabled General Weygand, without referring to his message sent at 16.00 the previous day, that acting in liaison with some British Army units he would launch an attack to seize a departure base along the Marquion–Bois de Bourlon–Cambrai line with the intention of prolonging the attack in the general direction of Bapaume during Sunday i.e. the following day. 5. On receipt of the above telegram from General Blanchard, General Weygand replied with the following

---

58 General Pierre Héring, Governor of Paris. He will be the one to call on the Government to leave for Bordeaux.

telegram: "I approve your plan and I am pleased that despite the situation described in my telegram the previous day, you considered that you were in a position to launch an attack. 6. On arrival in Paris at noon General Weygand received a senior commissioned officer from General Blanchard's staff headquarters, who had left these quarters the previous day at noon. The officer showed him a map with the current positions of the army groups. 7. General Weygand despatched the senior officer back to General Blanchard and cabled him saying that in the difficult situation he faced, of which everyone was aware, only General Blanchard could decide what action to take and that the honour of nations was in his hands".

17.00 I jot down the following: "We have to make peace as long as we have an army. When we have none left, the peace that will be imposed on us will be catastrophic – but in the end will Germany even accept it? Italy does not wish us to be completely crushed, but it will only be able to play a role in this as long as we still have cards up our sleeves. Conclusion: take action towards Rome to agree the necessary sacrifices if this is still possible".

18.10 Campbell arranged for the following message he had received from Churchill to be taken to Mr Paul Reynaud:

> "My telegram last night informed you of all that we know here and so far we have heard nothing from Lord Gort to contradict it – but I have to tell you that an officer from Staff Headquarters has submitted a report to the War Office confirming the withdrawal of two divisions from the Arras area, which was mentioned in your telegram. General Dill, who must currently be with Lord Gort, was instructed to send over by air an officer from Staff Headquarters. As soon as we know the outcome, we will let you know in full. It is clear, however, that the northern army is almost completely surrounded and that their communications have been cut except for Dunkirk and Ostend".

Late into the evening I visited the Prime Minister together with Baudouin and Leca. I explained the reasons why I believed it was necessary, as a matter of urgency, for Italy to act as mediator but I added that such a power would not agree with just a sweetener". It needs something more substantial. As far as we know and according to logic, its deepest aspirations are the means of its independence rather than any expansion of its territory. It wishes to ensure above all that it has free access to both entries to the Mediterranean. Hence it was essential to convince the British to make a sacrifice in this respect.

After a long discussion, Paul Reynaud decided to leave with me the following day for London. Having been advised of the visit over the telephone, Churchill replied that he awaited the Prime Minister. I then proceeded to collect until midnight the necessary information from Colonel Bourget[59] and various officers. None of them seemed too sure of their figures, often hesitating on essential points.

Next day, 26 May, at 5.00 pm, in a restricted meeting for the first time of the five politicians that made up the War Cabinet, a detailed discussion was held about approaching Signor Mussolini. The record of these discussions is the basis of Chapter 4. It was also the day that the French Prime Minister visited London. It is worth noting that Attlee had not only studied the Italian Renaissance at Oxford, but spoke fluent Italian. Italy was a country he knew much about.

De Villelume records[60] the visit to London of the French Prime Minister Reynaud:

Sunday 26 May
On early arrival at the Prime Minister's private residence I had the unpleasant surprise to find de Margerie there. He had come to seek authorisation to accompany us to London, whereas he had stated yesterday that I alone would travel with Paul Reynaud.

---

59 Colonel P-A Bourget: Chief of Staff and Principal Private Secretary to Weygand.
60 Recent English translation from Paul de Villelume, *Journal d'une défaite (23 août 1939 – 16 juin 1940)*. Preface de René Rémond (Grandes Études Contemporaines Villelume, Fayard, 1976) pp 355–6.

It was quite a long journey via the south of the Seine. We were escorted by six fighter aircraft.

Whilst the Prime Minister was talking with Corbin[61] in his office, I went into an adjoining room to write a note. The object was to show Paul Reynaud that we should not have any scruples opposite the British and provide him with a number of replies to Churchill. I reminded him of our grievances with regard to our allies: German rearmament; breach by Britain on 7 March 1936 of its obligations under the Treaty of Locarno, even though this had been ratified and recorded; separate negotiation with Italy in 1938 during which some of our interests were treacherously sacrificed; failure of the negotiations with Russia; direct action in 1939 at the breakout of the war; failure of the expedition in Norway; breach of the agreements of 27 April; lack of action by Gort to Weygand's orders; derisory air support. It would be reasonable for Britain to make substantial concessions to Italy at Suez and Gibraltar to compensate for so many errors and disloyalties.

I took this note to the Prime Minister who was in Corbin's office and I left immediately. Unfortunately, Paul Reynaud cannot decipher my scribble. He called me just as I was at the door to ask me to read it out loud. I was rather put out as it is somewhat inelegant to disturb our host so directly. Moreover, the ambassador's reactions were restrained.

Shortly afterwards the President left to dine in private with Churchill. After this he had to attend a war meeting at the War Office in 10 Downing Street.

Whilst the above was in progress, I dined at the Embassy. De Margerie did the same. On leaving the table I had a conversation with Corbin, which lasted several hours. My impression, maybe incorrectly, was that I had led him to support some of my ideas, or at least, to consider them less scandalous than they had seemed at first sight.

At about four o'clock, Paul Reynaud returned to the Embassy. He told us that Halifax was the only one to have shown some understanding; Churchill as prisoner of the swashbuckling

---

61   French Ambassador in London.

attitude he always takes in front of his ministers was decidedly negative. I asked the Prime Minister if he had threatened him to reach a separate peace. He replied to me positively but stated that it had served no purpose. I gained the impression that Paul Reynaud had only dangled the threat, if Italy were to enter the arena as the result of a lack of British concessions. Furthermore, it would appear that his sole objective in these negotiations was to determine the means likely to prevent Mussolini from declaring war. I believe that mine, which was on a par with his, was completely neglected.[...]

We returned with a fourth passenger, namely Spaak, Minister for Foreign Affairs of Belgium, as well as another member of the Belgian Government. Whilst flying over Lisieux, with the intention of landing at Chartres, we received at the last minute a radio-telegraphic message from staff headquarters to abort and fly on to Le Bourget. It appeared that German fighter aircraft were present around Évreux.

On 27 May Spears wrote from Paris to Churchill having had a long talk with Reynaud, who "I thought rather yellow at the gills ... He added that he himself would go on to the end but he could not disguise the fact that if the Germans really advanced on the Seine others ready to negotiate would replace him ... I have located the nigger on the fence [sic] as far as Reynaud is concerned, the pessimist who, fat and sly, sits next door to him pouring defeatism in his ears. It is Lt Col de Villelume ... If [Villelume] is half as dishonest and furtive as he looks, he has Fagin beat by furlongs ... The French people are not angry yet. They are resolute and calm but bewildered."[62]

There is little doubt from some of Villelume's comments and interpretation of history that he was not averse to stirring the pot of Anglo-French relations. But the real strains in relations were to emerge later in June as surrender loomed. Meanwhile the War Cabinet ministerial meetings on an approach to Italy were due to start on 26 May.

---

62 PREM 3/188/6.

4

The Hidden Agenda

Minutes of the War Cabinet

"Future generations may deem it noteworthy that the supreme question of whether we should fight on alone never found a place on the War Cabinet agenda. It was taken for granted and as a matter of course by these men of all parties in the state, and we were much too busy to waste time on such unreal, academic issues."

Winston Churchill, *The Second World War, Vol. 2: Their Finest Hour*
(London, 1949)

That categorical assertion at the start of Chapter Nine of *Their Finest Hour* is described by professor David Reynolds "... strictly correct yet seriously misleading. There are no items of the Cabinet minutes headed 'Surrender' or 'Negotiated Peace'."[1] But when Churchill wrote that chapter he was writing the most significant cover-up in the book. In 1949 he was Leader of the Opposition and a general election was due after the five-year limit for a parliament had almost been reached. Prime Minister Attlee held a massive majority and Churchill knew that the 1950 election would be very difficult to win. He made the decision to exclude the details of the Cabinet meetings as a politician, not an historian. It suited his election strategy for he cast himself as the indomitable figure, resolute, uncompromising for victory whatever the cost. He was being censored by Whitehall to conceal secrets – for example, he was not allowed to describe

---

1 *Command of History* (Penguin: 2005, p.169).

'Enigma' or the work of the Bletchley Park code breakers – and he censored his comments on people like de Gaulle, Eisenhower and Tito whom he expected to meet again when back in government, so a little censorship concerning his own image was not so reprehensible. As someone commented, Churchill fought the war twice over, first as Prime Minister and then as its premier historian. We can understand why he distorted history, but we must not forget that he did distort it. This record of nine highly secret ministerial meetings, from 26 to 28 May 1940 reveals the truth. Churchill was the leader of a War Cabinet in which his voice was powerful, but not all-powerful.

As Churchill wrote, "Those of us who were responsible at the summit in London understood the physical structure of our island strength and were sure of the spirit of the nation. The confidence with which we faced the immediate future was not founded, as was commonly supposed abroad, upon audacious bluff or rhetorical appeal, but upon a sober consciousness and calculation of practical facts." It was in no sense "academic". Here are the facts, and here are the sober calculations for you, the reader, to make your own assessment.

The following Chapter has been arranged so that on the left hand side, on even page numbers, you can read a continuous account of seven confidential ministerial War Cabinet meetings. On the opposite right hand side, on odd page numbers, you can read the actual documents the ministers had before them at the time.

This pattern is followed for the majority of the chapter, until page 156, when a series of documents available to Cabinet ministers run alongside the arguably most essential read for ministers 'British Strategy in the Near Future'. The Eighth Meeting of Ministers (page 193) is directly followed by the Ninth Meeting (page 196). The chapter ends on a series of recollections and diary extracts from the later writings of Dalton, Amery and Churchill.

Defence Committee Meeting at Admiralty
(Cabinet papers 69/1)

25 May 1940
10 p.m.

The Prime Minister directed that a Meeting of the War Cabinet should be held at 9 o'clock on the morning of Sunday, 26 May. (DO:) At that meeting the following extract of the minutes was read out to the ministers from the Defence Committee of the previous day.

March to the Coast

The Prime Minister summed up the plans outlined in discussion as follows:—
    (1) Lord Gort should march north to the coast, in battle order, under strong rearguards, striking at all forces between himself and the sea.
    This plan should, if possible, be prepared in conjunction with General Blanchard, and the Belgians should be informed.
    (2) A plan should at once be prepared on these lines, and the Navy should prepare all possible means for re-embarkation, not only at the ports but on the beaches.
    (3) The RAF should dominate the air above the area involved.
    (4) The warning telegram should at once be sent by the War Office to Lord Gort to draw up a scheme on these lines, on the assumption that the march would start on the night of the 26th/27th, but informing him not to give effect to this plan without further orders from the War Cabinet.
    (5) The first six Divisions now in this country should be mobilised, i.e., brought to full strength and provided with equipment.
    (6) The stores at Le Havre, Rouen, Rennes, St Nazaire and Nantes, or at least a proportion of them, should be evacuated.

Documents seen by War Cabinet Ministers

SPECIAL DISTRIBUTION AND WAR CABINET.

To: FRANCE.

Cipher telegram to Sir R. Campbell, (Paris).

Foreign Office. 24th May, 1940. 7.40 p.m.

No. 195. DIPP.

- - - - - - -oOo - - - - - - -

[Illegible] IMMEDIATE.

Your telegrams Nos. 241 [of May 21st], 255 and 262 [both of May 23rd. possible approach to Italy].

The idea now put forward by the French Prime Minister and Minister for Foreign Affairs viz. to approach Signor Mussolini through the President of the United States is welcome to His Majesty's Government, who have themselves been contemplating the possibility of taking action in this sense. His Majesty's Government would see no objection to an enquiry being addressed to Signor Mussolini on the lines suggested in paragraph 2 of your telegram No. [Illegible], provided that this was done on the President's own responsibility.

2. At the same time it would be useful, in the opinion of His Majesty's Government, if President Roosevelt were to convey to Signor Mussolini the sense of the last two paragraphs of the statement we had in mind to make concerning Italy (see my telegram No. 406 to [Illegible] action on which has been suspended), omitting the question of contraband control which, as Your Excellency knows, is now being dealt with separately in Rome through the Master of the Rolls. In other words, we would suggest that the President might inform Signor Mussolini that "he had reason to believe

First Meeting of Ministers

War Cabinet: Confidential Annex
(Cabinet papers, 65/13)

26 May 1940
10 Downing Street
9 a.m.

The Prime Minister informed the War Cabinet that the
previous night he had received a letter from General
Spears, describing an interview he had had with what
had been to all intents and purposes a War Council of
France, and also a message from M. Reynaud.

He read these two documents to the War Cabinet.
The letter from General Spears may be summarised as
follows:—

(i)   The suggestion that Lord Gort had fallen back
      on the 24th May without warning and without
      orders had been cleared up. General Weygand
      had apologised with good grace.

(ii) On the strength of a report brought in from
      General Blanchard by Commandant Fauvelle,[1]
      General Weygand had been inclined to alter his
      instructions to General Blanchard in the sense
      of inviting him to fall back to the Channel
      harbours, but in view of the fact that he had
      later information from General Blanchard,
      he had finally determined to allow General
      Blanchard to use his own discretion.

(iii) General Weygand did not consider that attacks
      to the southward by the Blanchard group of
      armies could serve any other purpose than
      to gain breathing space to fall back to a
      line covering the harbours. (It had been the

---

1 Commandant (Major) Fauvelle, a Staff Officer from General Blanchard's Group
of Armies. Reynaud had written: 'According to him there was no longer any hope of
Blanchard being able to carry out the offensive movement that Weygand had ordered'
(*In the Thick of the Fight*, page 374, footnote 2).

that the following represented the attitude of the
Allied Governments" :-

That the Allied Governments

(a) were aware that the Italian Government entertains
certain grievances in regard to the Italian
position in the Mediterranean.
(b) were prepared to consider reasonable Italian
claims at the end of the war.
(c) would welcome Italy's participation at the peace
conference with a status equal to that of the
belligerents.

3. This offer would be more attractive to the
Italian Government if the United States Government could
not only sponsor but guarantee it, and His Majesty's
Government would accordingly suggest that the President
should be asked to make the following statement in
addition : -

That the United States Government for their part
would be prepared to guarantee the fulfilment of the
Allied promise, but that they would only do so - thus
ensuring that Italian claims would be dealt with as part
of the general settlement of Europe - provided always
that in the meantime Italy had not joined in the war
against [remainder of page cut off].

4. Please endeavour to obtain the early concurrence
of the French Government in these proposals. So soon
as I [Illegible] that they are in agreement, I would
propose to telegraph Washington in this sense, and would
suggest that the French Government should take similar
action.

Addressed to Paris No. 198 DIPP.

Repeated to Rome No. 465 and Washington No. 869.

original intention to try and break through
with a force of five French and two British
Divisions, but one of the British Divisions
had since had to be put into the line between
Menin and Ypres to resist a thrust from the
East.)

(iv)   There seemed no chance whatever of any French
attack from the south across the Somme to
disengage the Blanchard group. There were only
eight Divisions spread over a very wide front.

(v)   Commandant Fauvelle has been extremely
pessimistic. The Blanchard group has lost
all their heavy guns; they had no armoured
vehicles; and movements were very much
hampered by refugees.

The message from M. Paul Reynaud set out the
conclusions which had been reached at the meeting which
General Spears had attended. The principal point was
that discretion was given to General Blanchard as to his
action.

The Prime Minister also read a telegram received
from Sir Roger Keyes relating to the evacuation of the
King of the Belgians, which could be summarised as
follows:—

The King was being urged by his Ministers to fly with
them, but he was determined not to desert his army
at a time when a stern battle was in progress. If
the King were to leave, this would inevitably hasten
the capitulation of the Belgian Army and endanger
the BEF. King Leopold had written to King George VI
to explain his motive in remaining with his army and
people if the Belgian Army became encircled and the
capitulation of the Belgian Army became inevitable.

The Prime Minister said that the above
communications and other information which had been
received had been considered at a meeting the previous
night of the Service Ministers and Chiefs of Staff.
General Karslake, who had seen General Swayne, reported
that the latter thought that the French seemed unlikely
to take any effective action from the south. M. Reynaud
had telegraphed that he was arriving in this country

THIS DOCUMENT IS THE PROPERTY OF HIS BRITANNIC MAJESTY'S
GOVERNMENT

Printed for the War Cabinet. May 1940.

MOST SECRET.
Copy No. 33

W.P. (40) 168.
(Also C.O.C. (40) 390.)
May 25, 1940.

TO BE KEPT UNDER LOCK AND KEY.

It is requested that special care may be taken to
ensure the secrecy of this document.

WAR CABINET.

_____

BRITISH STRATEGY IN A CERTAIN EVENTUALITY.

_____

REPORT BY THE CHIEFS OF STAFF COMMITTEE.

THE object of this paper is to investigate the
means whereby we could continue to fight single-handed
if French resistance were to collapse completely,
involving the loss of a substantial proportion of the
British Expeditionary Force, and the French Government
were to make terms with Germany. The assumptions we have
made are contained in Appendix A of the Annex. Of these
the two most important are that:-

(i)   United States of America is willing to give us
      full economic and financial support, *without
      which we do not think we could continue the war
      with any chance of success.*

(ii) Italy has intervened against us.

2. In particular we have asked ourselves two
questions:-

that day and wished to meet the Prime Minister alone, or
perhaps with one other Minister present only. It seemed
from all the evidence available that we might have to
face a situation in which the French were going to
collapse, and that we must do our best to extricate the
British Expeditionary Force from northern France.

The Prime Minister read to the War Cabinet the
conclusions which had been reached at the meeting of
Ministers and Chiefs of Staff the previous night. On
the basis of these conclusions a telegram had been
despatched to Lord Gort, warning him that he might
be faced with a situation in which the safety of the
British Expeditionary Force would be the predominant
consideration, and that every endeavour would be made to
provide ships for the evacuation, and aircraft to cover
it. Preliminary plans were accordingly to be prepared at
once.

The Prime Minister expressed the opinion that,
although we could not foresee the outcome of the battle,
there was a good chance of getting off a considerable
proportion of the British Expeditionary Force. We must,
however, be prepared for M. Reynaud in his interview
that day to say that the French could not carry on the
fight. He would make every endeavour to induce M. Reynaud
to carry on, and he would point out that they were at
least in honour bound required to provide, as far as lay
in their power, for the safe withdrawal of the British
Expeditionary Force. He asked the War Cabinet to be
ready to meet again at 2 p.m. to receive his report
of his discussions with M. Reynaud. He hoped that M.
Reynaud would be willing to meet the War Cabinet. There
was some indication that M. Reynaud might bring with him
a military expert, in which case the discussions might
be extended in their scope.

In order to be prepared to meet all eventualities he
had asked the Chiefs of Staff to consider the situation
which would arise if the French did drop out of the war,
on the following terms of reference:—

‘In the event of France being unable to continue
in the war and becoming neutral, with the Germans

(a) Could the United Kingdom hold out until
    assistance from the Empire and America made
    itself felt? And

(b) Could we ultimately bring sufficient economic
    pressure to bear on Germany to ensure her defeat?

We summarise our conclusions and recommendations
below. As regards the latter *there are a large number of
measures which we consider should be carried out at once
irrespective of whether a French collapse is or is not
likely*.

We attach our detailed appreciation as an Annex.

CONCLUSIONS.

3. There are three ways in which Germany might break
down the resistance of the United Kingdom - unrestricted
air attack aimed at breaking public morale, starvation
of the country by attack on shipping and ports, and
occupation by invasion.

Air Factor.

4. The vital fact is that our ability to avoid
    defeat will depend on three factors:-

(a) Whether the morale of our people will withstand
    the strain of air bombardment;

(b) Whether it will be possible to import the
    absolute essential minimum of commodities
    necessary to sustain life and to keep our war
    industries in action;

(c) Our capacity to resist invasion.

All of these depend primarily on whether our
fighter defences will be able to reduce the scale of
attack to reasonable bounds. This will necessarily mean
the replacement of casualties in personnel and aircraft
on a substantial scale. Our capacity to resist invasion
may, however, depend also to a great extent on the
maintenance of an effective air striking force.

These factors cannot be assessed with certainty,
and it is impossible to say whether or not the United

holding their present position, and the Belgian army being forced to capitulate after assisting the British Expeditionary Force to reach the coast; in the event of terms being offered to Britain which would place her entirely at the mercy of Germany through disarmament, cession of naval bases in the Orkneys etc.; what are the prospects of our continuing the war alone against Germany and probably Italy. Can the Navy and the Air Force hold out reasonable hopes of preventing serious invasion, and could the forces gathered in this Island cope with raids from the air involving detachments not greater than 10,000 men; it being observed that a prolongation of British resistance might be very dangerous for Germany engaged in holding down the greater part of Europe.'

The Prime Minister said that peace and security might be achieved under a German domination of Europe. That we could never accept. We must ensure our complete liberty and independence. He was opposed to any negotiations which might lead to a derogation of our rights and power.

The Secretary of State for Foreign Affairs[2] suggested that in the last resort we should ask the French to put their factories out of gear.

The Lord President of the Council[3] felt that whatever undertakings of this character we might extract from the French would be worthless, since the terms of peace which the Germans would propose would inevitably prevent their fulfilment.

The Prime Minister agreed. It was to be expected, moreover, that the Germans would make the terms of any peace offer as attractive as possible to the French, and lay emphasis on the fact that their quarrel was not with France but with England.

---

2 Lord Halifax.
3 Neville Chamberlain.

Kingdom could hold out in all circumstances. We think
there are good grounds for the belief that the British
people will endure the greatest strain, if they realise
- as they are beginning to do - that the existence of
the Empire is at stake. We must concentrate our energies
primarily on the production of fighter aircraft and
crews, and the defence of those factories essential to
fighter production should have priority. At the same
time it is clear that we cannot afford to neglect our
bomber force or to expend it on operations that are not
of first importance.

Civil Defence.

5. As long as the present quasi-peacetime
organisation continues, it is unlikely that this country
can hold out. The present Home Security Organisation was
constituted to deal with air attack only by aircraft
operating from bases in Germany; it is not sufficient
to grapple with the problems which would arise as a
result of a combination of heavy air attack from bases
on a semi-circle from Trondheim to Brest, invasion, and
internal attack by the "Fifth Column."

Land Forces.

6. Germany has ample forces to invade and occupy
this country. Should the enemy succeed in establishing
a force, with its vehicles, firmly ashore - the Army in
the United Kingdom, which is very short of equipment,
has not got the offensive power to drive it out.

Naval Forces.

7. Our first naval task is to secure the United
Kingdom and its seaborne supplies against naval attack.
We have sufficient Naval forces to deal with those that
the enemy can bring against us in Home Waters, and we
can provide naval security for our seaborne supplies.
Our ability to defeat at sea a seaborne attack on this
country is dependent on the extent to which our Naval
forces can operate in the face of heavy air attack
on both ships and bases, and it is of the greatest
importance to strengthen our systems of intelligence and

On 26 May 1940 Churchill lunched with Reynaud at Admiralty House, before going to 10 Downing Street for a further meeting of the War Cabinet.

Second Meeting of Ministers

War Cabinet: Confidential Annex
(Cabinet papers, 65/13)

26 May 1940
10 Downing Street
2 p.m.

The Prime Minister said that he did not think that M. Reynaud would object to the British Expeditionary Force being ordered to march to the coast, although this matter had not yet been finally settled with him.

The Prime Minister then gave an account of M. Reynaud's discussion with him over lunch.

M. Reynaud had given an exposé of France's position. Apart from the troops in the Maginot Line, including the fortress troops, the French had 50 divisions between Malmédy and the coast. Against these the Germans could put 150 divisions. The French Ministers had asked General Weygand for his views on the position. They would defend Paris as long as possible, but if Paris was taken they would retire to the south-west. General Weygand had made it clear, however, that the Germans with their superiority of numbers and tanks, could pierce the line and pass through it. While he would obey orders and fight it out as long as he was told to do so, and would be prepared to go down fighting for the honour of the Flag, he did not think that France's resistance was likely to last very long against a determined German onslaught.

The French Ministers therefore concluded that, with 50 divisions against 150, it was clear that the war could not be won on land. On sea we had good fleets which had established a superiority over Germany; but if Germany had command of resources from Brest to reconnaissance to ensure early and accurate warning of enemy intentions is obtained.

Seaborne Supplies.

8. We have adequate shipping to meet our requirements, but again the provision of air security is the main problem. We may have to abandon our ports on the South and East Coasts for trade purposes, and our ability to carry on the war will then depend on West Coast ports entirely. These, therefore, must be adequately defended. All unimportant imports must be eliminated. If we can maintain 60 per cent of our present imports we can obtain enough food for the population and raw materials to continue essential armament production.

Overseas.

9. On a long-term view, Germany, in concert with Italy, will strive to overthrow our position in Egypt and the Middle East.

10. The immediate effect of a French collapse would be the loss of naval control in the Western Mediterranean. Italy would be able to concentrate all her strength against Malta, Gibraltar and Egypt. Malta could probably withstand one serious assault. We could continue to use Gibraltar as a naval base until Spain became hostile. Even then Gibraltar should hold out for 60 days.

11. To contain the Italian Fleet and secure Egypt a capital ship fleet should be based on Alexandria. In due course a heavy scale of attack could be mounted on Egypt from Libya, and we might have to withdraw the Fleet through the Suez Canal to Aden and block the Canal. Preparations to do this should be undertaken as soon as the contingency considered in this paper arises.

12. The retention of Singapore is very important for economic control, particularly of rubber and tin. To counter Japanese action in the Far East, a fleet, adequately supported by air forces, is necessary at Singapore. It is most improbable that we could send any naval forces there, and reliance would have to be placed upon the United States to safeguard our interests.

Vladivostok it did not look as though the blockade could win the war. It was clear that this country would take a long time to build up a big army, and that we could not make a big effort in 1941 on land.

This left the Air. If the Germans took Paris they would have the air factories in that neighbourhood, as well as those in Belgium and Holland.

What of the United States of America? The munitions industry in that country was feeble.

Where, then, could France look for salvation? Someone had suggested that a further approach should be made to Italy. This would release 10 French divisions. There were said to be a number of people in Italy, such as Grandi[4] and Balbo,[5] and the like, who thought that to stab France in the back when she was in mortal struggle with Germany was rather too like the action which Russia had taken in regard to Poland.

If an approach was made to Italy, what sort of terms would Italy ask? Probably the neutralisation of Gibraltar and the Suez Canal, the demilitarisation of Malta, and the limitation of naval forces in the Mediterranean. Some alteration in the status of Tunis would also be asked for, and the Dodecanese would have to be put right. The Prime Minister said that he had not understood what was meant by this.

Apparently the French suggestion was that the offer of such terms might keep Italy out of the war.

M. Reynaud realised that the Germans would probably not keep any terms which they agreed to. He had hinted that he himself would not sign peace terms imposed upon France, but that he might be forced to resign, or might feel that he ought to resign.

The Prime Minister said that he had then put the

<hr />

4 Dino Grandi, 1895–1988. Born at Mordano (Bologna). On active service, 1915–18. Foreign Minister, 1929–32. Italian Ambassador in London, 1932–9. Member of the Fascist Grand Council. Minister of Justice, Rome, 1939–43. On 24 July 1943 he moved the resolution in Fascist Grand Council which was the direct cause of the overthrow of Mussolini.

5 Italo Balbo, 18896–1940. Minister of Aviation, 1936, and subsequently Governor of Libya. He opposed Italy's alliance with Hitler and urged Mussolini not to enter the war in 1940.

13. We should endeavour to maintain our position in all our overseas possessions.

Ability to defeat Germany.

14. Germany might still be defeated by economic pressure, by a combination of air attack on economic objectives in Germany and on German morale and the creation of widespread revolt in her conquered territories.

15. We are advised in the following sense by the Ministry of Economic Warfare. We cannot emphasise too strongly the importance of substantial accuracy of this forecast, since upon the economic factor depends our only hope of bringing about the downfall of Germany.

16. In spite of immediate economic gains obtained from her conquests, Germany will still be very short of food, natural fibres, tin, rubber, nickel and cobalt. Above all, even with Roumanian supplies, she will still have insufficient oil.

17. Given full Pan-American co-operation, we should be able to control all deficiency commodities at source. There will be no neutrals except Japan and Russia.

18. The effect of a continued denial of overseas supplies to Germany will be:-

   (a) By the winter of 1940-41, widespread shortage of food in many European industrial areas, including parts of Germany.

   (b) By the winter of 1940-41, shortage of oil will force Germany to weaken her military control in Europe.

   (c) By the middle of 1941, Germany will have difficulty in replacing military equipments. A large part of the industrial plant of Europe will stand still, throwing upon the German administration an immense unemployment problem to handle.

19. Air attacks on Germany's oil centre will be an important contribution to the enemy's defeat and to the reduction of the intensity of his air offensive.

The pressure we could exert by air action will be extremely limited for some time owing to the effects other side of the case, and suggested that as soon as the situation in North-eastern France had been cleared up, the Germans would make no further attacks on the French line and would immediately start attacking this country. M. Reynaud thought that the dream of all Germans was to conquer Paris, and that they would march on Paris.

The Prime Minister had said that we were not prepared to give in on any account. We would rather go down fighting than be enslaved to Germany. But in any case we were confident that we had a good chance of surviving the German onslaught. France, however, must stay in the war. If only we could stick things out for another three months, the position would be entirely different. He had asked M. Reynaud if any peace terms had been offered to him. M. Reynaud had said 'No', but that they knew they could get an offer if they wanted one. He repeated that General Weygand was prepared to fight on, but could hold out no hope that France had sufficient power of resistance.

The Prime Minister said that he suggested that the Foreign Secretary should now go over and see M. Reynaud, who was at Admiralty House, and that he himself, the Lord President of the Council and the Lord Privy Seal[6] should come over a few minutes later.

A short further discussion ensued on whether we should make any approach to Italy.

The Foreign Secretary favoured this course, and thought that the last thing that Signor Mussolini wanted was to see Herr Hitler dominating Europe. He would be anxious, if he could, to persuade Herr Hitler to take a more reasonable attitude.

The Prime Minister doubted whether anything would come of an approach to Italy, but said that the matter was one which the War Cabinet would have to consider.

The Minister without Portfolio[7] said that if we

---

6 Neville Chamberlain and Clement Attlee.

7 Arthur Greenwood, The Minister without Portfolio, evaluated in a memorandum for the War Cabinet that day, 26 May 1940 (War Cabinet Paper 171 of 1940 'British Strategy in the Near Future'), that Germany could be harmed by a 'tight economic

of the enemy's attacks and the need to conserve our
striking power to deal with the contingency of invasion.

20. The territories occupied by Germany are likely to
prove a fruitful ground for sowing the seeds of revolt,
particularly when economic conditions deteriorate.

21. Finally, we emphasise once more that these
conclusions as to our ability to bring the war to a
successful conclusion depend entirely upon full Pan-
American economic and financial co-operation.

22. In view of our terms of reference and the
speculative nature of the problem, we have not
considered whether the Empire can continue the war if
the United Kingdom were defeated.

RECOMMENDATIONS.

23. The following recommendations were drafted before
the Bill conferring on the Government complete power of
control over persons and property for the prosecution
of the war was passed. We have not had the opportunity
of studying the details of this Bill, so some of our
recommendations are no doubt covered by its provisions.

We recommend that the following measures should
be carried out NOW, irrespective of events in France.
These measures are confined to those which we consider
necessary for the security of this country against
attack during the critical period that may arise in the
next few months:-

(i)   We should do our utmost to persuade the
      United States of America to provide aircraft,
      particularly fighters, as soon as possible and in
      large numbers, including those from stocks now
      held by the United States Army and Navy.

(ii) Measures should be taken to ensure the strictest
      economy in A.A. ammunition expenditure.

(iii) The most ruthless action should be taken
      to eliminate any chances of "Fifth Column"
      activities. Internment of all enemy aliens and
      all members of subversive organisations, which
      latter should be proscribed.

(iv) Alien refugees are a most dangerous source of

could maintain the struggle for some further weeks he thought that we could make use of our economic power in regard to raw materials, textiles, and oil. Stocks in Germany were very depleted. In any event, he hoped that France would take steps to see that valuable stocks and manufacturing capacity in France did not fall into German hands.

The Prime Minister said that he thought the only point to be settled that day was to persuade M. Reynaud that General Weygand should be instructed to issue orders for the BEF to march to the coast. It was important to make sure that the French had no complaint against us on the score that, by cutting our way to the coast, we were letting them down militarily. At the same time it was important that the orders for the march to the coast should be issued as soon as possible. He asked the Secretary of State for War[8] to prepare a draft telegram for despatch, which should be brought over to Admiralty House at 3.15 p.m.

(Greenwood continued) blockade' and her war effort thereby bolstered through co-operation with the United States. He wrote: 'I suggest that immediate steps should be taken through diplomatic channels to press for active economic assistance and that a strong mission should be sent out to America without delay to secure economic and financial allies for the prosecution of the blockade with the utmost vigour' (Cabinet papers 66/8).

8 Anthony Eden.

subversive activity. We recommend that the number of refugees admitted to this country should be cut to the minimum and that those admitted should be kept under the closest surveillance.

(v)   In order to ensure the necessary co-operation between the Civil and Military Authorities, operational control of all Civil Defence Forces, including county and borough police, &c., should be vested in the Ministry of Home Security and exercised through Regional Commissioners.

(vi)   Any evacuation which the Government intends to carry out in emergency should be carried out now. We recommend that a modification of the scheme for reception areas, in view of the dangers of invasion, should be carried out.

(vii)   Immediate steps to be taken to obtain destroyers and M.T.Bs. from the United States of America.

(viii) Every possible measure should be directed to obtaining the active support of Eire, particularly with a view to the immediate use of Berehaven.

(ix)   Our intelligence system to be strengthened with a view to getting early warning of German preparations for invasion of this country.

(x)   Dispersal of stocks of raw materials to free our West Coast ports to deal with the heavy increase in imports should now be made.

(xi)   So far as is practicable distribution of food reserves throughout the country with a view to meeting the disorganisation of transport which may occur.

(xii)   Bunkering facilities and other arrangements necessary to deal with a heavy volume of merchant shipping in West Coast and Irish ports should be organised.

(xiii) All unimportant and luxury imports to be cut out.

(xiv)   Finally we consider that the time has come to inform the public of the true dangers that confront us and to educate them on what they are

Churchill, Neville Chamberlain and Arthur Greenwood left 10
Downing Street for Admiralty House to see Reynaud, who was
already with Lord Halifax. After Reynaud had left for France, they
continued with their discussion.

Third Meeting of Ministers

War Cabinet: Confidential Annex
(Cabinet papers, 65/13)

26 May 1940
Admiralty House
5 p.m.

The Prime Minister said that we were in a different
position from France. In the first place, we still had
powers of resistance and attack, which they had not.
In the second place, they would be likely to be offered
decent terms by Germany, which we should not. If France
could not defend herself, it was better that she should
get out of the war rather than that she should drag us
into a settlement which involved intolerable terms.
There was no limit to the terms which Germany would
impose upon us if she had her way. From one point of
view, he would rather France was out of the war before
she was broken up, and retained the position of a strong
neutral whose factories could not be used against us.

The Lord Privy Seal[9] said that Herr Hitler was
working to a time-limit, and he had to win by the end of
the year.

The Lord President of the Council[10] thought that he
would have to win by the beginning of the winter.

The Lord Privy Seal said that if France now went out
of the war, Herr Hitler would be able to turn on us the
sooner.

The Prime Minister said that he hoped that France
would hang on. At the same time we must take care not

---

9 Attlee.
10 Chamberlain.

required to do and what NOT to do, if the country is invaded.

(Signed)   C.L.N. NEWALL.
DUDLEY POUND.
A. E. PERCIVAL,
A.C.I.G.S (for C.I.G.S.).
*Richmond Terrace, S.W.*1

to be forced into a weak position in which we went to
Signor Mussolini and invited him to go to Herr Hitler
and ask him to treat us nicely. We must not get tangled
in a position of that kind before we had been involved
in any serious fighting.

The Foreign Secretary[11] said that he did not disagree
with this view, but that he attached perhaps rather more
importance than the Prime Minister to the desirability of
allowing France to try out the possibilities of European
equilibrium. He was not quite convinced that the Prime
Minister's diagnosis was correct and that it was in Herr
Hitler's interest to insist on outrageous terms. After
all, he knew his own internal weaknesses. On this lay-out
it might be possible to save France from the wreck. He
would not like to see France subjected to the Gestapo.

The Prime Minister did not think that Germany was
likely to attempt this in regard to France.

The Foreign Secretary said that he was not so sure.

The Prime Minister had said that it was undesirable
that France should be in a position to say that we had
stood between her and a tolerable settlement.

He referred to the Prime Minister's statement that
we might be better off without France. That meant,
provided we could obtain safeguards on particular
points. This was certainly a point of view which
deserved serious consideration.

The Prime Minister thought that it was best to
decide nothing until we saw how much of the Army we
could re-embark from France. The operation might be a
great failure. On the other hand, our troops might well
fight magnificently, and we might save a considerable
portion of the Force. A good deal of the re-embarkation
would be carried out by day. This would afford a real
test of air superiority, since the Germans would attempt
to bomb the ships and boats.

The Prime Minister said that his general comment on
the suggested approach to Signor Mussolini was that it
implied that if we were prepared to give Germany back
her colonies and to make certain concessions in the

---

11 Halifax.

Foreign Office.
May 25th, 1940.

Sir,
        I asked the Italian Ambassador to call this
afternoon.
        2. I told His Excellency that I wished to
speak to him because I had reason to think that
a misunderstanding had arisen with regard to the
possibility of some statement being made by His
Majesty's Government about the political issues between
our two countries. It was quite true that we had
intended to make and approach, in appropriate form, to
certain political questions, following on the approach
which we had made to questions concerning contraband
control; and in any such approach we should have wished
to make plain our desire that Italy should naturally
take her proper place at a peace conference by the side
of the belligerents. I had, however, hesitated to make
the approach in question because of the discouraging
nature of the reply which Signor Mussolini had sent
through Count Ciano to a personal communication from the
Prime Minister, which had led me to doubt whether any
useful purpose would be served by our trying to define
our position more closely to the Italian Government.
In view, however, of the misunderstanding which seemed
to have arisen, I wished to take the opportunity of
saying that while we fully recognised the special
relations in which Italy stood to Germany, we had
always been quite willing to discuss any questions
between our two countries and to endeavour to reach
solutions satisfactory to both sides. His Majesty's
Government would be willing at any time to propose such
a discussion to the Italian Government if we could
have some assurance that we should not be rebuffed. If
and when we should ever receive an indication that our
approach might be received with due consideration, we
should be prepared to carry the matter further and deal
with it in greater detail. Personally I should hope, and
I felt sure that this would be the view of His Majesty's
Government, that the measure of success which we were

Mediterranean, it was possible for us to get out of
our present difficulties. He thought that no such option
was open to us. For example, the terms offered would
certainly prevent us from completing our re-armament.

The Foreign Secretary said that, if so, the terms
would be refused, but he felt sure that Signor Mussolini
must feel in a most uncomfortable position.

The Prime Minister said that Herr Hitler thought
that he had the whip hand. The only thing to do was to
show him that he could not conquer this country. If,
on M. Reynaud's showing, France could not continue,
we must part company. At the same time, he did not
raise objection to some approach being made to Signor
Mussolini.

During the latter part of this discussion the Prime
Minister was called out of the room to speak to Sir
Roger Keyes, who had a message from the King of the
Belgians. The King was determined to stay with his
Army. There was, perhaps, a chance that he might be
persuaded to leave at the last minute. The Belgians
were determined to act as the left flank to assist our
re-embarkation. Sir Roger Keyes said there was still
nothing in Ostend to prevent it being taken. The Menin
Gate 'was being shelled that afternoon'.[12] He had been at
Lord Gort's headquarters when orders had come to march
to the coast. It was clear that these orders had been
received with acclamation at GHQ, where it was held that
the march to the South held out no prospect of success.

The Lord President of the Council[13] asked what
information should be given to the Dominions.

The Prime Minister thought that nothing should
be said to them in regard to the discussions with M.
Reynaud. At the same time, they should be told that
we had now obtained the formal assent of the French
Government to falling back on the coast, and that the
position was a serious one.

---

12 The Menin Gate at Ypres had been rebuilt as a memorial to British war dead who
had no grave.
13 Chamberlain.

in the way of achieving as regards the difficulties
connected with contraband control might serve to open
the way to the treatment of other questions, always
provided that we could approach these questions on the
basis of the frankest recognition of the rights and
necessities of both parties.

3. I told His Excellency that I had thought that I
ought to give him this message in order that I might
feel, and perhaps His Excellency also, that, so far as
we were concerned, nothing had been left undone that
could help to avoid any misunderstanding, or something
worse, between our two countries.

4. Signor Bastianini thanked me very much for my
communication. He said that he had no knowledge of the
exchange of letters between Signor Mussolini and the
Prime Minister, but that he would of course immediately
pass on what I had said to his Government. It had,
however, always been Signor Mussolini's view that the
settlement of problems between Italy and any other
country should be part of a general European settlement,
and His Excellency asked me whether he might inform his
Government that His Majesty's Government considered it
opportune now to examine the questions at issue between
our two countries within the larger framework of a
European settlement.

5. I said that I had always thought, if any
discussions were to be held with a view to solving
European questions and building a peaceful Europe,
that matters which caused anxiety to Italy must
certainly be discussed as part of the general European
Settlement.

6. Whether or not it might be possible to bring
matters, which caused anxiety to Italy, to solution
while the war was still in progress would no doubt
depend upon the nature of the issues raised, and upon
the course which any discussions might take.

7. Signor Bastianini then said that he would like
to know whether His Majesty's Government would consider
it possible to discuss general questions involving not
only Great Britain and Italy, but other countries. On
my saying that it was difficult to visualise such wide

Author's Note

The upcoming document ('British Strategy in the Near Future', pp. 156, 158, 160) was essential reading for ministers and of a different level of importance to other documents seen by them. This is why it influenced continuous narrative of Mussolini discussions available to some on the 26th and read by others only on the 27th. It was the first document under the signature of Dill, having taken over from Ironside, and its optimism, that despite all the problems the Chiefs believed Britain could hold its own alone after the fall of France, must have arrived on Ministers' desks like 'manna from heaven'. Politicians are usually optimists, military men less so. All the time the question in the minds of politicians would have been whether Britain could make it. Halifax was the most doubtful. Even for those politicians brought into the Government since 13 May, the news for a fortnight had been unremittingly awful. Now a new Chief of the Defence Staff was bringing hope to the table. This 'Near Future' paper is referred to in Chapter 5, pp. 216–217.

discussions while the war was still proceeding, the Ambassador replied that once such a discussion were begun, war would be pointless.

8. Signor Mussolini, said the Ambassador, was interested in European questions - the Ambassador mentioned Poland - and was always concerned to build a European settlement, that would not merely be an armistice, but would protect European peace for a century. I said that the purpose of His Majesty's Government was the same, and they would never be unwilling to consider any proposal made with authority that gave promise of the establishment of a secure and peaceful Europe. I added that I thought I could say that this would also be the attitude of the French Government.

9. The Ambassador warmly agreed with an observation that I had made to the effect that when we come to such discussions, Signor Mussolini would have an absolutely vital part to play. Signor Mussolini was always ready to help in securing a wider European settlement because he saw the solution of Italian problems only within the framework of the solution of all the problems of all other European countries.

10. His Excellency said that he would like to be able to inform Signor Mussolini that His Majesty's Government did not exclude the possibility of some discussion of the wider problems of Europe in the event of the opportunity arising. This I told His Excellency he could certainly do, for plainly the secure peace in Europe that both Signor Mussolini and we desired to see established could only come by the finding through frank discussion of solutions that were generally acceptable and by the joint determination of the Great Powers to maintain them.

(Signed)   HALIFAX.

26 May 1940

THIS DOCUMENT IS THE PROPERTY OF HIS BRITANNIC MAJESTY'S
GOVERNMENT

TO BE KEPT UNDER LOCK AND KEY.

It is requested that special care may be taken to ensure
the secrecy of this document.

SECRET.

W.P. (40)169.   COPY NO. 17

(Also Paper No.

C.O.S. (40) 397).

26th MAY 1940.

WAR CABINET.

BRITISH STRATEGY IN THE NEAR FUTURE.

_____

Report by the Chiefs of Staff Committee.

    We have reviewed our Report on "British Strategy in
a Certain Eventuality" (Paper No. W.P. (40) 168) in the
light of the following Terms of Reference remitted to us
by the Prime Minister.

    "In the event of France being unable to continue
in the war and becoming neutral with the Germans holding
their present position and the Belgian army being forced
to capitulate after assisting the British Expeditionary
Force to reach the coast; in the event of terms being
offered to Britain which would place her entirely at
the mercy of Germany through disarmament, cession of
naval bases in the Orkneys etc; what are the prospects
of our continuing the war alone against Germany and
probably Italy. Can the Navy and the Air Force hold out
reasonable hopes of preventing serious invasion, and
could the forces gathered in this Island cope with raids
from the air involving detachments not greater than
10,000 men; it being observed that a prolongation of

OUTWARD TELEGRAM

[This Document is the Property of His Britannic
Majesty's Government
and should be kept under Lock and Key.]

(R.6198/G)

SPECIAL DISTRIBUTION AND WAR CABINET

TO: UNITED STATES OF AMERICA

Cypher telegram to The Marquess of Lothian (Washington)
Foreign Office 25th May, 1940.   7.30 p.m.

No. 887 DIPP.

————————

MOST IMMEDIATE

My telegram to Paris No. 198 [of May 24th: possible
approach to Italy].
　　　　French Government concur and are instructing
French Ambassador in Washington in this sense so soon
as Monsieur Daladier has enlisted support of United
States Ambassador in Paris which he has, we understand,
done today. Please therefore approach the President at
once in the sense of my telegram under reference. You
need not wait until your French colleague has received
instructions.
　　　　Repeated to Paris 206, Rome 471.

British resistance might be very dangerous for Germany engaged in holding down the greater part of Europe."

2.   Our conclusions are contained in the following paragraphs.

3.   While our air force is in being our Navy and air force together should be able to prevent Germany carrying out a serious seaborne invasion of this country.

4.   Supposing Germany gained complete air superiority, we consider that the Navy could hold up an invasion for a time, but not for an indefinite period.

5.   If with our Navy unable to prevent it and our air force gone, Germany attempted an invasion, our coast and beach defences could not prevent German tanks and infantry getting a firm footing on our shores. In the circumstances envisaged above our land forces would be insufficient to deal with a serious invasion.

6.   The crux of the matter is air superiority. Once Germany had attained this, she might attempt to subjugate this country by air attack alone.

7.   Germany could not gain complete air superiority unless she could knock out our air force, and the aircraft industries, some vital portions of which are concentrated at Coventry and Birmingham.

8.   Air attacks on the aircraft factories would be made by day or by night. We consider that we should be able to inflict such casualties on the enemy by day as to prevent serious damage. Whatever we do, however, by way of defensive measures and we are pressing on with these with all despatch, we cannot be sure of protecting the large industrial centres, upon which our aircraft industries depend, from serious material damage by night attack. The enemy would not have to employ precision bombing to achieve this effect.

<u>**TO BE KEPT UNDER LOCK AND KEY.**</u>
It is requested that special care may be taken to ensure
the secrecy of this document.

S E C R E T.
W.P. (40)171.
COPY NO. 20
<u>26TH MAY, 1940</u>

<u>WAR CABINET.</u>

<u>BRITISH STRATEGY IN THE NEAR FUTURE.</u>

<u>Notes by the Minister without Portfolio[1] on Report
By Chiefs of Staff (W.P. (40???68).</u>

The memorandum on "British strategy in a certain
eventuality" envisages the steps which should be taken
"if French resistance were to collapse completely". As
seems desirable to consider now the proposals of the
Chiefs of Staff.

This paper is confined to the economic aspects of
the problem.

In the section of the memorandum dealing with
our ability to defeat Germany it is said that "Germany
might still be defeated by economic pressure, by a
continuation of air attack on economic objectives
in Germany and on German morale and the creation
of widespread revolt in her conquered territories"
(paragraph 14).

In paragraph 15 it is stated that "upon the
economic factor depends our only hope of bringing about
the down-fall of Germany."

Whilst, as a result of her conquests, Germany
may have secured new economic assets, she will suffer

---
1 Arthur Greenwood.

9.   Whether the attacks succeed in eliminating the
aircraft industry depends not only on the material
damage by bombs but on the moral effect on the workpeople
and their determination to carry on in the face of
wholesale havoc and destruction.

10.   If therefore the enemy presses home night attacks
on our aircraft industry, he is likely to achieve such
material and moral damage within the industrial area
concerned as to bring all work to a standstill.
11.   It must be remembered that numerically the
Germans have superiority of four to one. Moreover,
the German aircraft factories are well dispersed and
relatively inaccessible.

12.   On the other hand, so long as we have a counter-
offensive bomber force, we can carry out similar attacks
on German industrial centres and by moral and material
effect bring a proportion of them to a stand-still.

13.   To sum up, our conclusion is that _prima facie_
Germany has most of the cards; but the real test is
whether the morale of our fighting personnel and civil
population will counter balance the numerical and
material advantages which Germany enjoys. We believe it
will.

         J.G. DILL.   (Signed)   C.L.N. NEWALL.
         T.S.V. PHILLIPS.   DUDLEY POUND.
         R.E.C. PEIRSE.   EDMUND IRONSIDE.
[The Chiefs of Staff have not had an opportunity to see
this Report in its final form and reserve to themselves
the right to suggest such modifications as they may wish
to put forward.]

certain economic and political disabilities in consequence.

Though she may have obtained new resources as, for example, Iron ore, her ability to utilise them effectively for war purposes depends upon the possession of non-ferrous metals, which she must obtain from abroad.

Moreover, for the effective prosecution of the war she requires further supplies of food, rubber, oil, and fibres for clothing and footwear. For these there is no adequate source of supply close at hand.

Therefore, given a tight economic blockade, Germany can be strangled, her war effort seriously reduced, and her industrial manpower made impotent. In this connection, it is vital, as the memorandum under consideration points out, that we must take the necessary steps to secure allies to assist us in this direction. The memorandum sets out two important assumptions in the plan of the Chiefs of Staff for facing a desperate situation. The first is that "the United States of America is willing to give us full economic and financial support, <u>without which we do not think we could continue the war with any chance of success.</u>"

In paragraph 17 it is asserted that "given full Pan-American co-operation, we should be able to control all deficiency commodities <u>at source</u>". Paragraph 21 emphasises the view that the conclusions as to our ability to bring the war to a successful conclusion "depend entirely upon full Pan-American economic and financial co-operation".

It is vital, therefore, whether the French resistance is weakened or not, that steps should be taken to secure this co-operation.

I suggest that immediate steps should be taken

Fourth Meeting of Ministers, Starting in War Cabinet

War Cabinet: minutes
(Cabinet papers, 65/7)

27 May 1940
11.30 a.m.

Various suggestions had been made that we should cede some of our possessions in the New World to the United States in part payment of our war debt, but suggestions of this kind had always been discouraged by President Roosevelt.

Lord Lothian[14] thought that we should consider making a formal offer to the United States Government that, while we were not prepared to discuss any question of sovereignty, we were prepared to lease to the United States landing grounds on British territory, in view of the importance of such facilities to USA security. Lord Lothian mentioned particularly Trinidad, Newfoundland and Bermuda.

Lord Lothian believed that an offer of this kind made by us would make a deep impression in the United States and add to our security. If we acted quickly, our action would have the advantage also of spontaneity. If this proposal were to be pursued, it was very desirable that Congress should vote the necessary appropriations before its adjournment in early June.

The Prime Minister said that he would be opposed to a proposal that we should offer such facilities except as part of a deal. The United States had given us practically no help in the war, and now that they saw how great was the danger, their attitude was that they wanted to keep everything which would help us for their own defence.

---

14 The ambassador in Washington. In his telegram No. 814 from Washington, sent on 24 May 1940.

through diplomatic channels to press for active economic
assistance and that a strong mission should be sent
out to America without delay to secure economic and
financial allies for the prosecution of the blockade
with the utmost vigour.

Our position will be strengthened by maintaining
control as far as possible of the output of the overseas
Empires of France, Holland and Belgium.

Further questions are raised in Paragraph 33 of
the memorandum which reads as follows :-

> 35.   Plans have already been prepared to divert
> all shipping to West Coast ports and, provided
> we can maintain approximately 60 per cent of
> our present imports, we believe that we should
> be able to obtain enough food to support the
> population and sufficient raw materials to
> continue our essential armament production,
> although at a reduced rate. We again draw
> attention to the importance of reducing now
> the unimportant imports (such as bananas and
> children's toys), so that the maximum import
> of important raw materials may be available
> to increase our stocks of these essentials.
> Moreover, even if our imports were reduced to
> a mere trickle, we should still be able to
> tide over a critical period of a few weeks by
> drawing on our reserve stocks, which have been
> accumulated to meet a crisis of this nature. To
> increase our ability to hold out in a critical
> period, we should now put into operation plans
> for drastic rationing and distribution of
> stocks. Nevertheless, our ability to carry
> on the war is absolutely dependent upon the
> eventual maintenance of supplies through the
> West Coast ports, and we would point out that
> this will raise major problems of labour
> transference. Moreover, the West Coast ports
> themselves will be subjected to air attack,

War Cabinet: Confidential Annex
(Cabinet papers, 65/13)

27 May 1940
11.30 a.m.

The Prime Minister said that at the meeting with M. Reynaud the previous afternoon, complete agreement had been reached that the British Expeditionary Force must be withdrawn to the coast. The BEF was being pressed on both flanks, and the Germans had made a break in the line East of Courtrai. It was clear that we could not allow the security of our Army to be compromised in order to save the First French Army. He asked the Chief of the Imperial General Staff[15] to make the position in this respect clear to Lord Gort.

The Prime Minister thought that it would be as well that he should issue a general injunction to Ministers to use confident language. He was convinced that the bulk of the people of the country would refuse to accept the possibility of defeat.

The Prime Minister dealt with the main Report by the Chiefs of Staff first.[16] In his opinion this Report did not give a true picture of the position. In particular he challenged the Tables of the British and German air strengths, which gave a misleading impression. He had caused a statistical examination of the comparative position of the two Air Forces to be made, and although it had been extremely difficult to arrive at a true comparison, there were certain observations which he wished to make.

(i)   During the last three years, according to the figures provided by the Air Ministry, the Germans had turned out 25,000 aircraft and we had produced 15,000 i.e. a ratio of 5 to 3. On this basis it was quite misleading to say that the Germans had a superiority of 4 to 1 over us. Either we credited the Germans with getting a

---

15 Sir John Dill.
16 See Document 1, page 135.

although possibly on a lesser scale to that on
the East and South Coasts.

It should be possible to maintain approximately
60% of our present imports, provided there is not
abnormal waste and provided also that the importation
of commodities not required for the prosecution of
the war is prohibited. To make the scheme effective
consideration must be given to harbour accommodation, to
the dispersal of raw materials and foodstuffs, and to
rail and road transport both of which would be called
upon to meet substantially increased demands.

Finally the situation demands the most drastic
action regarding both home production and consumption.
All kinds of production which can be postponed should
be damped down and every effort concentrated on two
objectives:- (1) the needs of the fighting and civil
defence services and (2) the maintenance of the civil
population under wartime conditions.

This will necessitate the re-allocation of raw
materials and the transfer of labour.

It is also of great importance to restrict
unnecessary consumption. This appears to be essential if
the country is to be put on a war footing.

These considerations require further exploration.

This aspect of the question is not dealt with
in the memorandum of the Chiefs of Staff, but it is an
integral part of the problem which now confronts us.

This memorandum is purely personal and has been
drafted by me after considering memorandum W.P. (40)168,
without consultation with my colleagues or with any of
the officers concerned.

(Intld.)   A.G.

much greater operational strength out of a given
production than ourselves, or we made insufficient
allowance for all the difficulties which, if our
own experience was to be any guide, they must
have encountered in expanding their air force.

(ii) We knew the very large requirements of our own
training establishments and formations. If the
German Air Force was really four times as large
as ours, presumably their training requirements
must similarly be four times as great and would
amount to an enormous total. Unless we believed
that the Germans succeeded in carrying out their
training with a far smaller proportion of wastage
than ourselves (which seemed unlikely), we must
accept the fact that training requirements made
far greater inroads into their operational
strength than was shown in the tables.

(iii) In January, 1940, the Air Ministry had estimated
that Germany was turning out 2,000 aircraft per
month. A detailed examination of this estimate
had been carried out by the Ministry of Economic
Warfare, however, and as a result of this the Air
Ministry had finally accepted a very much lower
estimate of only 1,000 aircraft per month. Our
whole policy might depend on our assessment of
the German air strength, and it was therefore
essential that all estimates should be subjected
to the most detailed scrutiny.

With regard to the figures for the Metropolitan
Air Force given in Appendix 'C', the late
Secretary of State for Air[17] had given as his
forecast of first-line strength on the 30th June,
1940, a figure of 2,150 aircraft. The figure given
in the Tables, however, amounted only to 1,256,
to which must be added some 200 to 300 aircraft
in France, a total of, say, 1,550. If these
figures were correct, they would imply that we had
lost two-fifths of our effective force since active

17 Kingsley Wood. Conservative MP for Woolwich West, 1918–1943. Secretary of State
for Air, 1938–40. Chancellor of the Exchequer from May 1940 until his death.

NOTE: Since writing the above I have shown a copy to the Lord Privy Seal who concurs in the view expressed.

A.G.

Treasury Chambers, S.W.1.

operations had begun on Western Front. The figures
of our losses up to the 24th May were 360, but
against this must be offset the new intake since
May 12th of 610 machines.

The Prime Minister said that he proposed to go into
these Tables of comparative strengths himself and try to
obtain agreed figures on a truly comparable basis. The
German bombing force might be four times as great as
ours, but he did not believe the ratio was anything like
so great in respect of our total air force.

The Vice Chief of the Air Staff[18] agreed that
Appendices 'B' and 'C' were not drawn up on comparable
bases. The British figures referred to operational
strength, and the German figures to first-line strength.
An attempt had been made to arrive at a true basis
of comparison, and he handed to the War Cabinet a
comparative Table drawn up on these lines.

The Prime Minister observed that from this Table it
appeared that the odds against us were only 2½ to 1. If
our airmen were shooting down 3 to 1, the balance was on
our side.

The Chief of the Air Staff[19] pointed out that at
night the balance would be very much less favourable for
us. It was only in the day fighting that we were able to
inflict such heavy losses on the enemy.

The Secretary of State for Air[20] drew attention to
the importance of the factors of morale and superior
equipment. One of our fighter squadrons operating from
Kent had given battle to a crack German squadron
equipped with MC.110s. The Germans had fought extremely
well, but their losses had been very much greater than
ours.

The Prime Minister paid tribute to the skill of the
Air Ministry's designers which had produced such a fine
fighting machine as the Hurricane.

Continuing, he observed that the Chiefs of
Staff Report was based on the assumption that French

---

18 Air Marshal Richard Peirse.
19 Air Chief Marshal Sir Cyril Newall.
20 Sir Archibald Sinclair.

TO BE KEPT UNDER LOCK AND KEY

It is requested that special care may be taken to ensure the secrecy of this document.

SECRET.
COPY No. 10
W.P. (40) 170.
26th May, 1940.

WAR CABINET.

SUGGESTED APPROACH TO SIGNOR MUSSOLINI.
Memorandum by the Secretary of State for Foreign Affairs.

By direction of the Prime Minister, I circulate this statement which shows briefly what has passed between His Majesty's Government and the French Government on the subject of the possibility of securing mediation in some form by the Italian Government.

Monsieur Reynaud came to London today and explained the critical situation in which France finds herself.

He enquired whether His Majesty's Government would join with the French Government in making a direct approach to Signor Mussolini on the following lines.

A frank explanation of position in which Signor Mussolini will be placed if the Germans establish domination in Europe.
Great Britain and France will fight to the end for the preservation of their independence: and they will be helped by the resources of other nations now outside the war.
If Signor Mussolini will co-operate with us in securing a settlement of all European questions which safeguard the independence and security of the Allies, and could be the basis of a just and durable peace for Europe, we will undertake at once

resistance would collapse completely, and that we
should be exposed at short range to the concentrated
attack of the whole of the German naval and air forces,
operating from bases extending from Norway to the
North-west of France. If France went out of the war,
it did not necessarily follow that his assumption was
correct; France might become a neutral, and it was not
certain that Germany would insist on retaining all the
ports in Northern France. She might be so anxious to
divide France from us that she would offer France very
favourable terms of peace.

to discuss, with the desire to find solutions, the
matters in which Signor Mussolini is primarily
interested.

We understand that he desires the solution
of certain Mediterranean questions; and if he will
state in secrecy what these are, France and Great
Britain will at once do their best to meet his
wishes, on the basis of co-operation set out above.

Meanwhile, His Majesty's Ambassador in Washington
telegraphed on May 26th at 12.54 a.m. that he had
agreed with his French colleague the text of a joint
communication to the President of the United States.

The text reads as follows:

"The Allied Governments suggest the President
on his own initiative should ask Signor Mussolini
for the reasons which apparently induce him to
contemplate an immediate entry into the war against
the Allies and that he should further state that if
Signor Mussolini will inform him of his grievances
or claims against the Allies he will immediately
communicate them to the Allied Governments in order
to leave nothing undone to prevent an extension of
the war.

They suggest the President should inform Signor
Mussolini that he had reason to believe that
the attitude of the Allies towards the Italian
Government can be defined as follows.

(a) The Allied Governments are aware that the
   Italian Government entertains certain grievances
   in regard to the Italian position in the
   Mediterranean.

(b) The Allied Governments would welcome Italian
   participation at the Peace Conference with a
   status equal to that of the belligerents.

(c) Signor Mussolini would thus be invited by the
   President to notify him for transmission to the
   Allies the claims of Italy the fulfilment of
   which would in his view ensure the establishment

Fifth Meeting of Ministers

War Cabinet: Confidential Annex
(Cabinet papers, 65,13)

27 May 1940
4.30 p.m.

The Prime Minister said that the Foreign
Secretary's Note[21] set out the kind of approach to Signor
Mussolini which M. Reynaud wanted the French and British
Governments to make. While M. Reynaud was prepared to
fight on for honour's sake, he was afraid that France was
in danger of collapsing. If Italy undertook to stay out
of the war, the French could remove ten Divisions from
the Italian front. An attack by Italy at this juncture
would give the *coup-de-grâce* to their existence. If
France collapsed, Germany would probably give her good
terms, but would expect the French to have the kind of
Ministers who were acceptable to the Germans.

The Prime Minister said that it might be argued
that an approach on the lines proposed by M. Reynaud
was not unlike the approach which we had asked President
Roosevelt to make to Signor Mussolini. There was,
however, a good deal of difference between making the
approach ourselves and allowing one to be made by
President Roosevelt ostensibly on his own initiative.

The Lord President thought that the completely
misleading account of military operations in Northern
France, coupled with the share of praise which the
French were claiming for themselves in connection with
events in which they had taken no part, must have some
explanation. Was it that they intended to say that the
French had had a magnificent scheme, but that, owing
to the withdrawal of the BEF, they had been unable to
carry it out and the poor French had been let down by
their allies and must take the best chance available
to them to get out of things. It would be unfortunate
if they were to add to this that we had been unwilling

---

21 War Cabinet No. 170 of 1940. See Document.

in the Mediterranean of a new order guaranteeing
to Italy satisfaction of Italian legitimate
aspirations in that sea, if the negotiations
succeeded the President would then formally
record

    (a) the agreement thus arrived at
    (b) the undertaking of the Allies to execute
        the agreement at the end of the war.
    (c) The assurance of Signor Mussolini that
        the claims of Italy would be satisfied
        by the execution of this agreement.
        The agreement thus arrived at to be
        dependent of course on Italy not
        entering the war against the Allies."

Lord Lothian was this morning authorised to make
this communication to the President, with his French
colleague, and he should have made it this afternoon.

Yesterday, I saw the Italian Ambassador, and I
annex a record of my conversation with him.

Monsieur Reynaud was not given any definite
reply, before returning to Paris, on the subject of his
present proposal. In the actual circumstances it holds
out only a very slender chance of success, and that
chance would seem to depend principally on the degree of
discomfort which the prospect of a Europe dominated by
Hitler may cause to Mussolini.

It was understood that we should endeavour to
give Monsieur Reynaud a reply tomorrow.

P.S.

Since drafting the above, I have seen the Master
of the Rolls, who has just returned from Rome. He
tells me that Sir P. Loraine had been informed by the
United States Ambassador that President Roosevelt's
last attempt to deter the Italian Government had been
bitterly resented by Signor Mussolini as unwarrantable

even to allow them the chance of negotiations with
Italy.

The Prime Minister said that the Lord President's
argument amounted to this, that nothing would come of
the approach, but that it was worth doing to sweeten
relations with a failing ally. He read the following
telegram, which he had received from M. Reynaud that
morning (No. 283 DIPP):—

> 'I thank you for your cordial welcome and for your
> telegram. Your friendship is precious to me. As
> for Italy, that (?ultimate)[22] argument which to my
> mind carries most weight is that the assistance
> given by your country to mine through the approach
> we are making at this tragic hour will help to
> strengthen an alliance of hearts which I believe to
> be essential.'

The Prime Minister said that he was increasingly
oppressed with the futility of the suggested approach
to Signor Mussolini, which the latter would certainly
regard with contempt. Such an approach would do M.
Reynaud far less good than if he made a firm stand.
Further, the approach would ruin the integrity of our
fighting position in this country. Even if we did not
include geographical precision and mentioned no names,
everybody would know what we had in mind. Personally
he doubted whether France was so willing to give up
the struggle as M. Reynaud had represented. Anyway, let
us not be dragged down with France. If the French were
not prepared to go on with the struggle, let them give
up, though he doubted whether they would do so. If
this country was beaten, France became a vassal State;
but if we won, we might save them. The best help we
could give to M. Reynaud was to let him feel that,
whatever happened to France, we were going to fight it
out to the end. This manoeuvre was a suggestion to
get France out of the difficulty that she might have to

---

22 Words that could not be properly or fully deciphered were indicated this way in the
War Cabinet's minutes, with a bracket and a question mark.

interference with Italy's private affairs. He further
reports that Sir P. Loraine's judgement is that any
further approach would only be interpreted as a sign of
weakness and would do no good.

The Master of the Rolls, however, was disposed to
think that the situation could hardly be made worse by
the approach suggested by Monsieur Reynaud, and that the
first consideration there set out must be very present
to Signor Mussolini's mind.

FOREIGN OFFICE,
          26th May, 1940.

make a separate peace, notwithstanding her bargain not to do so.

At the moment our prestige in Europe was very low. The only way we could get it back was by showing the world that Germany had not beaten us. If, after two or three months, we could show that we were still unbeaten, our prestige would return. Even if we were beaten, we should be no worse off than we should be if we were now to abandon the struggle. Let us therefore avoid being dragged down the slippery slope with France. The whole of this manoeuvre was intended to get us so deeply involved in negotiations that we should be unable to turn back. We had gone a long way already in our approach to Italy, but let us not allow M. Reynaud to get us involved in a confused situation. The approach proposed was not only futile, but involved us in a deadly danger.

The Secretary of State for Air[23] thought that it might help matters if the Prime Minister were to go to Paris and see other French Ministers.

The Prime Minister said that General Spears was in Paris. France had got to settle this matter for herself. It was a question of her word and her army's honour. He had heard that day that there had been some change for the better in the fighting spirit of the French troops. There might be some hope in this. Otherwise everything would rest on us. If the worst came to the worst, it would not be a bad thing for this country to go down fighting for the other countries which had been overcome by the Navy tyranny.

The Secretary of State for Foreign Affairs[24] said that he saw no particular difficulty in taking the line suggested by the Lord President. Nevertheless, he was conscious of certain rather profound differences of points of view which he would like to make clear.

In the first place, he would have thought that, if we could persuade them to do so, there would have been some positive value in getting the French Government

---

23 Sinclair.
24 Halifax.

THIS DOCUMENT IS THE PROPERTY OF HIS BRITANNIC MAJESTY'S
GOVERNMENT

TO BE KEPT UNDER LOCK AND KEY.
It is requested that special care may be taken to ensure
the secrecy of this document.

S E C R E T.
C. O. S. (40) 394.
COPY NO. 33
26th MAY. 1940.

WAR CABINET.

CHIEFS OF STAFF COMMITTEE.

_____

BRITISH STRATEGY IN A CERTAIN EVENTUALITY.

Note by the Secretary.

The Report which the Chiefs of Staff approved
yesterday, the 25th May, on the above subject has been
circulated this morning as a War Cabinet Paper.

2.   At this morning's (26th May) Meeting of the
War Cabinet the Prime Minister remitted the following
additional Terms of Reference, and directed that the
Chiefs of Staff Committee and the Vice Chiefs of Staff
should together examine them and report at once.

"In the event of France being unable to continue
in the war and becoming neutral with the Germans holding
their present position and the Belgian army being forced
to capitulate after assisting the British Expeditionary
Force to reach the coast; in the event of terms being
offered to Britain which would place her entirely at
the mercy of Germany through disarmament, cession of
naval bases in the Orkneys etc; what are the prospects
of our continuing the war alone against Germany and
probably Italy. Can the Navy and the Air Force hold out

to say that they would fight to the end for their independence.

In the second place, he could not recognise any resemblance between the action which he proposed, and the suggestion that we were suing for terms and following a line which would lead us to disaster. In the discussion the previous day he had asked the Prime Minister whether, if he was satisfied that matters vital to the independence of this country were unaffected, he would be prepared to discuss terms. The Prime Minister had said that he would be thankful to get out of our present difficulties on such terms, provided we retain the essentials and the elements of our vital strength, even at the cost of some cession of territory. On the present occasion, however, the Prime Minister seemed to suggest that under no conditions would we contemplate any course except fighting to a finish. The issue was probably academic, since we were unlikely to receive any offer which would not come up against the fundamental conditions which were essential to us. If, however, it was possible to obtain a settlement which did not impair those conditions, he, for his part, doubted if he would be able to accept the view now put forward by the Prime Minister. The Prime Minister had said that two or three months would show whether we were able to stand up against the air risk. This meant that the future of the country turned on whether the enemy's bombs happened to hit our aircraft factories. He was prepared to take that risk if our independence was at stake; but if it was not at stake he would think it right to accept an offer which would save the country from avoidable disaster.

The Prime Minister said that he thought the issue which the War Cabinet was called upon to settle was difficult enough without getting involved in the discussion of an issue which was quite unreal and was most unlikely to arise. If Herr Hitler was prepared to make peace on the terms of the restoration of German colonies and the overlordship of Central Europe, that was one thing. But it was quite unlikely that he would make any such offer.

reasonable hopes of preventing serious invasion, and
could the forces gathered in this Island cope with raids
from the air involving detachments not greater than
10,000 men; it being observed that a prolongation of
British resistance might be very dangerous for Germany
engaged in holding down the greater part of Europe."

(Signed)
L.C. HOLLIS.

The Foreign Secretary said he would like to put the following question. Suppose the French Army collapsed and Herr Hitler made an offer of peace terms. Suppose the French Government said 'We are unable to deal with an offer made to France alone and you must deal with the Allies together.' Suppose Herr Hitler, being anxious to end the war through knowledge of his own internal weaknesses, offered terms to France and England, would the Prime Minister be prepared to discuss them?

The Prime Minister said that he would not join France in asking for terms; but if he were told what the terms offered were, he would be prepared to consider them.

THIS DOCUMENT IS THE PROPERTY OF HIS BRITANNIC MAJESTY'S
GOVERNMENT

TO BE KEPT UNDER LOCK AND KEY.
It is requested that special care may be taken to ensure
the secrecy of this document.

S E C R E T.
C. O. S. (40) 391.
COPY NO. 33
26th MAY. 1940.

WAR CABINET.
CHIEFS OF STAFF COMMITTEE.

VISIT OF M. REYNAUD ON 26th MAY. 1940.

Aide Memoire.

We have been instructed to prepare an Aide
Memoire for the Prime Minister on the assumption that
the object of M. Reynaud's visit on 26th May is to say
that the French wish to make a separate peace.

2.   We put forward our views under the following
headings:-
   (a) Arguments to deter the French capitulation.
   (b) Arguments to strengthen the French will to
       continue the fight.
   (c) Measures which we should press the French to take
       if M. Reynaud is determined to capitulate.

Arguments to deter the French from capitulation.

3.   M. Reynaud is at once reminded that the French
and British Governments have given a solemn undertaking
not to conclude a separate peace. Even if the French
decide to capitulate we shall continue the fight single-
handed.

Sixth Meeting of Ministers

War Cabinet: minutes
(Cabinet papers, 65/7)

27 May 1940
10 Downing Street
10 p.m.

The Prime Minister informed the War Cabinet that a
message had been received from Sir Roger Keyes to the
effect that the King of the Belgians had ordered his
Commander-in-Chief to send a plenipotentiary to the
Germans to ask for an armistice for the Belgian Army to
take effect from midnight that night.

News of this had been received in Paris and General
Spears had rung up to say that General Weygand had
advised the French Government to dissociate themselves
from the Belgians in this matter and to order General
Blanchard and Lord Gort to fight on. He had asked for the
Prime Minister's support in this advice.

The Prime Minister said that he had acceded
immediately to this request.

The Prime Minister said that he had telegraphed to
Sir Roger Keyes in the early hours of that morning that
the British Expeditionary Force was withdrawing towards
the ports, and that we should do our best to evacuate
such of the Belgian Army as could get back to the coast.
He had emphasised the importance of ensuring the King's
safety, and had made it clear that we should fight on
to the end. This message should not have affected the
King's determination to continue the struggle, although,
perhaps, he could not altogether be blamed now for the
action he was taking. Nevertheless, he had been very
precipitate in seeking an armistice. Apparently the
collapse of the Belgians was due to the heavy bombing to
which they had been subjected that day. Any grounds for
recrimination lay rather in the Belgian action on the
outbreak of war than in the more immediate past. At the
time when there had been only fifteen German divisions on

4.   However attractive the conditions which Germany may offer to France, in order to get her out of the war, while she deals with Great Britain, there is not the faintest chance of these conditions being kept when it no longer suits the German book. Thus by capitulating France will become a vassal, if not a slave, to Germany.

5.   The only way we can defeat Germany if we fight alone, will be by instituting a virtual blockade of the whole of Europe, <u>including France</u>. This we should immediately do. We should forthwith acquaint the United States of America with the facts of the situation and seek their full cooperation. In the present economic state of Europe, the effects of the blockade would be to cause widespread starvation in Europe this year.
       The French Colonial Empire would be entirely cut off from France by this blockade.

6.   France could not escape the military measures we should have to take against German forces on French soil. Our necessity would compel us to treat the whole of French European and North African territories as hostile. If the military situation so dictated we should have no hesitation in bombing French cities.

7.   Italy would certainly exploit the situation to her advantage and satisfy her claims against France.

8.   Whatever peace terms the French may accept at German hands, these will by no means be final. There need be no illusion as to the ultimate fate of France.

<u>Arguments to strengthen the French will to continue the fight.</u>

9.   The German economic position is already known to be serious. The commitments involved in holding down the territories already conquered must be placing further strain on German economic resources.

10.   At the present moment Germany is staking her

their Western frontier, and the bulk of the German Army
had been engaged in Poland, if Belgium had then invited
us to enter their country, we could have established
ourselves in a strong defensive position or invaded
Germany. The King's action was certainly not heroic.
Presumably, he would now make a separate peace with the
Germans and carry on as a puppet monarch. This might
well be the best that he could do for his country, but
we had to face the fact that it had the most serious
consequences for the British Expeditionary Force. It
was possible, of course, that the four divisions in the
Lille area might manage to draw back and cut their way
out to the coast. Our formations were practically intact
and the troops were in excellent heart. They did not
realise the plight in which they had been placed.

The Chief of the Imperial General Staff[25] said that
the collapse of the Belgians would undoubtedly place
the British Expeditionary Force in the most serious
peril. Lord Gort had no troops with which to close the
gap and prevent the Germans breaking through to Dunkirk.
No information had yet been received by the War Office
as to the casualties which our Army had suffered. Some
personnel had been withdrawn from France that day, but
a ship leaving Dunkirk that afternoon had been heavily
attacked from the air and had suffered some casualties
from machine-gun fire.

The Prime Minister said that General Spears had
reported that the feeling in Paris was better than
it had been a short time ago. This might perhaps be
attributed in part to the results of M. Reynaud's visit
to London the previous day. As for the effect of the
Belgian defection on French resistance, the French
had probably already written off Blanchard's army as a
dead loss. The action of the Belgians might sting the
French to anger, in which case they would be very much
more formidable opponents to the Germans than in their
present stunned and bewildered state.

Our chief preoccupation now was to get off as
much of the British Expeditionary Force as possible.

---

25 Dill.

all on a desperate throw with a view to making a quick
decision. The intense effort she is now making she cannot
hope to sustain. If only we can stop and hold the present
onslaught we shall be well on the way to precipitating
an early German collapse. The greater the determination
we can show in the face of heavy odds, the greater the
chances will be of obtaining American support.

11.   Moreover, Germany's own military difficulties
should not be overlooked. So far she has staked the pick
of her forces both human and material. The forces which
we have not yet seen are probably of lower fighting
value.

Measures which we should press the French to take if M.
Reynaud is determined to capitulate.

12.   Before capitulation, the French should be pressed
-

(a) To make a supreme effort to extricate the British
    Expeditionary Force and the Advanced Air striking
    Force from the situation in which it has been
    placed by the virtual collapse of the French
    Army.

(b) To despatch the whole of the French Mercantile
    Marine to British or Dominion ports.

(c) To remove all gold and bearer securities to the
    United States of America.

13.   As soon as the French capitulate, they should
agree -

(a) To send the French Navy to British ports.

(b) To transfer what is left of their Air Force to
    British bases.

(c) To destroy as far as possible all military
    equipment, particularly anti-aircraft and long-
    range guns.

(d) To destroy all British secret equipment (e.g.
    R.D.F., Asdics), and burn all secret documents
    related to policy and plans.

14.   It would of course be highly desirable from the

There would be very confused fighting in the area of operations. The bombers on both sides would be able to do little, as the opposing troops would be very much intermingled. The German bombers, however, would get their opportunity when our men reached the coast.

The Minister of Information[26] suggested that a statement should be issued referring to the gallant defence by the British troops.

The Prime Minister agreed, but thought that for the sake of relatives no names of regiments should be given at present.

The Minister of Information suggested that the public should be given some indication of the serious position in which the BEF had been placed. The French communiqués still had a cheerful tone. There was no doubt that the public were, at the moment, quite unprepared for the shock of realisation of the true position.

The Prime Minister thought that the seriousness of the situation should be emphasised; but he would deprecate any detailed statement or attempt to access the results of the battle, until the situation had been further cleared up. The announcement of the Belgian Armistice would go a long way to prepare the public for bad news.

The Minister of Information said that he realised the danger of announcements which appeared to contradict the French communiqués, and he thought that it would be as well to remind the public of the constant German efforts to drive a wedge between the two peoples. At the same time editors could be asked to tone down the French announcements. The Prime Minister thought that it would be necessary for him to make a full statement in Parliament, although it might be another week before the situation had cleared sufficiently to allow him to do so. He proposed to say that the essential dangers which had menaced this country in the first days of the war had not been greatly increased by what had happened. Our means

---

26 Duff Cooper.

military point of view that the French should stipulate
that their territory should not be used by the enemy
as a base of operations against ourselves. We feel,
however, that even if the French were to attempt to
obtain a guarantee of this nature and the Germans
nominally subscribed to it the guarantee itself would be
utterly worthless.

(Signed)	C.L.N. NEWALL
"	DUDLEY POUND.
"	EDMUND IRONSIDE.

Cabinet War Room.

of meeting them, on the other hand, had increased since
the beginning of the war; moreover, we could take heart
from the superior quality and morale of our Air Force
which had been so clearly demonstrated.

Winston S. Churchill: statement
(Hansard)

28 May 1940
House of Commons

WAR SITUATION

The Prime Minister (Mr Churchill): The House will
be aware that the King of the Belgians yesterday sent
a plenipotentiary to the German Command asking for a
suspension of arms on the Belgian front. The British
and French Governments instructed their generals
immediately to dissociate themselves from this procedure
and to persevere in the operations in which they are
now engaged. However, the German Command has agreed to
the Belgian proposals and the Belgian Army ceased to
resist the enemy's will at four o'clock this morning.
I have no intention of suggesting to the House that we
should attempt at this moment to pass judgement[1] upon
the action of the King of the Belgians in his capacity
as Commander-in-Chief of the Belgian Army. This Army has
fought very bravely and has both suffered and inflicted
heavy losses. The Belgian Government has dissociated
itself from the action of the King and, declaring itself
to be the only legal Government of Belgium, has formally
announced its resolve to continue the war at the side of
the Allies who have come to the aid of Belgium at her
urgent appeal. Whatever our feelings may be upon the
facts so far as they are known to us, we must remember
that the sense of brotherhood between the many peoples
who have fallen into the power of the aggressor, and
those who still confront him, will play its part in
better days than those through which we are passing.
The situation of the British and French Armies

---

1 This phrase had been suggested to Churchill by Lieutenant-Colonel G. M. O.
Davy. Brought into the War Cabinet to give an account of the Belgian capitulation, he
persuaded Churchill to 'cut all references to treachery and the absence of warning'. After
Churchill redrafted his statement, he eventually said 'How about that, Colonel Davy?'
'That's better, Sir,' he replied, and everyone laughed. The PM smiled.

Seventh Meeting of Ministers

War Cabinet: minutes
(Cabinet papers, 65/7)

28 May 1940
10 Downing Street
11.30 a.m.

The Prime Minister said that the Belgian Army
had ceased fire at 0400 hours that morning. He invited
Admiral Sir Roger Keyes, who had just returned from
Belgium, to give the War Cabinet his appreciation of the
present situation.

Sir Roger Keyes said that the Belgian Army had
been completely demoralised by incessant bombing from
large numbers of German aircraft. The Germans appeared
to have maintained a ring of fighter patrols round the
battle area and, although our fighters had been seen in
many engagements with the German fighters, they had been
unable to break through the ring in order to attack
the German bombers, which had circled round at low
altitudes, bombing the Belgian troops with impunity.

Sir Roger Keyes commented on the precipitate flight
of the Belgian Government. King Leopold had said that he
wished to have nothing more to do with them. In his (Sir
Roger Keyes's) view the Belgian Government were entirely
responsible for the chaos caused by the evacuation of
the civil population, who had been told that asylum
would be found for them in England or France. It had
been noticeable that the Local Authorities had in most
cases been the first to get away.

The Prime Minister expressed the War Cabinet's warm
appreciation of what Sir Roger Keyes had done in such
difficult and dangerous circumstances. He did not think,
however, that Sir Roger Keyes should return to Belgium,
at any rate for the moment.

(At this point Sir Roger Keyes withdrew).

The Prime Minister said that the King of the
Belgians would now presumably become the puppet of

now engaged in a most severe battle and beset on three sides and from the air, is evidently extremely grave. The surrender of the Belgian Army in this manner adds appreciably to their grievous peril. But the troops are in good heart, and are fighting with the utmost discipline and tenacity, and I shall, of course, abstain from giving any particulars of what, with the powerful assistance of the Royal Navy and the Royal Air Force, they are doing or hope to do. I expect to make a statement to the House on the general position when the result of the intense struggle now going on can be known and measured. This will not, perhaps, be until the beginning of next week.

Meanwhile, the House should prepare itself for hard and heavy tidings. I have only to add that nothing which may happen in this battle can in any way relieve us of our duty to defend the world cause to which we have vowed ourselves; nor should it destroy our confidence in our power to make our way, as on former occasions in our history, through disaster and through grief to the ultimate defeat of our enemies.

Hitler, and might possibly obtain better treatment
for his people than if he had left the country and
continued to resist from foreign soil. No doubt history
would criticise the King for having involved us and the
French in Belgium's ruin. But it was not for us to pass
judgement on him.

The Prime Minister then read to the War Cabinet the
terms of the armistice which the Belgians had agreed
with the enemy, as follows:—

    (1) All Belgian troop movement forbidden. Belgian
        troops must line up on the side of the road to
        await orders. They must make known their presence
        by means of white signs, flags, &c.

    (2) Orders must be given forbidding destruction of
        war material and stores.

    (3) German troops must be allowed to proceed to the
        coast.

    (4) Free passage to Ostend is demanded and no
        destruction permitted.

    (5) All resistance will be overcome.

The Minister of Information read to the War Cabinet a
message he had just received from Sir Walter Monckton[1]
pressing for a frank statement of the desperate
situation of the British Expeditionary Force. He feared
that, unless this was given out, public confidence would
be badly shaken and the civil population would not be
ready to accept the assurances of the Government of the
chances of our ultimate victory. The Minister suggested
that he should make a short statement in the 1 o'clock
news of the BBC.

The Prime Minister said that he would also make a
statement in the House of Commons in the afternoon.

---

1 Walter Turner Monckton, 1891–1965. Educated at Harrow and Balliol College,
Oxford. Director General Ministry of Information, 1940–1; British Propaganda and
Information Services, Cairo,1941–2. Solicitor-General, 1945. Conservative MP for
Bristol West, 1951–7. Minister of Labour and National Service, 1951–5. Minister of
Defence, 1955–6. Paymaster-General, 1956–7. Created Viscount, 1957.

Eighth Meeting of Ministers

War Cabinet: Confidential Annex
(Cabinet papers, 65/13)

28 May 1940
4 p.m.

The Foreign Secretary[1] said that Sir Robert
Vansittart[2] had now discovered what the Italian Embassy
had in mind, namely, that we should give a clear
indication that we should like to see mediation by
Italy.

The Prime Minister said that it was clear that the
French purpose was to see Signor Mussolini acting as
intermediary between ourselves and Herr Hitler. He was
determined not to get into this position.

The Foreign Secretary said that the proposal which
had been discussed with M. Reynaud on Sunday had been
as follows: that we should say that we were prepared
to fight to the death for our independence, but that,
provided this could be secured, there were certain
concessions that we were prepared to make to Italy.

The Prime Minister thought that the French were
trying to get us onto the slippery slope. The position
would be entirely different when Germany had made an
unsuccessful attempt to invade this country.

The Foreign Secretary said that we must not ignore
the fact that we might get better terms before France
went out of the war and our aircraft factories were
bombed, than we might get in three months' time.

The various possibilities now under development of
countering night-bombing were referred to.

The Prime Minister then read out a draft which
expressed his views. To him the essential point was that
M. Reynaud wanted to get us to the Conference-table with
Herr Hitler. If we once got to the table, we should then

---

1 Halifax.
2 Robert Gilbert Vansittart, Chief Diplomatic Adviser to the Foreign Secretary,
1938–41.

find that the terms offered us touched our independence and integrity. When, at this point, we got up to leave the Conference-table, we should find that all the forces of resolution which were now at our disposal would have vanished. M. Reynaud had said that if he could save the independence of France, he would continue the fight. It was clear, therefore, that M. Reynaud's aim was to end the war.

The Foreign Secretary said that M. Reynaud also wanted the Allies to address an appeal to the President of the United States.

The Prime Minister thought that a paragraph might be added to the draft outlined by the Lord President[1] to the effect that we were ready in principle to associate ourselves with such an appeal.

The Minister without Portfolio[2] thought that M. Reynaud was too much inclined to hawk round appeals. This was another attempt to run out.

The Prime Minister said that he came back to the point that the French wanted to get out of the war, but did not want to break their Treaty obligations to us. Signor Mussolini, if he came in as mediator, would take his whack out of us. It was impossible to imagine that Herr Hitler would be so foolish as to let us continue our re-armament. In effect, his terms would put us completely at his mercy. We should get no worse terms if we went on fighting, even if we were beaten, than were open to us now. If, however, we continued the war and Germany attacked us, no doubt we should suffer some damage, but they also would suffer severe losses. Their oil supplies might be reduced. A time might come when we felt that we had to put an end to the struggle, but the terms would not then be more mortal than those offered to us now. The Foreign Secretary said that he still did not see what there was in the French suggestion of trying

---

1 Neville Chamberlain.
2 Arthur Greenwood.

out the possibilities of mediation which the Prime
Minister felt was so wrong.

The Lord President said that, on a dispassionate
survey, it was right to remember that the alternative to
fighting on nevertheless involved a considerable gamble.

The War Cabinet agreed that this was a true
statement of the case.

The Prime Minister said that the nations which went
down fighting rose again, but those which surrendered
tamely were finished.

The Foreign Secretary said that nothing in his
suggestion could even remotely be described as ultimate
capitulation.

The Prime Minister thought that the chances of
decent terms being offered to us at the present time were
a thousand to one against.

At this point the War Cabinet broke off its discussion, to enable
Churchill to meet the full Cabinet, a meeting that had been arranged
earlier in the day.

Ninth Meeting of Ministers

War Cabinet: Confidential Annex
(Cabinet papers, 65/13)

28 May 1940
7 p.m.

The Prime Minister said that in the interval he
had seen the Ministers not in the War Cabinet. He had
told them the latest news. They had not expressed
alarm at the position in France, but had expressed the
greatest satisfaction when he had told them that there
was no chance of our giving up the struggle. He did
not remember having ever before heard a gathering of
persons occupying high places in political life express
themselves so emphatically.

The Foreign Secretary again referred to the
proposed appeal to the United States. It appeared that
Mr Bullitt[1] had told M. Reynaud that he favoured the
plan, but thought that Lord Lothian should be consulted
before anything was done. This differed somewhat from
what M. Reynaud had said.

The Prime Minister thought that an appeal to the
United States at the present time would be altogether
premature. If we made a bold stand against Germany,
that would command their admiration and respect; but a
grovelling appeal, if made now, would have the worst
possible effect. He therefore did not favour making any
approach on the subject at the present time.

---

1 William Christian Bullitt, 1891–1967. Entered the State Department, 1917. President
Wilson's special emissary to Russia, 1919. United States Ambassador to the Soviet
Union, 1933–6; to France, 1936–41. President Roosevelt's special representative in the
Far East, 1941. Special Assistant Secretary of the Navy, 1942–3. Served as a Major in the
French armed forces, 1944.

Winston S. Churchill to Paul Reynaud
(Churchill papers, 4/152)

28 May 1940
11.40 p.m.
By telephone

I have with my colleagues examined with
the most careful and sympathetic attention the
proposal for an approach by way of precise offer
of concessions to Signor Mussolini that you
have forwarded to me today, fully realising the
terrible situation with which we are both faced
at this moment.

2. Since we last discussed this matter
the new fact which has occurred, namely the
capitulation of the Belgian Army, has greatly
changed our position for the worse, for it is
evident that the chance of withdrawing the armies
of Generals Blanchard and Gort from the Channel
ports has become very problematical. The first
effect of such a disaster must be to make it
impossible at such a moment for Germany to put
forward any terms likely to be acceptable and
neither we nor you would be prepared to give up
our independence without fighting for it to the
end.

3. In the formula prepared last Sunday by
Lord Halifax it was suggested that if Signor
Mussolini would co-operate with us in securing
a settlement of all European questions which
would safeguard our independence and form the
basis of a just and durable peace for Europe, we
would be prepared to discuss his claims in the
Mediterranean. You now propose to add certain
specific offers, which I cannot suppose would have
any chance of moving Signor Mussolini, and which
once made could not be subsequently withdrawn,
in order to induce him to undertake the role of
mediator, which the formula discussed on Sunday
contemplated.

4. I and my colleagues believe that Signor Mussolini has long had it in mind that he might eventually fill this role, no doubt counting upon substantial advantages for Italy in the process. But we are convinced that at this moment when Hitler is flushed with victory and certainly counts on early and complete collapse of Allied resistance, it would be impossible for Signor Mussolini to put forward proposals for a conference with any success. I may remind you also that the President of the USA has received a wholly negative reply to the proposal which we jointly asked him to make and that no response has been made to the approach of Lord Halifax, made to the Italian Ambassador[1] here last Saturday.

5. Therefore, without excluding the possibility of an approach to Signor Mussolini at some time, we cannot feel that this would be the right moment and I am bound to add that in my opinion the effect on the morale of our people, which is now firm and resolute, would be extremely dangerous. You yourself can best judge what would be the effect in France.

6. You will ask, then, how is the situation to be improved. My reply is that by showing that after the loss of our two armies and the support of our Belgian Ally, we still have stout hearts and confidence in ourselves, we shall at once strengthen our hands in negotiations and draw to ourselves the admiration and perhaps the material help of the USA. Moreover, we feel that as long as we stand together, our undefeated Navy and our Air Force which is daily destroying German fighters and bombers at a formidable rate, afford us the means of exercising in our common interest a continuous pressure upon Germany's internal life.

7. We have reason to believe that the Germans

---

1 Giuseppe Bastianini.

too are working to a timetable and that their
losses and the hardships imposed on them together
with the fear of our air raids is undermining
their courage. It would indeed be a tragedy if
by too hasty an acceptance of defeat we throw
away a chance that was almost within our grasp of
securing an honourable issue from the struggle.

8. In my view if we both stand out we may
yet save ourselves from the fate of Denmark
or Poland. Our success must depend first on our
unity, then on our courage and endurance.

War Cabinet: minutes
(Cabinet papers, 65/7)

29 May 1940
11.30 a.m.

The Prime Minister said that the latest information from the Admiralty was that 40,000 troops from the BEF had so been landed in this country, and that evacuation was now taking place at the rate of about 2,000 an hour.

*Winston S. Churchill: note to Cabinet Ministers and
senior officials*
(Premier papers, 4/68/9)

29 May 1940
10 Downing Street
Strictly Confidential

In these dark days the Prime Minister would be
grateful if all his colleagues in the Government, as
well as high officials, would maintain a high morale in
their circles; not minimising the gravity of events, but
showing confidence in our ability and inflexible resolve
to continue the war till we have broken the will of the
enemy to bring all Europe under his domination.

No tolerance should be given to the idea that
France will make a separate peace; but whatever may
happen on the Continent, we cannot doubt our duty and we
shall certainly use all our power to defend the Island,
the Empire and our Cause.

Recollections of May 1940

From *The Second World War Diary of Hugh Dalton 1940–45*, edited by Ben Pimlott[1]

28 May 1940

In the afternoon all ministers are asked to meet the PM. He is quite magnificent. The man, and the only man we have, for this hour. He gives a full, frank and completely calm account of events in France. When the Germans broke through on the Meuse, French morale for the moment collapsed. Therefore, he flew to France and saw Reynaud and Gamelin. The latter said, 'We have been defeated by German superiority in numbers, in material and in methods.' Churchill said, 'What then are you going to do?' Gamelin merely shrugged his shoulders. Churchill said, 'Will you please leave the room', and then, alone with Reynaud, they went into everything, including the High Command. The French, before this war, had given up all ideas of the offensive. They were hypnotised by the Maginot Line. General Billotte commanding the forces north of the Somme, including our own, had given no important or significant order for four days! Since then he had been killed in a motor accident and succeeded by Blanchard. The French had failed to make a push northwards from the Somme. They had had too few Divisions between the sea and Amiens and their communications had been badly bombed. Therefore, though we had done our best from the north, it had been impossible to close the gap, and we were in grave danger of being surrounded. Now, therefore, it was necessary to fight our way through to the Channel Ports and get away all we could.

The act of the King of the Belgians had opened our flank, but this was not so grave as might have been supposed, owing to the inundations on the Ysère, which were perhaps a better defence than the Belgian Army! How many would get away we could not tell. We should certainly be

---

1 Pimlott writes in an editorial note that 'Although there is an entry for virtually every day for much of the period of the Coalition, Dalton did not compose his diary daily. His usual practice was to dictate a week's material at a single sitting.' From internal evidence, this entry for 28 May was written at least two days later.

able to get 50,000 away. If we could get 100,000 away, that would be a magnificent performance. Only Dunkirk was left to us. Calais had been defended by a British force which had refused to surrender, and it was said that there were no survivors. We could only use the beaches east and west of Dunkirk in addition to the port itself. Dunkirk was under a great pall of black smoke, to which our ships were adding artificial smoke so as to screen our embarkations from the air. The Air Force were maintaining the most powerful possible fighter patrols over this scene, and the Germans were suffering immense losses in the air, as on the ground, in their attempts to interfere with the embarkation. The superiority of our fighters was once again being manifested, and on two occasions great flights of German bombers had turned away and declined battle when they saw our fighter patrols.

The PM went on to say that our clawing-down rate was gradually rising, taking an average of one day with another, to 3:1, to 4:1, and lately to 5:1. It was clear that we had killed off most of the best Nazi pilots, unless, which seemed unlikely, they had been holding some of their best in reserve. 'They're cold meat,' our airmen say.

He was determined to prepare public opinion for bad tidings, and it would of course be said, and with some truth, that what was now happening in Northern France would be the greatest British military defeat for many centuries. We must now be prepared for the sudden turning of the war against this island, and prepared also for other events of great gravity in Europe. No countenance should be given publicly to the view that France might soon collapse, but we must not allow ourselves to be taken by surprise by any events. It might indeed be said that it would be easier to defend this island alone than to defend this island plus France, and if it was seen throughout the world that it was the former, there would be an immense wave of feeling, not least in the USA which, having done nothing much to help us so far, might even enter the war. But all this was speculative. Attempts to invade us would no doubt be made, but they would be beset with immense difficulty. We should mine all round our coast; our Navy was immensely strong; our air defences were much more easily organised from the island than across the Channel; our supplies of food, oil, etc., were ample; we had good troops in this island, others were on the way by sea, both British Army units coming from remote garrisons and excellent Dominion troops, and, as to aircraft, we were now more than making good our current losses, and the Germans were not.

It was idle to think that, if we tried to make peace now, we should get better terms from Germany than if we went on and fought it out. The Germans would demand our fleet – that would be called 'disarmament' – our naval bases, and much else. We should become a slave state, though a British Government which would be Hitler's puppet would be set up – 'under Mosley[2] or some such person.' And where should we be at the end of all that? On the other side, we had immense reserves and advantages. Therefore, he said, 'We shall go on and we shall fight it out, here or elsewhere, and if at last the long story is to end, it were better it should end, not through surrender, but only when we are rolling senseless on the ground.'[3] There was a murmur of approval round the table, in which I think Amery, Lord Lloyd and I were loudest. Not much more was said. No one expressed even the faintest flicker of dissent. Herbert Morrison asked about evacuation of the Government, and hoped that it would not be hurried. The PM said certainly not, he was all against evacuation unless things really became utterly impossible in London, 'but mere bombing will not make us go'.

It is quite clear that whereas the Old Umbrella[4] – neither he nor other members of the War Cabinet were at this meeting – wanted to run very early, Winston's bias is all the other way. When we separate, several go up and speak to him, and I, patting him on the shoulder, from my physically greater height, say, 'You ought to get that cartoon of Low showing us all rolling up our sleeves, and frame it and stick it up in front of you here.' He says, with a broad grin, 'Yes, that was a good one, wasn't it.' He is a darling!

2 Oswald Ernald Mosley, 1896–1980.
3 Dalton later set down another version of Churchill's words in the margin of this diary entry: 'If this long island story of ours is to end at last, let it end only when each one of us lies choking in his own blood upon the ground.'
4 Neville Chamberlain.

From *The Empire at Bay: The Leo Amery Diaries of 1929–45*

28 May 1940

Down to the House and presently attended a meeting of Cabinet Rank Ministers outside the War Cabinet convened by Winston to tell us the situation. ... We heard in the morning that King Leopold had capitulated with his Army, refusing to follow his government outside Belgium. Roger Keyes told me that it was mainly because he could not bear the sufferings of his people who were being mercilessly bombed in every direction. All the same it was an extraordinary step and was lacking in loyalty to his Allies actually in the field. Winston told us the whole story very clearly and dramatically in no way minimising the extent of the disaster or of further disasters which might follow such a successful German march on Paris and a French surrender.[1] One thing he was clear about was that there could be no greater folly than to try at this moment to offer concessions to either Italy or Germany, the powers which were out to destroy us. There was nothing to be done at any rate until we have turned the tide, except fight all out and then he drew a picture of the encouraging side of the position. We had a little question and answering after that which then left all of us tremendously heartened by Winston's resolution and grip of things. He is a real war leader and one whom it is worthwhile serving under.

29 May 1940

Got in a short walk around the Park before leaving the office and dined with Clem Davies to meet Attlee and Greenwood. We had a good talk ranging over almost every aspect of the War Cabinet business. Both Attlee and Greenwood said that Ironside had been quite splendid during the last three weeks and that his appointment to the Home Command was not a shelving but on the contrary appointing him to the job for which he is ideally fitted while Dill is probably better as

---

1 ˙'He told us he did not expect to get more than 50,000 away from Dunkirk' (later holograph note). ˙

CIGS. *I should think they were right. Was interested to find that Attlee is a bit of a Classic and still quotes his Horace.*

30 May 1940

Presently went to the War Room and was immensely cheered by hearing that over 100,000 of our men and some 5,000 of the French had been got away. Later in the evening Winston told me that the figure was over 120,000. Walked round the park and then dined with what was originally the Economic sub-Committee of Clem Davies' Action Group at the Reform Club, but now consisted almost entirely of Ministers! Much good talk and the dinner which we propose to continue is likely to afford a very useful meeting ground for discussing business.

From Winston S. Churchill's *Their Finest Hour*

28 May 1940

I had not seen many of my colleagues outside the War Cabinet, except individually, since the formation of the Government, and I thought it right to have a meeting in my room at the House of Commons of all Ministers of Cabinet rank other than the War Cabinet Members. We were perhaps twenty-five round the table. I described the course of events, and I showed them plainly where we were, and all that was in the balance. Then I said quite casually, and not treating it as a point of special significance:

'Of course, whatever happens at Dunkirk, we shall fight on.'

There occurred a demonstration which, considering the character of the gathering – twenty-five experienced politicians and Parliament men, who represented all the different points of view, whether right or wrong, before the war – surprised me. Quite a number seemed to jump up from the table and come running to my chair, shouting and patting me on the back. There is no doubt that had I at this juncture faltered at all in the leading of the nation I should have been hurled out of office. I was sure that every Minister was ready to be killed quite soon, and have all his family and possessions destroyed, rather than give in. In this they represented the House of Commons and almost all the people. It fell to me in these coming days and months to express their sentiments on suitable occasions. This I was able to do because they were mine also. There was a white glow, overpowering, sublime, which ran through our Island from end to end.

ALL BEHIND YOU, WINSTON

Cartoon by David Low, *Evening Standard*, 14 May 1940
Front row: Churchill, Attlee, Bevin, Morrison, and
Amery; second row: Chamberlain, Greenwood, Halifax,
Sinclair, Duff Cooper, A.V. Alexander, Eden

5

Speaking for All of Us

In trying to reconstruct the argumentation, wisdom and mistakes of May 1940, it is the questions over whether to negotiate or to fight that are central. Churchill, above all, could not live with surrendering what he believed was Britain's greatest strength, namely the country's readiness to fight. Weaken that new-found indomitable cross-party spirit, give the impression to Hitler that he, Churchill, was like the other leaders Hitler had conquered, and Britain would be finished. It could be tolerated that France would negotiate through Italy, and even for a non-combatant like the US President, but he, as Prime Minister, was not prepared to talk to Hitler through Italy or any other means. I do not believe his position on this ever shifted and, every bit as importantly, the same position was held by Attlee, Greenwood and Sinclair.

The meetings of May 1940 were not to discuss a re-run of the Munich negotiations. Whatever view readers take of Munich, it was, in essence, an attempt to prevent a war from starting. Whether to negotiate with Italy was about a war that had already been running for eight months. Would negotiating stop that war or ensure defeat? There is a duty on any Foreign Secretary to look all the time for negotiation opportunities for peace and ensure that serious alternatives to war are examined, even if rejected. Neither Reynaud nor Halifax, with their different roles, were acting irresponsibly in examining the Mussolini option.

The reader has, in Chapter 4, the chance to follow a continuous narrative of the nine meetings in three days, and to read alongside these all the key documents that were available to those Cabinet ministers at the time, uninterrupted by comment or information from me or others. The Minutes themselves are unusual: never before or since have Minutes so comprehensively covered a real political debate with such an animated account of the opinions of named individuals in so much detail, and recorded for posterity to examine. The Minutes provide a lesson about the strengths of collective responsibility in government, of the virtues of private discussion in Cabinet and of debate led by a Prime Minister who chooses only to reply on being *primus inter pares*.

It is the best practical argument for maintaining and enhancing Cabinet government of considerable relevance to the UK in 2016 after the failed Presidential models practised in their different ways by the three previous Prime Ministers, Blair, Brown and Cameron. In the Chilcot Report on the Iraq War of 2003, published on 6 July 2016, the Imperial Prime Ministership has been tried and found wanting, and the incompatibility of an executive President, as in the US, with British parliamentary democracy exposed for all to see; 1940 is a salutary lesson of what has been proven to work at the most critical period in our country's history, when we really did, from June 1940 to December 1941, stand alone. But the reader has to go beyond the inevitably inadequate wording to sense the nuances and the power play behind the varying approaches, shaped by background and experiences, of the five initial participants, six when joined on their fourth meeting by Sinclair. Leader of the Liberal Party, Sinclair had served as Churchill's second-in-command in France after Churchill took a leave of absence from Parliament in 1916 to fight on the Western Front for eighteen months, having been given the temporary British Army rank of lieutenant colonel to take command of the 6th Battalion of Royal Scots Fusiliers. Sinclair was anti-appeasement and a friend.

The coalition government was maintained up until the preparations for the 1945 election. Labour's contribution was a massive one, something which has been distorted over time by an impression of Churchill standing alone. He was in truth very rarely alone, and certainly not during these nine meetings of May 1940. After the end of the war in 1945, by allowing Churchill and his researchers to have full access to all the documents, which has been accepted practice for senior Cabinet members writing about events, and to write as though there had never been any discussion of a negotiated peace was to perpetuate a distortion of the truth that only ended with the publication of documents under the 30-year rule. The distortive effect of this has been brilliantly analysed by David Reynolds in his book *In Command of History*.

The crucial sentence on discussion of negotiated peace comes in the second confidential meeting of ministers when the French and M. Reynaud's views on the sort of settlement that might keep Italy out of the war are delineated.

{If an approach was made to Italy, what sort of terms would Italy ask? Probably the neutralisation of Gibraltar and the Suez Canal, the demilitarisation of Malta, and the limitation of Naval forces in the Mediterranean. Some alteration in the status of Tunis would also be asked for, and the Dodecanese [the islands in the SE of Greece near to Turkey] would have to be put right.}

At the third meeting Halifax favoured making an approach to Italy and thought

{the last thing that Signor Mussolini wanted was to see Herr Hitler dominating Europe. He would be anxious, if he could, to persuade Herr Hitler to take a more reasonable attitude.}

Churchill had already suggested Halifax should go over and see Reynaud who had flown in and was at Admiralty House but he

{doubted whether anything would come of an approach to Italy, but said that the matter was one which the War Cabinet would have to consider}

There is no question that every step Churchill took throughout these critical days was influenced by one overriding political factor: to ensure that the combined influence of Halifax and Chamberlain did not saddle him with a policy he could not live with. I do not believe that Churchill ever felt he could not handle Chamberlain or Halifax individually; it was their combination that he feared. He was not contemptuous of either and this is one of the reasons that, despite being highly hubristic, he never acquired what I have written about extensively and called Hubris Syndrome. He identified both men as potential obstacles to his plans and actions, to be moved when possible, but he was confident throughout that he could handle them. In handling them he flattered, cajoled, and maintained the illusion of potential shifts in his thinking, but without any real intention of shifting. All of these are legitimate techniques for influencing debate and discussion in a democracy and essential for any Prime Minister handling the egos around a Cabinet table. What anyone says in Cabinet is not always what they feel; you propose sometimes knowing you will lose, but in losing you hope or even expect to gain.

I think it was deliberate flattery when Churchill wrote to Chamberlain on 10 May that "to a large extent I am in your own hands", proudly quoted, as I am sure he knew it would be, by Chamberlain writing to his sisters (see Chapter 3, p. 80). Churchill used the same technique but to less effect on Halifax, who had shown he could be both a leader and an administrator as Viceroy of India, serving as Lord Irwin, as he was then called. Now Lord Halifax, he had chosen to return to the rough and tumble of British politics; having been appointed Viceroy whilst still young, he did not let the pomp and ceremony of India go to his head on his return and seemed to enjoy politics in the Lords as one well able to hold his own in political combat. Halifax was a schemer, but Churchill did not fear him nor did he believe Halifax capable of shaping events. In politics guts is everything, and when Churchill watched Halifax turn down Chamberlain's offer of the premiership he must have thought the lesser of him. Ambition to be the top man was second nature to Churchill; influencing from below had no appeal. He did not become First Lord of the Admiralty under Chamberlain to influence him, but to be better placed to take over from him. Staying quiet, as he claimed he did, unnaturally but deliberately and on good advice, Halifax used the Lords as an excuse, though Chamberlain knew membership of the House of Lords was not, at that stage in British democracy, an insuperable barrier. It is impossible to imagine had Churchill been in the Lords that he would have turned down such an offer from Chamberlain.

So Churchill using every political wile, skill and knowledge he had accumulated over the decades, was intent on one thing: prizing Chamberlain away from Halifax. As this book makes clear, I agree with much of Andrew Roberts's writing, but not the chapter heading 'Churchill as Micawber' in *The Holy Fox*. John Lukacs, whose scholarship and skill in *Five Days in London May 1940* I am hugely indebted to, specifically endorses this description, also mentioning Charles Dickens's book *David Copperfield*, explaining Micawber's hope that "something may turn up." I see no suggestion that Churchill was waiting on events, rather I submit there is every evidence that he, within the limits of his and the UK's powers, was shaping events tirelessly. Micawberism was never Churchill's style nor his attitude. Optimism he certainly had in abundance. But Churchill exploited the fact that a Prime Minister controls the Agenda of the Cabinet and authorises not only whether any paper goes to Cabinet but determines *when* – a considerable power. The memorandum written by Arthur Greenwood on 26 May, War Cabinet Paper 171 of 1940 'British Strategy in the Near Future', arguing for full economic co-operation with the United States, would not have been presented, let alone discussed that day, had not Churchill wanted it. Indeed, he may even have prompted Greenwood to write it. The memorandum was written quickly and personally by Greenwood as an economist and it was there on the agenda because it fitted in with Churchill's urgent need to get the War Cabinet focused on help from Roosevelt as soon as possible with military equipment. At every stage during these nine meetings, unspoken or not, Churchill had in his mind how any event or decision would play out in Washington.

Likewise, it was Churchill who had set the terms of the Chiefs of Staff's most important paper to be discussed over the nine meetings, 'British Strategy in the Near Future', finished late on 26 May. It was taken next day by the War Cabinet, but its terms of reference came from Churchill. It began: "In the event of France being unable to continue in the war and becoming neutral..." The report was built on their earlier and far more substantive report 'British Strategy in a Certain Eventuality' already circulated on 25 May and given a fairly wide circulation in a printed, not just typed, format. The term 'Certain Eventuality' was, of course, a disguise for the unmentionable, the fear that France would fall. There was in addition to formal papers a spate of letters, 'Actions this Day' instructions and memos, to say nothing of the constant day and night meetings with ministers, officials and a wide variety of people. All this speaks to Churchill working tirelessly and with huge innovation. No wonder by 28 June his wife thought it necessary to warn him of his "rough, sarcastic and overbearing manner" and "contemptuous attitude" that were not his normal behaviour. She was a quintessential 'toe holder' who prevents leaders like Churchill developing Hubris Syndrome.[1]

Churchill was a politician who made the 'weather' throughout his life but never more so than in May 1940. His decision to be Minister of Defence was very significant and a means by which he could justify calling meetings with military figures at every level without having to summon the Minister of War to be present – at that stage Anthony Eden – nor the First Lord of the Admiralty A.V. Alexander and Secretary of State for Air, Archie Sinclair. These direct messages were military to military encounters and sometimes rough and abusive as we have already glimpsed in Churchill's open challenge to Gort's handling of his forces in France.

Churchill loved the whole ambience of war. From day one on 10 May, he intervened over strategy and military appointments and wore the Chiefs of Staff to a frazzle over long alcoholic dinners that went into the early hours. Roosevelt was more hands off over detail but he, like Churchill, intervened as an effective wartime Prime Minister or President is bound to do. Both understood that the military, set on a single-minded mission of winning, can develop tunnel vision and miss the wider context in which the battlefield is placed. The role of the politician is to bring a clarity of perspective.

Lukacs brilliantly sets these nine meetings in their wider context. He refers often to opinion poll findings and they are interesting for an appreciation of the mood outside Whitehall though my focus is on the politicians sitting around that Cabinet table. I am dubious whether any of the War Cabinet, let alone Churchill, read any such findings during the three hectic days of their deliberations. Polling was many decades away from achieving the dominant position in

---

1   David Owen, *In Sickness and In Power* (Methuen, 2011), pp 453–462.

political decision-making it has today. Churchill knew only too well the risks of an invasion to his own life for he had no intention of going abroad. At one stage when an invasion seemed imminent, Ismay remembers him saying, "You and I will be dead in three months time" (see Chapter 6, p. 244).

Lukacs raised questions about a meeting that took place around 4.00 pm after Reynaud's departure, described as an informal meeting of the War Cabinet in Admiralty House. The record does not cover the first quarter of an hour during which the Secretary to the Cabinet, Edward Bridges, was not present. Lukacs has said of this meeting that, "Such conditions of secrecy has no precedent in the modern history of Britain."[2] That is, I suspect, an exaggeration. I can think of many occasions when a small group of ministers discussed matters before being joined by the Cabinet Secretary, usually filling in time with gossip and raw politics. They may have been updating each other since Churchill, Chamberlain and Greenwood had not been present when Halifax had developed talks with Reynaud.

There is an interesting diary entry from Halifax's chief diplomatic adviser, Cadogan, from 26 May, saying, Churchill by 5.00 pm, and having been with M. Reynaud most of the day, was coming around to thinking "we might almost be better off if France 'did' pull out and we could concentrate on defence here. Not sure he is right. He is against final appeal, which Reynaud wanted to Muss. He may be right there."[3] 'Muss' is, of course, his shorthand for Mussolini. Here in front of Halifax, Chamberlain, Attlee and Greenwood, Churchill is letting the chief diplomat know his feelings, and in the privacy of his diary Cadogan is questioning the view of his boss, Halifax. Cadogan on 28 May, as will be discussed later, becomes a crucial factor in talking Halifax out of resigning on this very issue of Mussolini. It was also Cadogan who two years earlier persuaded Halifax that his assessment of Hitler was wrong, which in turn led to Halifax opposing Chamberlain in Cabinet.

During the fourth meeting on 27 May, the six men including Sinclair, who had been added to the War Cabinet by Churchill to

---

2 John Lukacs, *Five Days in London, May 1940* (Yale University Press, 2001), p 113.
3 *Ibid*, p 119.

strengthen his own position, had the task of absorbing the two and a half typed pages of the convincing and concise Chiefs of Staff report on the 'Near Future'. Most of the report would have already been known to Churchill, and almost certainly to Sinclair, the majority of its facts having stemmed from the Air Ministry.

This is arguably the most important single military assessment put to the Prime Minister and his colleagues in the entire War. A number, I suspect, particularly Attlee and Greenwood, were somewhat surprised by its rational optimism, an extract of which is below (see Chapter 4, p. 156, for the full paper):

> 6. The crux of the matter is air superiority. Once Germany had attained this, she might attempt to subjugate this country by air attack alone.
>
> 7. Germany could not gain complete air superiority unless she could knock out Air Force, and the aircraft industries, some vital portions of which are concentrated at Coventry and Birmingham.
>
> 8. Air attacks on the aircraft factories would be made by day or night. We consider that we should be able to inflict such casualties on the enemy by day as to prevent serious damage. Whatever we do, however, by way of defensive measures and we are pressing on with these with all despatch, we cannot be sure of protecting the large industrial centres, upon which our aircraft industries depend, from serious material damage by night attack. The enemy would not have to employ precision bombing to achieve this effect.

A huge sense of relief must have been felt as they turned the page to read paragraphs 11 and 12. For Chamberlain, too, this must have been a moment when he started to question his hitherto broad support for Halifax's initiative over Mussolini. If Britain could hold out for a few months, all three of them must have thought, then a better negotiating position could be achieved.

> 11. It must be remembered that numerically the Germans have a superiority of four to one. Moreover, the German aircraft factories are well dispersed and relatively inaccessible.

12. On the other hand, so long as we have a counter-offensive bomber force, we can carry out similar attacks on German industrial centres and by moral and material effect bring a proportion of them to a standstill.

Then comes the final paragraph, which in its new brevity, clarity and force one can sense the influence of Dill on his first day in post having replaced Ironside. Dill, as the most senior military adviser to the Government, was definitely backing a fight and not a negotiating strategy. Urged on by Churchill, the report had been put together and influenced by his personal adviser General Ismay, but it had the stamp and authority of a new head of the Chiefs of Staff. As if to emphasise this new authority, the independence of the Chiefs is rightly asserted at the bottom below the all-important last paragraph 13 (see p. 160).

13. To sum up, our conclusion is that *prima facie* Germany has most of the cards; but the real test is whether the morale of our fighting personnel and civil population will counter-balance the numerical and material advantages which Germany enjoys. We believe it will.
[The Chiefs of Staff have not had an opportunity to see this Report in its final form and reserve to themselves the right to suggest such modifications as they may wish to put forward]

I was nearly two years old when those words were written for the War Cabinet. When I read them tears came to my eyes, as if I remembered the bombing of Plymouth, sleeping under the stairs or in the metal bomb shelters on the floor in Newport. Throughout the war my father was a doctor away fighting, first with the BEF in France and then the 8th Army in North Africa and Italy. I did not recognise him on his return in 1945. My mother told me when she was 80 with total conviction that she had never doubted we would win. Here, on 27 May 1940, our military leaders were anticipating victory in the air during the Battle of Britain that ran from 10 July until October 1940. That prediction and those crucial paragraphs ensured the War Cabinet's eventual determination that we should fight on and not negotiate.

Meanwhile, three days earlier, unbeknown to anyone in that room in London, Hitler was visiting the HQ of Colonel-General Gerd Bon Rundstedt, fifteen miles to the south of Dunkirk with the Panzer tanks that had spearheaded the Germans' invasion. He gave the order on 24 May that "the advance should be halted at that point and not proceed to Dunkirk itself." Hitler "later suggested that he had not wanted to destroy the British Army, the backbone of the British Empire".[4] This was no more than a face-saving rationalisation. In fact, he was merely following the advice of his field commander, Rundstedt, who had wanted to preserve his motorised units for the final push south to conclude the campaign. Far from wanting to preserve the British Army, Hitler was being advised by Göring, Commander in Chief of the German Air Force, that the Luftwaffe would finish it off.[5]

The War Cabinet's fifth meeting at 4.30 pm that same day, 27 May, focused in considerable detail on the Foreign Secretary's note about the approach to Signor Mussolini. Chamberlain was still standing alongside Halifax, but there was seemingly less enthusiasm. At one stage the minutes read:

{The Prime Minister said that the Lord President's [Chamberlain's] argument amounted to this, that nothing would come of the approach, but that it was worth doing to sweeten relations with a failing ally. He read the following telegram, which he had received from M. Reynaud that morning (No 283 DIPP)}

What carried most weight with Reynaud then was Chamberlain's conviction too, and the approach would help strengthen an alliance of hearts, which he believed to be essential. Given Chamberlain's later scathing criticism of the French military (page 82), Churchill sensed that Chamberlain's argument for negotiating was nuanced and not one of principled opposition nor even a really substantive point.

---

4 Ian Kershaw, *Fateful Choices. Ten Decisions That Changed The World 1940–1941* (Allen Lane, 2007), p 27. Also Ian Kershaw, *Hitler, 1936–1945. Nemesis* (Allen Lane, 2000), pp 295–6 and p 921 nn. 63 and 66. Also Heinz Magenheimer, *Hitler's War: Germany's Key Strategic Decisions 1940–1945*, (Cassell Military Paperbacks, 1998), p 24.
5 *Ibid*, p 27.

Lukacs's account of this fifth meeting contains two important assertions, which according to Roy Jenkins are not justified from the minutes of the evening procedures: "The one was that 'Chamberlain now sat on the fence'[6]; and the other was that 'Churchill, at least momentarily, thought that he had to make *some* kind of concession to Halifax'."[7] Roy Jenkins concludes, "The balance of likelihood, however, seems on Lukacs's side on both statements." [8] I would not be so sure, both Chamberlain and Churchill seem to me to be adopting tactical positions for a purpose, namely for hoping to bring Halifax around to the gathering consensus in the War Cabinet, which was quite simply against making a deal to preserve the Empire. Halifax, it is easy to forget, had been Viceroy of India and wielded monarchal power – an experience of empire far different from that of Churchill's fighting in South Africa. There were also underlying tensions between Halifax and Chamberlain, the roots of which lay in the infamous Munich deal. Churchill, though not in Chamberlain's Cabinet at that stage, was almost certainly aware of it. Parliament is a place of gossip and in the smoking room, which Churchill frequented, there would have been people even 'loyal' to Chamberlain who, having witnessed the scene in the Cabinet, would have passed on the story of Halifax turning against Chamberlain. Today the smoking room no longer exists, nor the same male dominance. What was influencing Churchill in managing Chamberlain was his assessment of the man; what lay behind his flaws and his virtues.

By 1938 Chamberlain had had his head turned by power. He saw himself as a man of destiny. His relations with Halifax deteriorated as his policies of appeasement were progressively discredited. Only a few months later in the House of Commons, on 5 October 1938, Churchill unleashed his full invective, calling the Munich settlement "a total and unmitigated defeat".[9] Now, less than 18 months later, Chamberlain was in a lesser position. If Hubris is acquired, so it can recede with less power. Chamberlain was now focusing on reputation.

---

6 John Lukacs, *Five Days in London: May 1940*, p 121.
7 *Ibid*, p 116.
8 Roy Jenkins, *Churchill: A Biography* (Pan Macmillan, 2002), p 603.
9 Geoffrey Best, *Churchill and War* (A & C Black, 2006), p 104.

Exhausted but not depressed the day after his heady return from Germany to Heston Airport, he admitted to his sisters that he had come nearer to a nervous breakdown "than I have ever been in my life".[10] His mood was then exultant, and he believed he had been successful in ending the prospect of war. He had acted throughout with a small inner Cabinet and had marginalised any anti-opinion in the full Cabinet. Apologists for Chamberlain had begun in 1940 to claim he gained time for UK rearmament, and though this probably was the result it was not his intended objective in 1938. He had deluded himself about Hitler's trustworthiness and underestimated his sinister ambitions. But now in May 1940, he wanted to restore his place in history. Chamberlain had just that opportunity in these discussions in the War Cabinet and Churchill sensed he might be able to persuade him to recognise that talk of negotiating with Mussolini was a front and that behind it lay the figure of Hitler. Because Chamberlain had made the wrong assessment of Hitler in 1938, now in a different situation he had the chance to put that right. So Halifax only nominally came in behind the Lord President Chamberlain's words and he was aggressive. Halifax's words are noteworthy he {saw no particular difficulty in taking the lines suggested by the Lord President. Nevertheless, he was conscious of certain rather profound differences of points of view he would like to make clear ... In the discussion the previous day, he had asked the Prime Minister whether, if he was satisfied that matters vital to the independence of this country were unaffected, he would be prepared to discuss terms. The Prime Minister had said that he would be thankful to get out of our present difficulties on such terms, provided we retain the essentials and the elements of our vital strength, even at the cost of some cession of territory.}

The fifth meeting (page 172) was important for Chamberlain in clarifying Churchill's sticking points. The Prime Minister had earlier said, "it might be argued that an approach on the lines proposed by M. Reynaud was not unlike the approach which we had asked President Roosevelt to make to Signor Mussolini. There was, however, a

---

10 David Reynolds, *Summits: Six Meetings That Shaped the Twentieth Century* (Allen Lane, 2007), p 91.

good deal of difference between making the approach ourselves and allowing one to be made by President Roosevelt ostensibly on his own initiative." Halifax would have been wiser to have accepted that distinction then. In which case he could have avoided the meeting ending on a very harsh exchange. Halifax clearly brought the differences to the surface.[11] He conveys more than a hint of an impending resignation in the phrase "doubted he would be able to accept the view now put forward by the Prime Minister".

{On the present occasion, however, the Prime Minister seemed to suggest that under no conditions would we contemplate any course except fighting to a finish. The issue was probably academic, since we were unlikely to receive any offer which would not come up against the fundamental conditions which are essential to us. If, however, it was possible to obtain a settlement which did not impair those conditions, he, for his part, doubted if he would be able to accept the view now put forward by the Prime Minister. The Prime Minister had said that two or three months would show whether we were able to stand up against the air risk. This meant that the future of the country turned on whether the enemy bombs happened to hit our aircraft factories. He was prepared to take that risk if our independence was at stake; but if it was not at stake he would think it right to accept an offer which would save the country from avoidable disaster.

The Prime Minister said that he thought that the issue which the War Cabinet was called upon to settle was difficult enough without getting involved in the discussion of an issue which was quite unreal and was most unlikely to arise. If Herr Hitler was prepared to make peace on the terms of the restoration of the German colonies and the overlordship of Central Europe, that was one thing. But it was quite unlikely that he would make any such offer.

The Foreign Secretary said he would like to put the following question. Suppose the French Army collapsed and Herr Hitler made an offer of peace terms. Suppose the French Government

---

11 Roy Jenkins, *Churchill* (Pan Macmillan, 2012), p 605.

222 CABINET'S FINEST HOUR

said, "We are unable to deal with an offer made to France alone and you must deal with the Allies together." Suppose Herr Hitler, being anxious to end the war through knowledge of his own internal weaknesses, offered terms to France and England, would the Prime Minister be prepared to discuss them?

The Prime Minister said that he would not join France in asking for terms; but if he were told what the terms offered were, he would be prepared to consider them.}

Some of the tension which lay within this exchange was that Halifax's position was by now seen by Churchill, Attlee, Greenwood and Sinclair as defeatist, and I suspect by Chamberlain too. John Colville, the Prime Minister's private secretary, who did not attend such meetings but was in very close contact with the notetakers who did, wrote in his diary that evening, "The Cabinet are feverishly considering our ability to carry on the war alone in such circumstances, and there are signs that Halifax is being defeatist. He says that our aim can no longer be to crush Germany but rather to preserve our own integrity and independence."[12] Significantly, he did not link Chamberlain's name with Halifax.

Within that meeting's exchange, Chamberlain must have sensed the degree of exasperation, even resignation, from Halifax; yet Chamberlain said nothing – a significant omission, for if he intended to resign, it could be argued he owed it to colleagues to at least indicate he shared some of the concerns of Halifax.

Cadogan's diary entry for that day is significant: "After the afternoon Cabinet H. asked W.S.C. to come into the garden with him. H. said to me, 'I can't work with Winston any longer.' I said, 'Nonsense: his rodomontades probably bore you as much as they do me, but don't do anything silly under the stress of that.' H. came to have tea in my room after. Said he *had* spoken to W., who of course had been v. affectionate! I said I hoped he really wouldn't give way to an annoyance to which we were all subject and that, before he did anything he would consult Neville. He said that of course he would

12 Kevin Jefferys, *War and Reform: British Politics during the Second World War* (Manchester University Press, 1994), p 44.

and that, as I knew, he wasn't one to take hasty decisions." Cadogan seemed to have sensed, although not present at the meeting, that Chamberlain was in a different position, not as wounded as Halifax and more conciliatory.

Halifax in his diary entry writes:

At the 4.30 Cabinet we had a long and rather confused discussion about, nominally, the approach to Italy, but also largely about general policy in the event of things going really badly in France. I thought Winston talked the most frightful rot, also Greenwood, and after bearing it for some time I said exactly what I thought of them, adding that if that was really their view, and if it came to the point, our ways must separate. Winston, surprised and mellowed, and when I repeated the same thing in the garden, was full of apologies and affection. But it does drive me to despair when he works himself up into a passion of emotion when he ought to make his brain think and reason.

By 7.00 pm Churchill was telling the Defence Committee that the situation for the BEF was desperate and they would have to fight their way to the coast. He felt:

{We had no need to reproach ourselves for the terrible ordeal which now faced the British Expeditionary Force. We had agreed unreservedly before the war to place the British Expeditionary Force under the orders of the French. Immediately the Germans invaded Holland and Belgium Lord Gort, under the orders of the French High Command, had moved forward into Belgium. Then had come the German breakthrough on the Meuse, and the complete inability of the great French Army to stem the German advance.}

The sixth meeting of the War Cabinet started at 10.00 pm on 27 May and went to around midnight. An extract from the minutes read:

{Apparently the collapse of the Belgians was due to the heavy bombing to which they had been subjected that day. Any grounds for recrimination lay rather in the Belgian action on the outbreak of war than in the more immediate past. At the time when there had been only fifteen German divisions on their Western frontier, and the bulk of the Germans had been engaged in Poland, if Belgium had then invited us to enter their country, we could have established ourselves in a strong defensive position or invaded Germany. The King's action was certainly not heroic. Presumably, he would now make a separate peace with the Germans and carry on as a puppet monarch. This might well be the best that he could do for his country, but we had to face the fact that it had the most serious consequences for the British Expeditionary Force.}

There was no recorded discussion about the Italian's adverse reaction to Roosevelt's message, but it was leaking out from Rome and Washington that there had been difficulty in fixing meetings and the unsatisfactory nature of the exchange had caused reluctance in the Americans to engage further. On the document which had Mussolini's hostile reply, and included in his diaries under the entry for 27 May, Cadogan wrote "of course Mussolini is not going to, and in fact dare not, make any separate agreement with the Allies, even if he wanted to. He is simply wondering how much of the general 'share-out' he will be allowed by his 'Ally' to take, and whether he will ultimately get more, or less, by soiling Italian blood for it. We can't tell which way he will jump, but I hope we shan't delude ourselves into thinking that we shall do ourselves any good by making any more 'offers' or 'approaches'".[13] This was a very different appreciation to that of Halifax and closer one suspects to Chamberlain's.

On 28 May at 11.30 am the War Cabinet met and Churchill read out the humiliating terms of the armistice, signed by the Belgians before proceeding to make a statement to the House of Commons. At no stage was there any further record in the minutes of what was happening to the Roosevelt initiative until at the end of the day, after two further War Cabinet meetings had taken place. Churchill's telephone call to M. Reynaud at 11.40 pm that evening had the following

---

13 Sir Alexander Cadogan, *The Diaries of Sir Alexander Cadogan, O.M., 1930–1945* (Putnam, 1972), p 291.

sentence included: "I may remind you also that that the President of the USA has received a wholly negative reply to the proposal which we jointly asked him to make and that no response has been made to the approach of Lord Halifax, made to the Italian Ambassador here last Saturday."[14] Nevertheless the War Cabinet knew from the memorandum 'Suggested Approach to Signor Mussolini' by Halifax on 26 May, which stated as a P.S. that Halifax was told when in conversation with the Master of the Rolls, who had just returned from Rome, "that Sir P. Loraine has been informed by the United States Ambassador that President Roosevelt's last attempt to [deter] the Italian Government had been bitterly resented by Signor Mussolini as unwarrantable influence with Italy's private affairs". He further responded that the British Ambassador Loraine thought "any further approach would only be interpreted as weakness and would do no good".

Halifax, at the eighth meeting of the War Cabinet at 4.00 pm on 28 May, opened the afternoon discussion by reporting that his chief diplomatic adviser, Sir Robert Vansittart

{had now discovered what the Italian Embassy had in mind, namely, that we should give a clear indication that we should like to see mediation by Italy. Churchill said that it was clear that the French purpose was to see Signor Mussolini acting as an intermediary between ourselves. He was determined not to get into this position.}

A wiser and more flexible Foreign Secretary than Halifax would by this moment have abandoned the whole concept, but he ploughed on reiterating Reynaud's stance which all the ministers knew from previous discussions. The minutes record him saying

{The Prime Minister thought that the French were trying to get us on to the slippery slope. The position would be entirely different when Germany had made an unsuccessful attempt to invade this country.}

14 Winston S. Churchill, *Their Finest Hour*, p 110.

Still Halifax blundered on reiterating old arguments that better terms were available now, before France went out of the war and our aircraft factories had been bombed. One can almost feel Halifax losing with every word a little more of Chamberlain's support. Greenwood weighed in saying, "Reynaud was too much inclined to hawk round appeals. This was another attempt to run out." Jenkins in his account noted that Greenwood "next to Churchill made most of the intransigent running" and was Churchill's "most articulate Cabinet ally".[15] Attlee was "laconically reliable". Chamberlain then said only

{that, on a dispassionate survey, it was right to remember that the alternative to fighting on nevertheless involved a considerable gamble. The War Cabinet agreed that this was a true statement of the case. The Prime Minister said that nations which went down fighting rose again, but those which surrendered tamely were finished.}

Once more, seemingly oblivious to the fact that he had by now clearly lost the debate, the Foreign Secretary said:

{nothing in his suggestion could even remotely be described as ultimate capitulation. The Prime Minister thought that the chances of decent terms being offered to us at the present time were a thousand to one against.}

At this point the War Cabinet broke off its discussions to enable the Prime Minister to attend a meeting of the full Cabinet that had been arranged earlier in the day. It was clear that Halifax was in a minority of one. The meeting had been convened some time before, possibly after Churchill had made very clear his position in reply to Halifax's first intervention at this meeting. The Prime Minister at any time could have simply passed a note to 'not convene' to the Cabinet Secretariat. Meetings of the full Cabinet were a fairly regular occurrence anyhow and a democratic way of ensuring the full Cabinet were kept abreast of the War Cabinet's thinking. By calling such a meeting Churchill was not pre-empting the War

---

15 Nichlaus Thomas-Symonds, *Attlee: A Life in Politics* (I. B. Tauris, 2012).

Cabinet, but he could sense that day that the mood of Chamberlain had shifted and Halifax was on his own.

The accounts of Amery and Dalton of their meeting with Churchill make it very clear that this was no normal meeting, the full texts of which are available in Chapter 4 (pp. 202–206). Churchill told the 25 ministers around the Prime Minister's room in the House of Commons that Britain was going to fight and not negotiate. It was, in effect, an eve of war battle cry, a culmination of eight very full meetings of the War Cabinet, made in the knowledge that he had won the support of Chamberlain and had the full support of Attlee, Greenwood and Sinclair. Dalton's rather florid account has Churchill saying, "It was idle to think that, if we tried to make peace now, we should get better terms from Germany than if we went on and fought it out."[16] That was the War Cabinet's decision and in the correct sequence it was now being endorsed by the full Cabinet. Churchill had ensured democratic debate had been on full display throughout.

No one came out of the nine War Cabinet meetings diminished. If a Foreign Secretary cannot with honour raise the arguments for negotiating for peace during war then it is a diminished Prime Minister and Cabinet that blocks such a discussion. Halifax showed courage in persisting when Churchill showed no enthusiasm and that was his democratic right. It went too far in terms of what he saw as his role of restraining Churchill from below.

There is no close historic precedent to what Halifax was trying to do. It was not like Haldane's Mission to Berlin in 1912 which I describe in *The Hidden Perspective: The Military Conversations 1906–1914*[17], which was a brave and innovative attempt by the then Secretary of State for War to respond to an invitation from the then German Chancellor, Bethmann-Hollweg, to Edward Grey, the Foreign Secretary, to come to Berlin. It could and should have been supported by Grey in Cabinet and had Grey done so the First World War might never have happened. Halifax was trying to *end* a war that had started, using the Cabinet forum to authorise his diplomacy.

16 Kevin Jefferys, *War and Reform: British Politics During the Second World War* (Manchester University Press, 1994), p 45.

17 David Owen, *The Hidden Perspective* (Haus Publishing, 2014), p 145.

The big problem Halifax had to contend with, and convince his War Cabinet colleagues on, was that Germany in 1940 was not just the aggressor but already occupied a significant part of France, and was engaged in a battle with British forces on the ground in France.

Despite the risk of an inaccurate evaluation, once the Chiefs of Staff communicated to the War Cabinet that despite all the problems Britain could repulse a German invasion, Halifax continued looking defeatist and, to some around the Cabinet table, even advocating surrender. He was making a calculation of risk at a time of war against the Chief of Staff's views. This was not the appeasement of Munich, which Halifax had supported initially with all the blind trust, self-deception and hubris that Chamberlain brought to that agreement. Halifax was perfectly entitled to continue the debate against the Chief's conclusions and in so doing face the judgement of history. He was proved wrong. The War Cabinet had objectively looked at the alternative as any responsible government should have done. A War Cabinet of mere placemen would never have had those vital discussions. Nevertheless, Halifax held to his views all through the eighth meeting and longer than he needed to, and was, in effect, disowned on 28 May by the War Cabinet and crucially, though gently, by Chamberlain. Halifax, rightly, did not resign, which would have been damaging at this moment of national peril. Was he perhaps holding to his position believing he would be proved right by history? Probably, but it is hard to be sure. As Attlee, famous for his capacity to sum someone up in a few words, said of him when looking back in September 1965: "Queer bird, Halifax. Very humorous, all hunting and Holy Communion."[18]

Churchill's judgement was wiser than Halifax's and he was fully entitled to in effect dismiss him at the end of 1940. Correctly, as Prime Minister, Churchill did not stop debate but arranged for the professional view of the Chiefs of Staff to be brought forward. He supported their view to the hilt. He evaluated Hitler's intentions from a political as well as a military position. He had consistently held through the years of the rise of Hitler that appeasement was particularly dangerous of such a man for whom it would feed his

18 Clem Attlee, The Granada Historical Records Interview, p 20.

ambition and his prejudices. In the War Cabinet he powerfully expressed the realities of what would happen if a negotiation was conceded, a most notable instance of which appears towards the end of the minutes for the eighth meeting:

> {M. Reynaud wanted to get us to the Conference table with Herr Hitler. If we once got to the table, we should then find that the terms offered us touched our independence and integrity. When, at this point we got up to leave the Conference table, we should find that all the forces of resolution which were now at our disposal would have vanished.}

In effect Churchill knew that had talks been entered into, there would have to be a ceasefire. When the talks showed Hitler's intransigence, he, Churchill, would never be able to lift the ceasefire and restart the war.

The ninth and final series of meetings of mainly just ministers took place at 7.00 pm on 28 May. Churchill reported on his meeting with the full Cabinet, and said:

> {They had not expressed alarm at the position in France, but had expressed the greatest satisfaction when he had told them that there was no chance of our giving up the struggle. He did not remember having ever before heard a gathering of persons occupying high places in political life express themselves so emphatically.}

Halifax raised again the proposed appeal to the United States but Churchill thought it

> {altogether premature. If we made a bold stance against Germany, that would command their admiration and respect, but a grovelling appeal if made now, would have the worst possible effect.}

This was almost certainly a veiled reference to a draft telegram which Churchill had been sent by Halifax to send to Roosevelt, and which Churchill had sat on and refused to send. Only the draft exists, undated. It detailed what Roosevelt might say to Hitler if Britain had been offered by Hitler terms "destructive of British Independence". The draft telegram would encourage Roosevelt to assert that such an offer would "encounter US resistance". It was however too defeatist in tone and ran counter to Churchill's deep belief that Roosevelt had to be convinced that Britain had the determination to fight and win. The Prime Minister was then charged with the task of telephoning M. Reynaud to relay what could reasonably be described as the Cabinet government decision, and not just that of the War Cabinet, to fight on.

Churchill could now return to his major concern – how to get Roosevelt away from the isolationists in America and readier to supply arms, equipment, ships and planes. He had been alarmed at Roosevelt's view on 24 May that Canada should urge the British fleet to sail for North America before it could become a bargaining counter in any surrender terms demanded by Hitler.[19] Churchill was not ready to queer his pitch of credible defiance with such a letter. He knew the Americans were not ready to make the details of the President's letter to Mussolini public and were acting as if they regretted it, and probably did so.

For the next few days Britain continued to face its greatest challenge on the beaches of Dunkirk where the withdrawal was still under way. On 31 May Churchill flew to Paris escorted by nine Hurricane planes and met at the Ministère de la Guerre at 2.30 pm with Reynaud. The atmosphere was bad, recriminations very near the surface. Pétain, looking all of his 84 years, took little part as they discussed Narvik and Dunkirk. Churchill wrote his own recollections in *Their Finest Hour*: "The young Frenchman, Captain de Margerie, had already spoken about fighting it out in Africa. But Marshal Pétain's attitude, detached and sombre, gave me the feeling that he would face a separate peace. The influence of his personality, his reputation, his serene acceptance of the march of adverse events, apart from any words he used, was almost overpowering for those under his spell."[20] Churchill was referring back to the fact that Pétain had been in charge of the defence of Verdun in 1916 and was Commander in

---

19 Ian Kershaw, *Fateful Choices: Ten Decisions that Changed the World, 1940–1941* (Penguin, 2013), pp 30–31.
20 Churchill, *Their Finest Hour*, p 100.

Chief from 1917–18 when he had impressed Churchill in his determination to throw back the German onslaught. Spears, accompanying Churchill and a fluent French speaker, said to Pétain, "I suppose you understand, M. le Maréchal, that that would mean blockade? ... That would not only mean blockade, but bombardment of all French ports in German hands."

It is worth recalling that Verdun was the longest battle in the First World War and when the Germans attacked on 21 February 1916, the Somme offensive, which was originally intended as a joint Franco-British operation with France providing 40 divisions and the British only 25, became a British battle. On the first day of the battle on 1 July 1916, 19,240 men were killed and another 37,000 were listed as wounded or missing in action. The battle continued for 140 days and by mid-November, as Sir David Reynolds writes, it had "muddied out", with the British having lost 420,000 men "killed, wounded or missing, in order to advance at most six miles". Reynolds continues "There were dissenters, not only on the radical Left, but also at the highest levels of government. In November, as the battle subsided into the mud, Lord Lansdowne, a former Foreign Secretary and now wartime minister, wrote a memo to his Cabinet colleagues 'imploring them to consider a negotiated peace. Generations will have to come and go before the country recovers from the loss which it sustained in human beings, and from the financial ruin and the destruction of the means of production which are taking place ... All this is no doubt our duty to bear, but only if it can be shown that the sacrifices will have its reward.' His pleas were brushed aside. Despite its private doubts, the Government closed ranks behind Haig".[21]

Against this historic background, let there be no doubt that Halifax as Foreign Secretary was right to ensure in May 1940 that a negotiated peace was extensively discussed in the War Cabinet, and none of his colleagues showed any signs of resentment that he had stimulated such a debate.

---

21 David Reynolds, *New Statesman*, 12–18 August 2016, p. 25.

6

Dunkirk and Defiance

The evacuation of Dunkirk was recorded by a total cumulative figure each day in Cadogan's diaries: 40,000 off the beaches by the end of 29 May at a rate of 2,000 an hour. On the 30 May, 102,000. By noon on 31 May, 164,000 – a figure Cadogan refers to as "a miracle", a word which was to become famously associated with Dunkirk in British history. At the Cabinet meeting at 11.30 am on 31 May the total figure was given as 224,000 and 34,000 Allies. What that figure would have been if the German Panzers had not been stopped outside Calais by Hitler and his field commander, one can only imagine. Had that miracle never happened Professor Hindsight, that well-known figure that haunts political history, would have told us Halifax had been right. But the air battle that lay ahead was the crucial factor and we might still have avoided invasion if we had got 100,000 men off at Dunkirk. The Battle of Britain may have been enough to bring eventual victory. Fortune favours the brave. Even so, a huge price was paid in the massive amounts of ammunition, equipment, vehicles and tanks lost.

The next political hurdle to cross was Churchill's letters of requests to Roosevelt, sent against the background of a Presidential Election due in November in an American mood still of isolationism and on which the President had yet to declare as a candidate. On 1 June, Churchill wrote to Roosevelt again on the question of aircraft asking for the release of 200 Curtiss P-40 fighters, saying at the present rate of comparative losses, they would account for something like 800 German machines.

It was not that letter but Churchill's speech to Parliament on 4 June that had the electric effect on Roosevelt and American public

opinion. The international broadcast had Churchill's voice imper-
sonated by Norman Shelley, as Churchill did not have time to repeat
what he had said. "Roosevelt's response was dramatic. He ordered
a reluctant War Department (where stubborn officials managed to
delay implementation for three weeks) until overwhelmed by direct
presidential instruction to fill British requests for, and to despatch
at once, 500,000 Enfield rifles, 900 75mm artillery pieces, 50,000
machine guns, 130 million rounds of ammunition, a million artillery
shells and large quantities of high explosives and bombs. The neu-
trality legislation was circumvented by selling this equipment and
ordnance to private corporations, which sold it on at once to the
British. Except for tanks, the British Army would be substantially
rearmed, albeit with twenty-year-old rifles and field pieces, within six
weeks of returning, shorn and waterlogged, from Dunkirk."[1]

On 5 June Churchill sent a Most Secret Message to the Canadian
Prime Minister Mackenzie King in which his anxiety about President
Roosevelt's view that the British Fleet might need to go to Canada
is revealed in stark language: "We must be careful not to let Americans view too complacently prospect of British collapse, out of which
they would get the British Fleet and the guardianship of the British
Empire, minus Great Britain. If United States were in the war and
England conquered locally, it would be natural that events should
follow line you describe. But if America continued neutral, and we
were overpowered, I cannot tell what policy might be adopted by a
pro-German administration such as would undoubtedly be set up.
Although President is our best friend, no practical help has been
forthcoming from the United States as yet. We have not expected
them to send military aid, but they have not even sent any worthy
contribution in destroyers or planes, or by a visit of a squadron of
their Fleet to Southern Irish ports. Any pressure that you can supply
in this direction would be invaluable".[2] Churchill ends by showing
his disappointment with America, thanking King "for destroyers

1 Conrad Black, *Franklin Delano Roosevelt: Champion of Freedom* (Weidenfeld &
Nicolson, 2003), pp 554–555.
2 Martin Gilbert, *The Churchill War Papers, Volume II: Never Surrender* (Heinemann,
1994), p 255.

which have already gone into action against a U-Boat" and also demonstrating his Minister of Defence role, aware of every development and engagement of the forces in effect under his direct command.

On 9 June Churchill wrote to Lord Lothian, Ambassador in Washington to guide him for a conversation he was due to have with the President:

> If Great Britain broke under invasion, a pro-German Government might obtain far easier terms from Germany by surrendering the Fleet, thus making Germany and Japan masters of the new world. This dastardly deed would not be done by His Majesty's present advisors, but, if Mosley[3] were Prime Minister or some other Quisling[4] government set up, it is exactly what they would do, and perhaps the only thing they could do, and the President should bear this very clearly in mind. You should talk to him in this sense and thus discourage any complacent assumption on United States part that they will pick up the debris of the British Empire by their present policy. On the contrary, they run the terrible risk that their sea power will be completely over-matched. Moreover, islands and naval bases to hold the United States in awe would certainly be claimed by the Nazis. If we go down, Hitler has a very good chance of conquering the world.

No tougher message could have been sent and Churchill must have calculated that when read out in the Oval Office it would have a significant impact.

On 10 June the Italians declared war. Cadogan wrote in his diary: "Am rather glad. Now we can say what we think of these purulent

---

3 Sir Oswald Mosley, principally known as the founder of the British Union of Fascists (BUF). MP for Harrow 1918–24 and Smethwick 1926–31. Chancellor of the Duchy of Lancaster in the Labour Government of 1929–31. Formed the New Party which merged with the BUF (also known as the Blackshirts) in 1932. Interned in 1940, released in 1943.
4 Vidkun Quisling was a Norwegian military officer and politician who became nominal head of government of Norway after the Nazi occupation. The puppet government, known as the Quisling regime, was dominated by ministers from Nasjonal Samling, the party he founded in 1933. After WW2, he was put on trial for high treason and executed in October 1945.

dogs."[5] When Ciano, the Foreign Minister, informed the British Ambassador, Loraine, of Italy's decision, Cadogan wrote that the Ambassador supposedly responded: "I have the honour to remind Your Excellency that England is not in the habit of losing her wars." Churchill's reaction was recorded by John Colville in his diary "People who go to Italy to look at ruins won't have to go as far as Naples and Pompeii in future." Roosevelt also took the opportunity that same day to condemn the choice of the Italian Government, in a speech delivered at the University of Virginia: "the hand that held the dagger has struck it into the back of its neighbour".

On 11 June Churchill wrote to Roosevelt having heard his speech the night before: "I have already cabled you about airplanes, including flying boats, which are so needful to us in the impending struggle for the life of Great Britain. But even more pressing is the need for destroyers. The Italian outrage makes it necessary for us to cope with a much larger number of submarines which may come out into the Atlantic and perhaps be based in Spanish ports. To this the only counters are destroyers". The next day Churchill told Lothian that he had just learned the President was not convinced and must be updated with figures concerning losses and damages.

On the 12 June Churchill wrote once again to Roosevelt: "I spent last night and this morning at the French GQG where the situation was explained to me in the gravest terms... The aged Marshal Pétain, who was none too good in April and July 1918, is I fear ready to lend his name and prestige to a treaty of peace for France. Reynaud on the other hand is for fighting on, and he has a young General de Gaulle who believes much can be done. Admiral Darlan declares he will send the French Fleet to Canada. It would be disastrous if the two big modern ships fell into bad hands."

On the 14 June German forces entered Paris and two further messages were sent in 24 hours to Roosevelt about France. On 15 June in yet another message Churchill asks: "Have you considered what offers Hitler may choose to make to France? He may say, 'surrender the Fleet intact and I will leave you Alsace-Lorraine', or alternatively,

5 Alexander Cadogan, *The Diaries of Sir Alexander Cadogan O.M. 1938–1945*. Ed. David Dilks (Cassell & Company Ltd, 1971), p 296.

'if you do not give me your ships I will destroy your towns'. I am personally convinced that America will in the end go to all lengths, but this moment is supremely critical for France." He goes on to indicate the possibility of a declaration that the United States would if necessary go to war. At 10.45 he sends another, "I am of course not thinking in terms of an expeditionary force, which I know is out of the question. What I have in mind is the tremendous moral effect such an American decision would produce, not merely in France, but also in all democratic countries in the world, and, in the opposite sense, on the German and Italian people."

At the War Cabinet on 22 June "The Prime Minister said that in a matter so vital for the safety of the whole of the British Empire we could not afford to rely on the word of Admiral Darlan. However good his intentions might be, he might be forced to resign and his place taken by another minister who would not shrink from betraying us. The most important thing to do was to make certain of the two modern battleships *Richelieu* and *Jean Bart*. If these fell into the hands of the Germans they would have a very formidable line of battle when the *Bismarck* was commissioned next August". Halifax thought "we should exhaust every means of persuasion before using force ... The Prime Minister agreed, but stressed that we must at all times keep in our view the main object, which was that in no circumstances must we run the mortal risk of allowing these ships to fall into the hands of the enemy. Rather than that, we should have to fight and sink them."[6]

On 23 June, the War Cabinet agreed in principle to the request from General de Gaulle to recognise a Council of Liberation (Comité National Français) and Churchill described him as a "fine fighting soldier, with a good reputation and a strong personality, and might be the right man to set up such a council". On 24 June, the War Cabinet agreed:

1. French shipping should not be allowed to sail from any British port
2. All French ships on the high seas should be diverted into British ports

---

6 Martin Gilbert, *The Churchill War Papers*, p 395.

The Cabinet also approved Churchill's reply to the Canadian Prime Minister Mackenzie King in a follow-up to Churchill's earlier message on 5 June. This telegram further expressed Churchill's position that "I see no reason to make preparation for or give any countenance to the transfer of the British Fleet. I shall myself never enter into any peace negotiations with Hitler but obviously I cannot bind a future Government which, if we were deserted by the United States and beaten down here, might very easily be a kind of Quisling affair ready to accept German overlordship and protection. It would be a help if you would impress this danger upon the President as I have done in my telegrams to him. All good wishes and we are very glad your grand Canadian division is with us in our fight for Britain."

"The real question at issue" however, "was what to do as regards the French ships at Oran", and in a Confidential Annex to the War Cabinet meeting of 27 June "the view was expressed that it was most important to take action to ensure that the French Fleet could not be used against us ... The Prime Minister summed up the discussion as follows: He thought that the War Cabinet approved in principle that the operation proposed should take place on 3 July. It might be combined with further operations in the Mediterranean, or with operations designed to secure the *Richelieu* and the *Jean Bart* ... The War Cabinet approved in principle the operation on the lines indicated by the Prime Minister".

No decision was more important in setting the tone of Churchill's defiance than on 2 July 1940 when the First Sea Lord, Sir Dudley Pound, sent a signal to Admiral Somerville which had been drafted by Churchill: "You are charged with one of the most disagreeable and difficult tasks that a British Admiral has ever been faced with, but we have complete confidence in you and rely on you to carry it out relentlessly." At 2.00 am on 3 July, Somerville's ships began shelling the French naval vessels at Mers-el-Kébir while aircraft from HMS *Ark Royal* dropped torpedoes. The French Navy lost 1,297 men, dead or missing. Churchill on this issue had stamped his authority ruthlessly and in a way that could allow no doubt anywhere in the world that the British Empire would fight on alone.

Just prior to a Secret Session, the Prime Minister made a statement to the House of Commons on 4 July on the War Situation and the French Fleet.

It is with sincere sorrow that I must now announce to the House the measures which we have felt bound to take in order to prevent the French Fleet from falling into German hands. When two nations are fighting together under long and solemn alliance against a common foe, one of them may be stricken down and overwhelmed, and may be forced to ask its Ally to release it from its obligations. But the least that could be expected was that the French Government, in abandoning the conflict and leaving its whole weight to fall upon Great Britain and the British Empire, would have been careful not to inflict needless injury upon their faithful comrade, in whose final victory the sole chance of French freedom lay, and lies.

As the House will remember, we offered to give full release to the French from their Treaty obligations, although these were designed for precisely the case which arose, on one condition, namely, that the French Fleet should be sailed for British harbours before the separate armistice negotiations with the enemy were completed. This was not done, but on the contrary, in spite of every kind of private and personal promise and assurance given by Admiral Darlan to the First Lord and to his Naval colleague the First Sea Lord of the British Admiralty, an armistice was signed which was bound to place the French Fleet as effectively in the power of Germany and its Italian following, as that portion of the French Fleet which was placed in our power when many of them, being unable to reach African ports, came into the harbours of Portsmouth and Plymouth about ten days ago. Thus I must place on record that what might have been a mortal injury was done to us by the Bordeaux Government with full knowledge of the consequences and of our dangers, and after rejecting all our appeals at the moment when they were abandoning the Alliance, and breaking the engagements which fortified it.

The House of Commons had one of its unique moments; both sides clapped – which is very rare (the last occasion was in 2016 after the killing of the young Labour MP Jo Cox on the street of her constituency) – cheered – which they often do – and some had tears in their eyes. As did Churchill. The Commons is a hugely sentimental place. It loves eulogising over members who have died and recognising Royal events. Here was Churchill, a Francophile to his core, a former naval person (First Sea Lord twice in two World Wars) who everyone knew had friends in the French Navy and had done everything in his power to avoid sinking the French Fleet; yet he had done his duty. That same recognition touched people worldwide. The former naval person in the White House understood its significance – the British were going to be resolute and utterly ruthless. General de Gaulle, in what was a difficult and courageous broadcast for him to the French people on 8 July 1940, said of the French Fleet, "There cannot be the slightest doubt that, on principle and of necessity, the enemy would have used them either against Britain or against our own Empire. I therefore have no hesitation in saying that they are better destroyed."[7]

On 5 July a very different moment of significance occurred. Gollancz published *Guilty Men* written under the pseudonym 'Cato'. The publication came at an unfortunate time for Churchill; he knew the Government was facing bigger challenges and he had no intention of supporting a witch-hunt against the appeasers. Indeed, back on 25 June Churchill, still on the alert for any sense of defeatism amongst those known appeasers, had written to Halifax on a sensitive issue relating to his Deputy Minister, Rab Butler:

It is quite clear to me from these telegrams and others that Butler held odd language to the Swedish Minister and certainly the Swede derived a strong impression of defeatism. In these circumstances would it not be well to find out from Butler actually what he did say. I was strongly pressed in the House of Commons in the Secret Session to give assurances that the present Government and all its Members were resolved to fight on to the death, and I did so taking personal responsibility for the resolve of all. I saw a

---

7 General de Gaulle, *War Memoirs: The Call to Honour 1940–1942*, trans. Jonathan Griffin (Collins, 1955), p 20.

silly rumour in a telegram from Belgrade or Bucharest and how promptly you stamped upon it, but any suspicion of lukewarmness in Butler will certainly subject us all to further annoyance of this kind.

The issue is dealt with fully by Butler's official biographer, Anthony Howard, where his letter of explanation to Halifax is printed in full:

I can see that in this case I should have been more cautious and I apologise. I now place myself in your hands ... Under the circumstances I await your and the Prime Minister's final opinion ...[8]

Halifax handled the incident well; he did not tell Churchill that Butler was ready to resign, and said he was "satisfied that there is no divergence of view ... I should be very sorry if you felt any doubt either about Butler's discretion or his complete loyalty..." What is significant is that Churchill was not looking for a political scalp. He had put a shot across both men's bows about defeatism, but that was all.

However, with the publication of *Guilty Men* came a very public criticism of those involved in the Munich Agreement. The book was a series of vitriolic character assassinations of originally fifteen appeasers, with the title from the French revolutionary writer Saint-Just. "The leader of the angry crowd replied 'The people haven't come here to be given a lot of phrases. They demand a dozen guilty men.'"[9] It was more than a bestseller, there were six impressions by the printer in one month, it sold over 210,000 copies, and was given huge coverage in newspapers and passed from hand to hand amongst soldiers and factory workers. The ODOB refers to its sensational sales as "reminiscent of a pornographic classic". Gollancz himself, on the left, had consulted friends about the advisability of publishing in case its message had a negative impact on morale. An addendum was published in the front by 'Cato' in block capitals, the first line of which was: At long last, the aeroplanes, the tanks, the arms of every kind are piling up.

---

8   Anthony Howard, *RAB: The Life of R A Butler* (Jonathan Cape, 1990), pp 96–100.
9   Simon Hoggart, David Leigh, *Michael Foot* (Hodder and Stoughton, 1981), pp 80–83.

The words inside were, however, very tough. Two former Foreign Secretaries were quoted. Sir John Simon: "I was not prepared to see a single ship sunk ... in the cause of Abyssinian independence"; Sir Samuel Hoare: "We are obsessed with the urgent necessity of doing everything within our power to prevent a European conflagration." Then how "Hoare passed from experience to experience, like Boccaccio's virgin, without any discernible effect on his condition." Baldwin, who had appointed a Minister for the Co-ordination of Defence, Thomas Inskip, a lawyer who admitted he had no qualifications, was chastised through a quote "by a famous statesman" (a reference to Churchill): "There has been no similar appointment since the Roman Emperor Caligula made his horse a consul." Chamberlain was quoted, when answering a question at a dinner party as to why Hitler should be trusted, as saying: "Ah, but this time he promised me." The actual authors were journalists all writing for Beaverbrook newspapers. One of them was Michael Foot who became Leader of the Labour Party from 1980–1983 and a close friend of Lord Beaverbrook. Somehow the authors were able to justify to themselves not branding Beaverbrook guilty despite his well-known period as an appeaser. The hardest jibe of all in *Guilty Men* was to remind readers that Chamberlain had said on 3 April 1940 that "Hitler had missed the bus" five days before he struck at Norway. The Government machine it appears was quietly guided by Churchill, through Duff Cooper, as Minister for Information, to push public criticism towards Baldwin, MacDonald and Simon as far as they could in an attempt to protect Chamberlain, Halifax and the then Chancellor of the Exchequer, Kingsley Wood. He, too, had been an appeaser, but here was the man who, so it is claimed, had advised Churchill in early May to keep silent when he met Chamberlain and Halifax, to sit it out and not proffer any view, to let Halifax speak for himself.

It was not just politicians but civil servants too who were branded. Sir Horace Wilson, a sinister figure, was named as a 'guilty man' and a Chamberlain confidant. He was a top civil servant seconded to Chamberlain and had a room at No. 10. When Churchill became Prime Minister, Wilson was politely told by Churchill that he was making changes to the rooms in No. 10 and was asked to vacate his. Wilson, called 'Sir H Quisling' by Labour, was still there by

6.00 pm, at which point Churchill turned to Brendan Bracken, "Tell that man, if his room is not cleared I will make him Minister for Iceland." Arthur Greenwood allegedly hated Wilson whom he had known for 20 years. Nevertheless, despite the objections Churchill allowed Wilson to stay on as the head of the Civil Service and head of the Treasury and he kept him in this post until July 1942, long after Chamberlain had left in the autumn of 1940. Such actions by Churchill again suggest he was a leader fearful of a coup, anxious about a potential uprising among appeasers.

Meanwhile, a different but more important piece of history was being assembled on 16 July at the Democratic Convention in Chicago. Senate Majority Leader and Chairman of the convention, Alben Barkley, ended a magnificent speech by referring at last with full authority to Roosevelt's intentions: "He wishes in all earnestness and sincerity to make it clear that all the delegates to this convention are free to vote for any candidate." As the convention, after a slight pause, gathered the full implication of the word 'any', the cry went up "we want Roosevelt." So Roosevelt was nominated for a third term and until November there was no chance that the President would give the isolationists any comfort by giving the slightest hint that he would take America into the Europeans' war. On 5 November Roosevelt won a third Presidential term, but though he defeated Wendell Willkie by five million votes, the electoral college margin had been close. All Roosevelt's caution, so frustrating to Churchill and the people of Britain, was fully justified. Had he taken on the isolationists in the full frontal way which many in Britain believed he should have, it is very likely he would have lost and Willkie won. Churchill, despite pleasure at Roosevelt's victory, knew he faced an even harder struggle to persuade the newly returned President for a third term to give help over military equipment at a faster pace, but at least he believed it would happen.

In addition to anxieties of securing military aid, Churchill had to sort out his own party and deal with the divisions that still rumbled on inside government, exacerbated by the publication of *Guilty Men*, as well as negotiate a substantial reshuffle to the Cabinet. Chamberlain had resigned on 29 September, suffering with cancer of the colon, and died on 9 November 1940, after declining the offer of a

Knight of the Garter and an Earldom. Churchill became leader of the party upon Chamberlain's death, attending a crowded meeting at Caxton Hall to be elected on 9 October and given a "tumultuous reception".[10] Significant additions were made to the War Cabinet; Churchill brought in Beaverbrook in August, and in October the Home Secretary Sir John Anderson became Lord President of the Council and a fully-fledged member of the War Cabinet, his role as Home Secretary assumed by Herbert Morrison. Ernest Bevin also became a member of the War Cabinet while remaining Minister of Labour, and was joined by Chancellor of the Exchequer Kingsley Wood.

Two months after this reshuffle to the War Cabinet, prompted by the resignation and death of Chamberlain, Lord Lothian, British Ambassador to the United States, died suddenly in December and provided the opportunity for Churchill to bring in Eden as Foreign Secretary and remove Halifax, who was offered the newly vacant role of British Ambassador to the US. It was a position of undoubted importance, but somewhat diminished when Field Marshal Dill went to Washington in December 1941. Nicknamed 'Dilly-Dally' by Churchill, there was respect between them and Dill had established friendships with the US military, particularly with General George Marshall. Churchill, correctly seeing this was now the all-important relationship, moved him to become head of the Joint Staff Mission and chose General Alan Brooke to take Dill's place as Chief of the Imperial General Staff and principal military adviser to the War Cabinet. Churchill knew that this tough-minded Northern Irishman was not going to be a pushover, nor was he. Throughout the war, Brooke resisted many of Churchill's ideas but also Marshall's. He was very cautious about invading France and even in 1944 had doubts about D-Day's success. His unexpurgated diaries are the best of all the war diaries. Unvarnished, expressing his often brutal opinions, they have a ring of truth.

Churchill had fully lived up to Hilaire Belloc's poem 'Lord Lundy' in his foreign postings, "My language fails! Go out and govern New

---

10 Jonathan Schneer, *Ministers at War: Winston Churchill and his War Cabinet* (Basic Books, 2014), p 38.

South Wales". He sent Hoare to Madrid, Malcolm MacDonald (Ramsay MacDonald's son) to Ottawa, and Duff Cooper to Singapore. Churchill had at first approached Lloyd George for the role of British Ambassador to the US which he turned down on 16 December. Beaverbrook then spoke unprompted, he claimed, to Halifax on 17 December about Washington, and told Churchill wrongly that Halifax would go if pushed a little. Halifax however never varied in his opposition to the whole idea, describing it as an "odious thought"[11] while Halifax's wife told Churchill to his face, "The day would come when he might need E's support". But Churchill held all the cards. It was not possible at that stage in the war for Halifax to be seen to refuse, and Churchill knew it. From Churchill's viewpoint there was an inexorable logic to the appointment and Lady Halifax was in essence right when she said he "wanted to get Edward out of the Government and that this gave him the chance of doing so and nothing would deter him." Churchill told the Cabinet of Halifax's appointment on 23 December.

The bitterness between Churchill and Halifax would linger. As David Reynolds reveals, in 1948 Churchill, when drafting his 'Provisional Final' version of *Their Finest Hour*, used these words about Halifax during the 26–28 May highly confidential War Cabinets: "'The Foreign Secretary showed himself willing to go a long way to placate ['buy off' in an earlier typescript] this new and dangerous enemy' ... and in clear contrast writes 'I found Mr Chamberlain and Mr Attlee very stiff and tough.'"[12] Reynolds then cites General 'Pug' Ismay as the mediating influence who urged discretion, conscious no doubt that Churchill was then having to work closely with Halifax as Opposition Leader of the Lords. "I feel sure that Halifax would be hurt by any inference that he was not as tough <u>during the war</u> as the rest of them, he wrote on the 17 September 1948". Ismay here referred to Halifax's diary, to which he had access, and quoted an extract "to the effect that Halifax did not believe anything could be

---

11 Andrew Roberts, *The Holy Fox, The Life of Lord Halifax* (Head of Zeus, 2014), pp 270–280.
12 David Reynolds, *In Command of History: Churchill Fighting and Writing the Second World War* (Penguin, 2005), p 171.

done to buy off Italy but wanted to avoid seeming 'too unsympathetic to Reynaud in his distress.'"Churchill, unconvinced, wrote in the margin by way of response "General P, You have not perhaps read Reynaud's account. I have however.'" Nevertheless, the incriminating references to Halifax, Reynolds notes, were removed and Churchill wrote merely "I found my colleagues very stiff and tough."[13] Churchill's telegram to Reynaud on 28 May 1940 however remains, with its revealing reference to "the formula prepared last Sunday by Lord Halifax suggesting that, if Mussolini would co-operate with us in securing a settlement of all European questions, which would safeguard our independence and form the basis of a just and durable peace for Europe, we should be prepared to discuss his claims in the Mediterranean".[14] Indeed, as Reynolds continues to note, such documents tell a story quite different to the auspicious and morale-boosting statements of Churchill's. This is poignantly highlighted in Ismay's recollection to Robert Sherwood of a talk between himself and Churchill on 12 June 1940 following the penultimate meeting with French leaders: "When Churchill went to the airport to return to England, he said to Ismay that, it seems 'we fight alone'. Ismay said that he was glad of it, that 'we'll win the Battle of Britain'. Churchill gave him a look and remarked, 'You and I will be dead in three months' time.'"[15]

In the summer of 1953 at a lunch given by the French Ambassador, Halifax said in Clementine Churchill's hearing unflattering comments about her husband to the effect that he, more than anyone else, had been responsible for India wanting to get rid of the British. She snapped back, "I don't know what you're getting at," continuing "if the country had depended on you we might have lost the war."[16] When Halifax asked her to apologise, Churchill said he hoped she would not.

On 29 December 1940 President Roosevelt gave one of his fireside chats on radio but this time the world, not just the nation, listened.

---

13 *Ibid.*
14 David Reynolds, *In Command of History: Churchill Fighting and Writing the Second World War*, p 172.
15 *Ibid.*
16 Andrew Roberts, *The Holy Fox*, p 299.

246 CABINET'S FINEST HOUR

"We must become the great arsenal of democracy" and "there can be no appeasement with ruthlessness" was matched by "no dictator, no combination of dictators." There was no pretence – the days of isolationism were over. Roosevelt had once explained to his close adviser Rexford Tugwell his attitude to people like General Slaughter, MacArthur and Joseph P. Kennedy, another eccentric leader, in his case in business: "We must tame these fellows and make them useful to us." He wanted them either where he could keep an eye on them or out of the way.[17] Roosevelt first appointed Kennedy to regulate the stock market on the basis that it takes a thief to catch a thief, and then made him Ambassador to Great Britain, cynically in order to keep the isolationists happy in America. In this role Kennedy is described in the Introduction to *The Patriarchy* as courting "new criticism in Washington and London, first as a toady for Prime Minister Neville Chamberlain and the Cliveden Set, then as a defeatist, a loud-mouthed Cassandra who believed the Nazis would easily conquer Europe and Great Britain."[18] He left the UK in October unloved and despised by most people. He formally resigned in December 1940. Roosevelt had shamelessly manipulated him right to the end, even getting his endorsement for President before his election. In reality Kennedy did not do Britain much harm because his advice was discounted and Roosevelt's relationship was direct to Churchill.

There is a particular analysis of the personalities of Churchill and Roosevelt that has never been exceeded in insight, coming from the vantage point of Washington during the war which lends it a peculiar intimacy. I refer to Isaiah Berlin's essay which appeared in 1949 in *The Atlantic Monthly* and the *Cornhill Magazine* under the title, 'Mr Churchill and FDR':

> Each was to the other not merely an ally, the admired leader of a great people, but a symbol of tradition and a civilisation; from the unity of their differences they hoped for a regeneration of the Western world ... Mr. Roosevelt was imaginative, optimistic,

---

17 Conrad Black, *Franklin Delano Roosevelt: Champion of Freedom*, p 320.
18 David Nasaw, *The Patriarch; The Remarkable Life and Turbulent Times of Joseph P Kennedy* (Penguin Press, 2012).

Episcopalian, self-confident, cheerful, empirically-minded, fear-less, and steeped in the idea of social progress; he believed that with enough energy and spirit anything could be achieved by man ... Mr. Churchill was imaginative and steeped in history, more serious, more intent, more concentrated, more preoccupied, and felt very deeply the eternal differences which would make such a structure difficult of attainment. He believed in institutions and permanent characters of races and classes and types of individuals ...

Berlin went on to identify "the peculiar degree to which they liked each other's delight in the oddities and humours of life and their own active part in it. This was a unique personal bond ... Mr Roosevelt's sense of fun was perhaps the lighter, Mr Churchill's a trifle grimmer."

Churchill wrote to Roosevelt after his broadcast: "With this trumpet call we march forward." Lend-Lease was on its way and with finance and military assistance. The year 1941 promised more than the bleakness of 1940 in which Britain had overcome the threat of invasion. It was to see the inexorable build-up in Japan for an act of infamy and the premeditated attack on Pearl Harbor at the end of the year, which would bring America into the war against Japan, and with Hitler's foolish decision to declare war on America, into the war on Germany. British power would never be as crucial or as strong again, but in May 1940 Britain paved the way for victory in 1945, first over Germany and then Japan, and in that process there was no weapon or military strategy more important than that of Cabinet government in a parliamentary democracy.

As Churchill had said to the House of Commons on 4 June, "Wars are not won by evacuations." Wars are won by the determination to fight, to lose and to fight again, and again. Had the British Cabinet decided not to fight on 28 May 1940 and instead to negotiate, it is a salutary thought that there would have been no victory celebration on 7 May 1945. Those who criticise Cabinet government today will argue that the wartime coalition government was exceptional and holds no lessons for why a more Presidential system of government, with a Prime Minister more authoritative than *primus inter pares*, is relevant in 2016. It came at a strange juxtaposition of historical circumstances, but in my judgement it is far from being irrelevant simply because it happened 76 years ago. There are modern lessons for Britain to learn about collective decision-making, just as there are lessons for the Labour Party over why Lansbury was removed as leader owing to a conviction that Labour would never win power with a pacifist leader. Lessons about alternative defence and foreign policies should also be learnt from Chamberlain's hubris over Munich in 1938, Eden's drug-induced hubris over Suez in 1956, and Blair's hubris over the invasion of Iraq and the horrendous incompetence in the handling of the aftermath. Time can bring fresh thinking, and a return of the old values to government. But first there must be recognition of why and where things have gone badly wrong in the Presidential style of Tony Blair and in the self-styled "heir to Blair", David Cameron, who resigned after the Brexit vote in 2016.

Underlying Cabinet government is a recognition of the value of a collective approach and the weaknesses of unbridled power. If, during the period of greatest peril our country has ever faced, Cabinet decisions were, as shown clearly in these pages, not only informed but enhanced, then such a model cannot be easily disparaged for the future. It is the strength of Churchill's period as wartime Prime Minister that he did not try to bypass either Cabinet or Parliament. Britain was facing dictatorships, authoritarian styles of government that led through Hitler to rampant anti-Semitism and to the genocide of the Jewish people. The brutal occupation of territory and the forced migration of people were crimes against humanity. A vital element in this fight – that democracy should not just be maintained but strengthened – was the readiness of people across political parties to come together, through the willingness of politicians, hitherto competing against each other for votes, to work together for victory. The history books continue to roll out of the post-Second World War period, but there has been a tendency to focus too much on Churchill as an individual leader and not on Churchill the collective leader. Under his leadership there was a deepening of democracy from 1940–45. He and his colleagues built the machinery to bring people together in a government of national unity, a spirit that continued in the UK through Attlee's peacetime Cabinet government.

7

Epilogue: Prime Minister to President – conflict and the post-war Cabinets

On 6 April 1955 Anthony Eden followed Churchill as Prime Minister. After calling a general election in May of the same year, he emerged with a majority of 58 seats in the Commons, a stunning personal victory. It could have been, and perhaps should have been, the start of a great Prime Ministership. However a combination of illness and temperament made it the worst period of governance in British Cabinet history until the Iraq War of 2003.

On 20 July 1956 President Nasser of Egypt nationalised the Suez Canal Company. Eden took this very personally, seeing it as a direct threat to British interests. He compared Nasser to Mussolini in the 1930s and declared he must not be allowed "to have his thumb on our windpipe". Despite active diplomacy and sanctions, Nasser was still in control of the Suez Canal nearly three months later. Before long there were grumblings in the Conservative Party about Eden's overall performance.

On Sunday 14 October 1956 Eden held what turned out to be a fateful meeting with the French Prime Minister Guy Mollet's emissaries, General Maurice Challe, a deputy Chief of Staff of the French Air Force, and Albert Gazier, France's acting Foreign Minister. Anthony Nutting, Eden's Minister of State for Foreign Affairs, was also present. The Challe plan, based on a conspiracy with Israel against Egypt, was presented and, ruinously, was adopted by Eden as the central policy instrument in his handling of the crisis.

Until this meeting with Mollet and Challe, Eden had had no inkling that the French were already deep in collusion with the

Israelis over Egypt. The plan was that Israel would invade the Suez Canal Zone on the agreed understanding that British and French forces would then intervene to separate the Israeli and Egyptian forces, posing to the world as peacekeepers between the combatants. The RAF would take out Egyptian planes that might otherwise have threatened Israeli territory.

To any Prime Minister, let alone Eden with his vast experience as Foreign Secretary, Challe's suggestion of collusion with Israel would have been viewed as fraught with political dangers at home and abroad. On his record, the cautious, pro-Arab Eden might have been expected to have ruled out involving Israel from the moment he first heard the idea. But Eden left the French in little doubt that he was desperate for a victory and would join them. Challe sensed that Eden was 'thrilled', Millard, his private secretary, felt he was merely 'intrigued'. Nutting, previously very close to Eden, asked "why did the man, whose whole political career had been founded on his genius for negotiation, act so wildly out of character?"[1] A war started in dishonour ended, not altogether surprisingly, in disaster and the man responsible for that, Eden, was in no fit condition to make a decision.[2]

Over the next few days Eden also decided that he would proceed without informing the United States of his intentions, foolishly believing he could keep Israeli involvement secret. In several respects this was a massive misjudgement. Eden allowed only two senior Foreign Office diplomats to be told of the collusion and specifically excluded the Foreign Office legal adviser, whom he knew would say the plan could not be justified by international law. Instead Eden was content to rely on advice from the Lord Chancellor, Lord Kilmuir, who maintained that intervention could be legally justified.[3] But constitutionally the Lord Chancellor is not the legal adviser to the Cabinet, that is the job of the Attorney General.

---

1 Anthony Nutting, *No End of a Lesson: The Story of Suez* (C.N. Potter, 1967).
2 Eden had high fevers because of his cholangitis, the result of a surgical mistake cutting his bile duct on 12 April 1953. Only a week before meeting Challe he had a fever of 107°F and rigors.
3 Geoffrey Marston, 'Armed Intervention in the 1956 Suez Canal Crisis: The Legal Advice Tendered to the British Government', *International and Comparative Law Quarterly* (1988), vol. 37, pp. 773–817.

Eden swept his Foreign Secretary Selwyn Lloyd off to Paris within hours of his having landed from UN meetings in New York. As far as one can determine, neither had had any formal or professional briefing from the Foreign Office, though Eden could rely on the support of the senior diplomat, Sir Ivone Kirkpatrick. His failure to consult the Foreign Office was but one of many examples of how personalised and unstructured Eden's decision-making had become in 10 Downing Street. Under Churchill during the Second World War the machinery of the War Cabinet had functioned fully, and different departments of state had had their input. Eden himself had always been a stickler for following due procedure. Now holding great power himself, he started to depend exclusively on his own political instinct. He was daily taking a mixture of a sedative to sleep and a stimulant (drinamyl) to counter the effect of the prolonged stress since the end of July. The quality of his political instinct and his decision-making abilities began to be noticed by his contemporaries as deteriorating, though they knew very little about his exact medical state.

Lord Home was a supporter of Eden's policy, serving on the all-important Egypt Committee, a form of War Cabinet. He was a generous and fair-minded man but even he has described Eden's conduct at such meetings as "probably not as methodically conducted as at times of lesser stress". [4] The permanent secretary at the Ministry of Defence, Sir Richard Powell, whom Eden continually rang up, described him as "very jumpy, very nervy, very wrought". He also described Eden as having "developed what one might call a pathological feeling about Nasser" and as being "in a state of what you might call exaltation ... He wasn't really 100 per cent in control of himself. Extraordinary, strange things happened."[5] Air Chief Marshal Sir William Dickson, chairman of the Chiefs of Staff Committee, speaking in April 1957 to John Colville, used the same word, 'exaltation', saying that Eden "during the final days was like a

---

4 *A Canal Too Far*, BBC Radio 3, 31 January 1987.
5 Transcript of interview with Sir Richard Powell, papers of the Suez Oral History Project 1989–91, Liddell Hart Centre for Military Archives, King's College, London, ref. SUEZOHP 16.

prophet inspired, and he swept the Cabinet and the Chiefs of Staff along with him, brushing aside any counter-arguments and carrying all by his exaltation". Dickson added that he "had never been spoken to in his life in the way the PM several times spoke to him during those tempestuous days".[6] The Chiefs of Staff were very reluctant to have the Israelis as allies.[7]

On 29 October Israeli paratroopers, led by the then unknown commander Ariel Sharon, later Prime Minister of Israel, dropped into Sinai. The following day the British and French, as agreed with the Israelis, issued their ultimatum demanding a ceasefire and threatening to intervene if this were not agreed. Gamal Abdel Nasser rejected the ultimatum and on 31 October Anglo-French military action began.

It is easy to be overly moralistic about what is done to win in times of war and collusion is certainly not unknown. By the time of the invasion Eden and Selwyn Lloyd were not alone amongst British ministers in being party to the collusion. It has been clear since January 1987 – when, under the thirty-year rule, the Eden Cabinet papers were first made public – that the Cabinet was told about the collusion with France and Israel on 23 October. An Annex reads "From secret conversations which had been held in Paris with representatives of the Israeli Government, it now appeared that the Israelis would not alone launch a full scale attack against Egypt. The United Kingdom and French Governments were thus confronted with the choice between an early military operation or a relatively prolonged operation." This was the moment for the Cabinet collectively to have challenged that collusion and Eden's judgement. So why didn't they? Why, despite some initial dissent, did they go along with the policy?

The short answer is that any Prime Minister, supported by the Foreign Secretary, has great influence on a Cabinet decision on international affairs and, seen as an expert on Egypt by his colleagues, Eden was in a special category. This power over international affairs is similar to but even greater than the power of a Prime Minister,

---

6 John Colville, *Fringes of Power: Downing Street Diaries 1939–1955*, rev. ed. (London: Weidenfeld & Nicolson, 2004), pp. 671–2.

7 Eden, *Clarissa Eden*, p. 250.

when supported by the Chancellor of the Exchequer, on domestic affairs. In addition, personal ambition and party manoeuvring played a crucial part, especially for Harold Macmillan, Chancellor of the Exchequer. Harold Wilson wittily described Macmillan's position on Suez as being that of 'first in, first out'. No reading of the many memoirs of the politicians and others closely involved in the Suez Crisis can possibly conclude that Eden was loyally supported throughout by his Chancellor.

In Cabinet, Macmillan was, superficially, committed to Eden's policy.[8] He advised Eden after privately seeing Eisenhower at the White House on 25 September that "Ike [Eisenhower] is really determined, somehow or other, to bring Nasser down. I explained to him our economic difficulties in playing the long hand and he seemed to understand." The British Ambassador, who had accompanied Macmillan and did not see his note to Eden at the time, later commented that he could see "no basis at all for Harold's optimism" about Eisenhower's support.

Eden's authority was never more brittle than on the morning of 6 November. He must then have sensed the possibility of an overt challenge from Macmillan, the one man who would have swayed a Cabinet that was not yet ready to disown Eden. But Eden moved first. He summoned the Cabinet to meet in his room in the House of Commons at 9.45 am. Aware that he could not expect to maintain a majority in the Cabinet for continuing the invasion, he said that owing to the Americans' likely support of economic sanctions in the Security Council later that day there was no alternative but to announce a ceasefire.

It was a diplomatic debacle. In Eisenhower's words, "I've just never seen great powers make such a complete mess and botch of things." It would have been better from Eden's personal point of view, and for British and French prestige in the Middle East, to have delayed calling the Cabinet together until 7 November, allowing time to take the whole Suez Canal while using the veto with the French on any UN sanctions resolution. There was no question that this is what

---

8 Alistair Horne, *Macmillan 1894–1956: Volume I of the Official Biography* (London: Pan Macmillan, 1998), pp. 420–

Guy Mollet, the French Prime Minister, and David Ben-Gurion, the Israeli Prime Minister, would have preferred, but Eden felt, for the sake of his own position, that he had to act quickly and pre-empt Macmillan upstaging him in the Cabinet as the advocate of accepting Eisenhower's position.

Later Mollet, meeting on 6 November with Konrad Adenauer, the German Chancellor, was told: "France and England will never be powers comparable to the United States ... not Germany either. There remains to them only one way of playing a decisive role in the world: that is to unite Europe ... We have no time to waste; Europe will be your revenge." The Treaty of Rome, the first step to creating the European Union, was signed by the original six continental European countries, with Britain remaining outside, the very next year, in 1957.

Had been there an inquiry into the Suez Crisis, as undoubtedly there should have been, lessons would have been learned that might have prevented many of the mistakes made later by Tony Blair over Iraq. The handling of such a complex international crisis from No. 10 was a recipe for disaster which, had it been fully exposed, might have emboldened civil servants, diplomats, military figures and even Cabinet ministers at the time of the Iraq Crisis to have challenged Blair's overall handling of the war. The invasions of Egypt and Iraq were initially militarily successful but the aftermath was a deep and public political failure. There were, however, crucial differences between 1956 and 2003. Blair was acting in support of a US President; Eden was doing quite the opposite. Blair was supporting an inexperienced and immature President; Eden was ignoring a proven military commander and level-headed leader. As time passes it is becoming ever clearer that Iraq was far more damaging to Britain's long-term interests than Suez.

Eden resigned from the House of Commons in early January 1957. There was a genuine feeling that his mishandling of the issue, of his colleagues and the paucity of Cabinet discussion was in large part due to his ill health. The Suez invasion, however, left lasting damage to Parliament's credibility in failing to bring the Cabinet's decision-making, judged illegal by its own law officers, to account. For many years very few people even knew Eden had lied to Parliament and there was a total refusal on the part of Parliament to learn the lessons, let alone to establish an official inquiry.

There was a measure of continuity and consensus in the post-war governments that is widely judged to have been broken by the arrival of Margaret Thatcher as leader of the Conservative Party in 1975. Not because she was a woman, though that helped, but because she had a political ideology very different from her post-war predecessors.

On the eve of becoming leader of the Conservative Party, Thatcher said on television: "All my ideas about [Britain] were formed before I was seventeen or eighteen." There is a good deal of truth in this comment. It explains her black-and-white view of life, which was part of her appeal, as well as the source of an off-putting certainty. On the day of her election as leader, she told ITN: "You don't exist as a party unless you have a clear philosophy and clear heritage."

On 31 March 1982, there came what Thatcher described as "the worst moment of my life". John Nott, her Defence Secretary, arrived bearing intelligence about an impending Argentinian invasion of the Falkland Islands. Thatcher's biographer, Charles Moore, offers a vivid reconstruction of a meeting that evening in the Prime Minister's room in the House of Commons. Nott and his permanent under-secretary, Frank Cooper, told her that the recapture of the Falkland Islands was all but impossible. She knew from her Foreign Office private secretary in No. 10 that this view was shared by the Chief of the General Staff. The then Chief of the Defence Staff, Admiral Sir Terence Lewin, was away in New Zealand but he was likely to be cautious. In the middle of the discussion, Admiral Sir Henry Leach, the First Sea Lord, arrived from Portsmouth in uniform. He had dropped in to his office in the Ministry of Defence to find a naval staff briefing on the Falklands that advised: 'Don't touch it.' But Leach was a man of resolution and intelligence, as I knew from my time as Navy Minister between 1968 and 1970 when he was head of naval plans. Leach asked the Prime Minister for political clearance to assemble a task force.

"What does that mean?" she asked.

Leach explained about ships, aircraft carriers and helicopters.

"How long can it take to assemble the task force?" she enquired.

"Three days," replied Leach.

"How long to get there?"

"Three weeks."

"Three weeks?" Thatcher exclaimed, with no idea of how far away the Southern Atlantic was. "Surely you mean three days?"

"No, I don't," Leach said.

"Can we do it?" she asked.

"We can, Prime Minister."

"Why do you say that?"

Leach replied: "Because if we don't do it, if we pussyfoot ... we'll be living in a different country whose word will count for little."

The retaking of the Falklands was the decisive event that changed the nature of Thatcher's premiership. Few British Prime Ministers would have reacted as she did and sent a naval task force to retrieve a small, distant archipelago of little strategic significance. She established a War Cabinet having consulted Harold Macmillan who advised her against the inclusion of the Chancellor of the Exchequer. Most of her Prime Ministership she ensured that the Cabinet as a whole was kept well informed. There was no abrogation of Cabinet government, though her later treatment of Cabinet colleagues left a lot to be desired. As I know from my own conversations with her during that war, while utterly determined, she was surprisingly cautious and in private she was more anxious than belligerent. Her 'rejoice, rejoice' statement on the steps of No. 10, following the landing of British troops on South Georgia, is often quoted as an example of hubris, but it was as much relief as exaltation.

The political tragedy for Margaret Thatcher is that she repeatedly pitted herself against her own source of power in Parliament, a group of pro-EEC Conservative MPs. She had reached a stage where not only was she not listening to her parliamentary colleagues but she appeared to enjoy deriding their European views. The Cabinet still functioned but it had been reduced in stature and in quality. People of substance, who well knew that Cabinet government was a great constitutional safeguard, allowed this to develop over the years to the detriment of the British democratic system. It was not just because Thatcher was a woman that the Cabinet had been so supine but it was a material factor. With the Cabinet too weak to act, it was left to the Conservative MPs to bring about Thatcher's political end. A leader who had won three general elections was removed by her own MPs, not by the nation's voters, and yet within the rules of our parliamentary democracy. For those who believe in representative democracy and decisive leadership it was an example of the parliamentary democratic control mechanisms acting as it should.

The successor to Margaret Thatcher was John Major, a low-key figure who benefited from being thought a eurosceptic but who turned out to be a committed supporter of the EU, though one who managed to negotiate an opt-out for the UK on the euro currency and from the Schengen open borders area. His seven years in office are marked by one high point, the military collaboration with President H W Bush during the first Gulf War of 1991, which comprised a multinational force, with Muslim countries participating and which successfully threw Saddam Hussein's Iraqi forces out of Kuwait. John Major was also somewhat responsible for restoring the Cabinet as a group with power to conduct policy from their own departments with less frequent interference from No. 10. Major was easy to depict as weak, but this was not as true as it appeared. It was nevertheless the way Blair sought to depict him when leader of the Opposition.

After the landslide victory of 1997, Blair at first governed cautiously, accepting the financial expenditure projections of his predecessor and, with the use of referenda, introducing Scottish and Welsh Parliaments. Cabinet government was still practised but early on there were signs of a dual Presidency emerging. Blair was concerned with overall image, the EU and foreign and defence policy whilst his Chancellor of the Exchequer, Gordon Brown, largely oversaw finance and domestic affairs at the expense of both the Prime Minister and his Cabinet colleagues. Blair's main achievement as Prime Minister was undoubtedly the Good Friday Agreement signed in April 1998, which built on the multi-party talks that had begun under John Major in June 1996.

When the will to take up arms in Afghanistan and later in Iraq returned to America after 11 September 2001, President Bush rightly seized the moment. He took military action in Afghanistan against its Taliban government that had for years been sheltering Al-Qaeda.

Other deeply dysfunctional states, such as Somalia and Sudan, had also allowed Al-Qaeda to operate within their borders, but the extent of Afghanistan's harbouring of international terrorist organisations had meant there was a strong case for pre-emptive action even before 9/11. Afterwards that case was overwhelming. Tony Blair was described by the Labour historian Lord Morgan in the immediate wake of 9/11 and afterwards:

> Blair seemed a political colossus, half-Caesar, half-Messiah. Equally, as times became tough following the Iraq imbroglio, he became an exposed solitary victim, personally stigmatised as in the 'cash for peerages' affair. Blair discovered, like Lloyd George and Thatcher before him, that British politics do not take easily to the Napoleonic style.

We know that, in the immediate aftermath of the 9/11 attacks, Tony Blair asked John Scarlett of MI6 and Stephen Lander, head of MI5, "Who's done this?" "The most likely is Osama bin Laden's organisation," Lander replied, adding that he felt bin Laden was most probably linked to Afghanistan's Taliban. Blair was apparently taken aback. "If it's coming from Afghanistan did I know about this?" A JIC report from 16 July sent to Blair had warned that Al-Qaeda, operating from bases in Afghanistan, was in the "final stages" of preparing an attack on the West, with UK interests "at risk, including from collateral damage in attacks on US targets". Understanding such reports fully and knowing when to call on the specialist expertise at your disposal is an issue for any President or Prime Minister. But Blair had never served in government, even as a junior minister. There is no escaping the conclusion his negligence in not questioning officials about the significance of the report demonstrated his lack of ministerial experience. Such experience would have instilled a readiness to order further studies from the briefing notes and intelligence reports. That was simply not done over Afghanistan in 2001, either in the White House or in No. 10. Nor over Iraq in 2002.

An article in *Management Today* in 2005 saw Blair wanting to act like a chief executive: "fast on his feet, flexible in his thinking and able to make quick decisions, often taken on the hoof, in shirt-sleeves, on the sofa, caffé latte in one hand, mobile phone in the other, running Great Britain plc as if it were a City investment company". But the role of Prime Minister is not that of a chief executive and the UK Government is not a company making profits for shareholders.

While Thatcher had sought to accrete more power in No. 10, she worked within the existing Cabinet structures to do so. She made considerable use of a personal foreign affairs adviser, Charles Powell, then a serving diplomat, but the Cabinet Secretary remained a powerful and independent figure. By contrast, Blair decided on a formalised and progressive destruction of the Cabinet system. Immediately on taking office he appointed a political Chief of Staff, Jonathan Powell. Exceptionally, both Blair's press secretary, Alastair Campbell, and Jonathan Powell were granted the powers of civil servants. This was a novel, far-reaching and ultimately disastrous change; a practice that should now be examined in light of the lessons learnt and arguably banned by the Civil Service Commission. Both Campbell and Powell progressively undermined the authority of the Cabinet Secretary and the new power structure undermined collective Cabinet responsibility. This was noted by Bernard Donoughue, Head of the Policy Unit in No. 10 under Harold Wilson and close advisor to James Callaghan, as early as 13 November 1997: "Met Jack (Cunningham) back from Cabinet and he said nothing of importance now happens there, quite different from 20 years ago. All policy decisions taken by Blair and Brown outside the Cabinet."[9]

In 2001, after winning the general election, Blair, with no prior parliamentary examination or scrutiny, changed the whole basis of Cabinet government as it had historically related to matters of foreign and defence policy. A Cabinet Office system which had evolved during the First World War was swept aside without a single serious objective study – no Green paper, no White paper, no Select Committee scrutiny. This was not modernisation but a hubristic act of vandalism for which, as Prime Minister, Blair alone bears responsibility. Shockingly there was little public or parliamentary

---

9   Bernard O'Donoughue, *Westminster Diary: A Reluctant Minister under Tony Blair*, 2016

recognition of the importance and significance of these changes.[10] If we are to learn from the mistakes that were made we need to examine how such changes could have been introduced without any parliamentary authority. This new structure was designed deliberately to ensure Blair could exercise similar powers to those of a US President over international policy. The Cabinet Office method of handling foreign and security matters had, until then, been designed to serve the Cabinet as a whole. From the summer of 2001 onwards, the key officials and their staff on foreign affairs, defence and the European Union were brought into the political hothouse atmosphere of 10 Downing Street in two new secretariats.[11] There they still remain, not serving the Cabinet.

The two diplomats chosen were David Manning, to deal with foreign affairs, like Iraq, and Stephen Wall, dealing with the European Union. Both exceptionally able but now untethered from departmental control, whether from ministers or Permanent Secretaries. One of the arguments used for this development was related to the UK's membership of the EU – the number of Presidents who attended meetings of the Heads of Government meant it was claimed as inevitable that No. 10 should develop this new structure. In 2016 the UK, having voted to leave the EU, it is a good time to reconsider Presidential Prime Ministerships and revert under Theresa May to a Cabinet Office structure which for a century served us well. It would be a welcome sign we were bringing back democratic control of our country.

A few months after these two secretariats were in place in No. 10 the new structure provided Blair with the means to project his very personalised response to 9/11. This directly and inexcusably led to the disastrous handling of the aftermath of the invasion of Iraq chronicled in the Iraq Inquiry. With few, if any, departmental papers circulated for debate, the War Cabinet system was bypassed in favour of informal agreement. The last time this was done so

---

10 Lord Owen 'The Ever-Growing Dominance of No. 10 in British Diplomacy since 5 April 1982', Graham Ziegner (ed.), *British Diplomacy. Foreign Secretaries Reflect* (London: Politico's, 2007) pp. 19–42.
11 David Owen, 'Two-Man Government', *Prospect*, December 2003; Owen, 'The Ever-Growing Dominance of No. 10 in British Foreign Policy since 5 April 1982'.

comprehensively was by Lloyd George after the Paris Peace Treaty until he was toppled by the 1922 Committee.

Blair was obsessed by presentation and needed to put himself visibly at the centre of events. This had already become evident when a private memo he wrote to his staff in 2000 was leaked. In it he urged them to search around for "two or three eye-catching initiatives ... I should be personally associated with as much of this as possible".[12] The biographer of another inexperienced Labour Prime Minister, Ramsay MacDonald, wrote of Blair's ten years in office:

> The true origin of his tragedy lies in an intellectual deformation that is becoming more and more prevalent in our increasingly paltry public culture. The best word for it is 'presentism' ... His fascination with fashionable glitz, his crass talk of a 'New Britain' and a 'Young Country' and his disdain for the wisdom of experts who had learned the lessons of the past better than he had were all part of the deadly syndrome.[13]

The world after 9/11 provided Blair with endless opportunities for such eye-catching initiatives as he indulged in considerable posturing and pursued a frenetic schedule. He held fifty-four meetings with foreign leaders, and travelled more than 40,000 miles on some thirty-one separate flights.

The British press were encouraged by No. 10, with its new foreign affairs and defence secretariats, to exaggerate the extent of the UK's early involvement in Afghanistan. The UK launched a few cruise missiles and made a contribution from its SAS. The attack was, however, first and foremost an American operation. Yet to reinforce the impression of his own central role, Blair flew into Kabul in early January 2002, just eight weeks after the Taliban-controlled capital had fallen to the Northern Alliance.

By now there was little pretence but that British foreign policy was being run from 10 Downing Street, with the Foreign Office and

---

12 Leaked memorandum of 29 April 2000 from Tony Blair to staff, reported in *The Times*, 18 July 2000.
13 David Marquand, 'A Man Without History', *New Statesman*, 7 May 2007.

Defence Ministry increasingly sidelined. The British Ambassador in Washington, Christopher Meyer, recorded this: "Between 9/11 and the day I retired at the end of February 2003, I had not a single substantive policy discussion on the secure phone with the Foreign Office. This was in contrast to many contacts and discussion with No. 10."[14]

The truth is the UK did not have to go to war in Iraq. Donald Rumsfeld made it very clear at a late stage that the United States was willing to go into Iraq alone, without the British. President Bush also offered to ease the way for any decision to not involve British troops in the invasion. Harold Wilson when Prime Minister had faced a similar choice on whether to contribute British forces to the Vietnam War. He chose not to, believing he would not have sufficient influence on the handling of that war because of President Johnson's nature. In December 1964 President Johnson wanted Wilson to send the Black Watch, a Scottish regiment, to Vietnam, for primarily presentational purposes. He revealed that to be his underlying attitude by actually saying to Wilson that even a few pipers would be better than nothing! Nevertheless, apart from measured criticism in a speech in the White House in February 1968, Wilson supported an American presence in Vietnam and knowingly risked the jibe that he was "the tail-end Charlie in an American bomber".[15]

No British Prime Minister in wartime, not Asquith, Lloyd George, Churchill or even Eden, let alone Major on the first invasion of Iraq, made strategic decisions as Blair did over Iraq, personally and without systematically involving senior Cabinet colleagues. There are important safeguards in the pre-circulation of strategy papers. It ensures the views of military commanders and key diplomats in the field are made known. There are considerable advantages to the Cabinet making collective decisions and a smaller group of ministers reporting regularly to the full Cabinet. This was the way Margaret Thatcher conducted the Falklands War in 1982, with a War

---

14 Christopher Meyer, *DC Confidential: The Controversial Memoirs of Britain's Ambassador to the US at the Time of 9/11 and the Iraq War* (London: Weidenfeld & Nicolson, 2006), p. 190.
15 Philip Ziegler, *Wilson: The Authorised Life of Lord Wilson of Rievaulx* (London: Weidenfeld & Nicolson, 1993), pp. 222–3.

Cabinet, and the way John Major took decisions over the Gulf War in 1991. It was not the way in which the Iraq War was conducted by Blair.

The Iraq Inquiry chaired by Sir John Chilcot was published in July 2016. Commonly referred to as the Chilcot Report, it provides both a history and a forensic analysis of the Iraq War. The Report considers there should have been collective decisions made on eleven specific occasions before the invasion.[16] But the full Cabinet was never properly informed, in effect acting only to rubber stamp decisions that Blair and a small coterie of selected colleagues and advisers had already taken in often unminuted meetings in No. 10 on strategic policy. What was even more unusual was that a somewhat similar procedure was operating out of 11 Downing Street, home of the Chancellor of the Exchequer, for many of Gordon Brown's decisions on economic policy. This 'dual President' arrangement, meekly accepted by the British Cabinet from 1997 but most markedly after the 2001 general election, meant that the Cabinet was comprehensively bypassed throughout Blair's premiership.

The deplorable decision-making of the Blair Government over Baghdad in the aftermath of the invasion of Iraq is chronicled in some detail in the Executive Summary of the inquiry's published findings, on pages 88 and 89. A more detailed account of the failure to move British troops from Basra to Baghdad can be read in the chapter on 'Bush, Blair and the War in Iraq' in my book *In Sickness and in Power*. Blair should have made a military deployment that would have impacted politically in Washington.[17]

The House of Commons should concentrate on Tony Blair's written statement issued on 6 July 2016 when the Chilcot Report was published. It cannot be left unchallenged. Defiance is the only way to describe his words: "If I was back in the same place with the same information I would take the same decision." A leading article in *The Times* published the following day charges that we went to war

---

16 The Report of the Iraq Inquiry, Executive Summary, 2016, pp. 58–59.
17 David Owen, *In Sickness and In Power*, pp. 370–375.

on the basis of intelligence on weapons of mass destruction that remained privy to the Prime Minister and his closest aides but which he insisted, in private as well as public, was incontrovertible. It was anything but. Still defiant 13 years on, Mr Blair insisted in a written statement that the Chilcot report alleged "no falsification or improper use of intelligence". In fact the report states that the intelligence "was not challenged and should have been". Many will conclude that amounts to improper use.[18]

It is for Parliament now to consider whether Blair's continued defiance brings Parliament into disrepute. In my view it does. The use Blair made of the available intelligence, quoting it inaccurately and ignoring caveats and concerns, should now be scrutinised carefully with a view to using the contempt procedure. The trouble is that MPs are, or many feel they are, complicit. They do not wish to appear to be scapegoating. So it may be that, in a dereliction of duty by MPs, it will be left to the civil courts to determine whether to hear a case from civil society. It seems fairly certain that the relatives of troops killed or injured in the Iraq War will assert that Blair committed 'misfeasance in public office' and the Report provides a saga of hubristic incompetence and levels of ignorance that will back such a charge up.

As long ago as February 1906 Lord Sanderson, just retired as the senior diplomat in charge of the Foreign Office, wrote an internal memorandum that touched on impeachment in circumstances with many parallels to those of almost a century later. Describing his call on the French Ambassador M. Chabon, which he had undertaken on the instructions of the Foreign Secretary Sir Edward Grey, and having with him Grey's own account of the meeting the previous day, Sanderson wrote:

> ...as I was no longer an official, I might speak to him quite freely ... on my own personal views ... I told him that I thought that if the Cabinet were to give a pledge which would morally bind the country to go to war in certain circumstances, and were not to mention this pledge to Parliament, and if at the expiration of

---

18 'Catalogue of Failure', 7 July, 2016.

some months the country suddenly found itself pledged to war in consequences of this assurance, the case would be one which would justify impeachment, and which might even result in that course unless at the time the feeling of the country were very strongly in favour of the course to which the Government was pledged.

On the face of it Tony Blair committed an impeachable offence in 2002 in his letter to President Bush of 28 July. He wrote "I will be with you, whatever." That both David Manning and Jonathan Powell advised him not to use those words showed they shared some of Sanderson's caution. It was only eight days after this expression of support from Blair to President Bush that the path to invasion had been set, if not in concrete terms at least in the minds of the key decision-makers in Washington and London. It can never have been constitutionally legitimate to exclude from meetings held before the Prime Minister wrote that note, not only the deputy Prime Minister, John Prescott, but also Lord Irvine of Lairg, the Lord Chancellor, and even perhaps the Home Secretary. A War Cabinet of six senior Cabinet ministers, the same number on which Churchill relied in May 1940, could easily have been formed and would have allowed Blair to exclude his Chancellor of the Exchequer, Gordon Brown, whom he already did not trust.

Other occasions, too, were identified by Chilcot in the investigations of important messages written or said to President Bush. In October 2015, a revealing cache of emails held on a private server belonging to Hillary Clinton, the former US Secretary of State, were released on orders from the US courts. One of them was written by Colin Powell, then US Secretary of State, in March 2002 to President Bush. Chilcot could not have expected this internal US document to have been available to him; he was promised only access to all UK documents, along with summaries of meetings and telephone conversations. The document is therefore both an unexpected and crucially important insight into Blair's commitment as early as April 2002. Headed 'Subject: Your meeting with United Kingdom Prime Minister Tony Blair, April 5–7 at Crawford' the key paragraph was the first:

Blair continues to stand by you and the US as we move forward on the war on terrorism and on Iraq. He will present to you the strategic, tactical and public affairs lines that he believes will strengthen global support for our common cause.

Whilst Tony Blair was right to put the decision to go to war in Iraq to the House of Commons in 2003, it was his conduct prior to that debate that showed he was oblivious to, or never knew about, the non-disclosure to the Cabinet of the Military conversations between Britain and France between 1906 and 1911. Had he known this history he might have thought twice about failing to impart necessary information to Cabinet about his commitment to Bush in 2002 or his failure to create an official War Cabinet. Instead he relied on ad hoc Cabinet meetings with no constitutional authority – their limitations clearly exposed by the way in which he went ahead regardless of the considerable reservations expressed by both Jack Straw and Geoff Hoon – and rarely any departmental papers. Whitehall stood by impotently.

The failures of intelligence prior to the invasion were made clear in the Butler Report of July 2004. Blair was apparently surprised that its conclusions were not more damaging, as were many others, but it was he who had deliberately limited its terms of reference. A former, loyal Cabinet colleague of Blair's sat on the inquiry's committee and Lord Butler, as chair, knew any criticism would have to be deftly drafted. Nevertheless the Butler Report, unusually, went beyond its remit into the area of intelligence failings before the war and commented on the nature of Blair's decision-making process. It singled out for criticism Blair's personalised sofa-style way of making key decisions, stating "We are concerned that the informality and circumscribed character of the Government's procedures ... risks reducing the scope for informed collective political judgement." The language of Whitehall concealed what a damning criticism that was. But the Blair spin machine swiftly defused the Report. The question Butler apparently most dreaded at his press conference was whether the Prime Minister should resign but the press and TV commentators never asked. Yet strangely much later in 2007 in the House of Lords I watched as Butler read out from a prepared passage the word "disingenuous" about what Blair had said to Parliament on the intelligence available to him, but never used that word in 2016.[19]

The most alarming circumstance of the first part of the 21st century is the way British Prime Ministers have started to assume some of the powers of a President, particularly those of a US President. This trend was checked in the debate on 29 August 2013 after which David Cameron became the first Prime Minister in 150 years to lose a vote in the House of Commons on an issue of military deployment. Along with the Chilcot Report, it is hoped this will prove a watershed moment in which Parliament is seen to reassert its authority. That vote, against bombing President Assad's forces in Syria without UN legal authority, may have done much to halt the growth of an imperial premiership. Perhaps the decision was to some extent inadvertent but the vote happened, and it needed to happen.[20]

The traditional right of the UK Prime Minister to declare war will never be the same again. It has become, in effect, a qualified power. There is now a political imperative to involve Parliament wherever possible. There will be democratic debate and in all but the most urgent and dire circumstances Parliament must vote before the UK goes to war. That is a major curtailment of the imperial premiership model. On the 24 June 2016, having promised to implement an EU referendum decision to leave, David Cameron publicly announced that he was going to cease to be Prime Minister as soon as the Conservative Party could elect a new leader. This was a contemptuous act which might have had bad effects on economic confidence had not Andrea Leadsom withdrawn from the leadership race, allowing Theresa May to become Prime Minister without nine weeks' constituency campaigning. Many of Cameron's dire economic predictions following Brexit did not happen but more might have done if such a drawn out leadership campaign had been allowed to take place. What has shocked people is the realisation that the Conservative Cabinet coalition undertook no comparable assessment of the economic

19 Hansard, HL Deb, 22 February 2007, vol. 689 col 1231.
20 SA Goodman, *The Imperial Premiership: The role of the modern Prime Minister in foreign policy making 1964–2015* (Manchester University Press, 2016).

modelling of leaving the EU before Cameron took the decision, at the end of 2013, that there would be an in-out referendum if he won an outright victory in the general election in 2015. Nor when he then won an outright victory was any Cabinet economic assessment made prior to the legislation for a referendum being carried through Parliament. A consequence of the bypassing of government studies of the economic impact of leaving the EU meant the referendum campaign was shriller than it need have been and the high watermark for referenda has passed. Personally I would doubt there will be any further referenda on such controversial political and constitutional issues, for a few decades at least.

When introducing the Chilcot Report David Cameron chose to highlight the creation of the National Security Council (NSC) by the coalition government in May 2010. This system, however, is yet to be tested in the face of a Prime Minister prepared to override existing conventions, or one determined not to operate under agreed NSC mechanisms. Chilcot did not consider whether, in the run up to the Iraq War, it could have been bypassed legally. Could it have met less frequently, or might its deliberations have been superseded by small ad hoc Cabinet Committees? Could the Chiefs of Staff have been prevented from bringing their concerns directly to the NSC? Could the Cabinet Secretary or senior civil servants have been prevented from doing likewise? These are just some of the fundamental questions that must be considered in the restoration of Cabinet government in the UK.

It was encouraging to see Theresa May, as her first major action on becoming Prime Minister in the wake of the Brexit vote, visit Edinburgh to talk to Nicola Sturgeon, Scotland's First Minister. Then Wales, Northern Ireland and inviting the Irish Prime Minister to No. 10. Of course there are important constitutional questions that arise from the UK leaving the EU and they are best sorted out through an all-party UK Constitutional Convention with a view to creating a new Second Chamber to replace the Lords, reflecting the emergence of a federal UK. That is the most appropriate democratic response to the decision to reject being sucked into a United States of Europe, which is the essence of Brexit.

An important debate that took place in the House of Lords in July

2016 stressed that good practices do not guarantee good decisions. Nor do they guarantee good behaviour, or prevent the participants succumbing to groupthink. Lord Bridges of Headley, Parliamentary Secretary for the Cabinet Office, and grandson of the Cabinet Secretary in 1940, concluded the debate, saying that in 2016 the Attorney General had become a member of the NSC as of right and would therefore be privy to all NSC discussions relating to conflict as well as other national security issues. That is a wise decision. A stabilisation unit has also been established for post-conflict work and will come under the NSC. A dedicated Conflict, Stability and Security fund will routinely support training, planning and the working together of officials from DFID and the MOD. Lord Bridges also spoke movingly of the importance of creating a culture and an environment in which politicians would welcome challenges, indeed provoke it themselves, and a framework that encourages both debate and deliberation. It is to precisely this culture we must now return – that of a government making collective decisions; only then will the presidential model that has proved so disastrous since 2001 be buried never to return, and will a Prime Minister uphold the practices of Cabinet government both in times of peace and war.

In his important book *The Myth of the Strong Leader*, Archie Brown, Emeritus Professor of Politics at the University of Oxford, writes of a much-needed check on the merits of charismatic leadership.[21] It ends: "Leaders who believe they have a personal right to dominate decision-making in many different areas of policy, and who attempt to exercise such a prerogative, do a disservice both to good governance and to democracy. They deserve not followers, but critics."[22]

The opportunity to exercise decisive and sometimes controversial leadership is one of the strengths of representative democracy and there is undoubtedly a need from time to time for boldness. But under the UK system representative democracy also demands that leaders' decision-making be open to democratic scrutiny in full Cabinet as

---

21 Archie Brown, *The Myth of the Strong Leader: Political Leadership in the Modern Age* (Bodley Head, 2014).
22 Archie Brown, *The Myth of the Strong Leader*, p. 362.

well as a War Cabinet. Also that during times of war, information be released to Parliament wherever possible. This system has operated well for this country, except for the last 15 years, and it is of paramount importance that after the referendum decision to leave the EU in 2016 the effective working of Cabinet government is restored.

Index

Note: Page numbers in **bold** indicate coverage on alternate pages.